The Politics of Crisis Management

Crisis management has become a defining feature of contemporary governance. In times of crisis, communities and members of organizations expect their leaders to minimize the impact of the crisis at hand, while critics and bureaucratic competitors try to seize the moment to blame incumbent rulers and their policies. In this extreme environment, policy makers must somehow establish a sense of normality, and foster collective learning from the crisis experience. In this uniquely comprehensive analysis, the authors examine how leaders deal with the strategic challenges they face, the political risks and opportunities they encounter, the errors they make, the pitfalls they need to avoid, and the paths away from crisis they may pursue. This book is grounded in over a decade of collaborative, cross-national case study research, and offers an invaluable multidisciplinary perspective. This is an original and important contribution from experts in public policy and international security.

ARJEN BOIN is an Associate Professor at Leiden University, Department of Public Administration. He is the author of *Crafting Public Institutions* (2001) and co-editor, with Rosenthal and Comfort, of *Managing Crises: Threats, Dilemmas, Opportunities* (2001).

PAUL 'T HART is senior fellow, Research School of Social Sciences, Australian National University, and Professor of Public Administration at the Utrecht School of Governance, Utrecht University. His publications include *Understanding Policy Fiascoes* (1996), *Beyond Groupthink* (1997), and *Success and Failure in Public Governance* (2001).

ERIC STERN is the Director of CRISMART, acting Professor of Government at the Swedish National Defence College, as well as Associate Professor of Government at Uppsala University. He is the author of *Crisis Decisionmaking: A Cognitive Institutional Approach* (1999).

BENGT SUNDELIUS is the Founding Director of CRISMART and Professor of Government at Uppsala University. He is Chief Scientist of the Swedish Emergency Management Agency and responsible for promoting research in the area of homeland security.

The Politics of Crisis Management

Public Leadership under Pressure

Arjen Boin

Paul 't Hart

Eric Stern

Bengt Sundelius

CAMBRIDGE UNIVERSITY PRESS

CAMBRIDGE
UNIVERSITY PRESS

University Printing House, Cambridge CB2 8BS, United Kingdom

Cambridge University Press is part of the University of Cambridge.

It furthers the University's mission by disseminating knowledge in the pursuit of education, learning and research at the highest international levels of excellence.

www.cambridge.org
Information on this title: www.cambridge.org/9780521607339

©Arjen Boin, Paul 't Hart, Eric Stern, Bengt Sundelius, 2005

First published 2005
16th printing 2016

Printed in the United States of America by Sheridan Books, Inc.

A catalogue record for this publication is available from the British Library

ISBN 978-0-521-84537-3 Hardback
ISBN 978-0-521-60733-9 Paperback

Contents

Figures and Table

FIGURES

TABLE

Acknowledgments

The writing of this book took place during the long aftermath of what is now simply known as "9/11." In the very last stages of rewriting this book, the tsunami catastrophe occurred. Whilst proof-reading, "7/7" shocked London. These crises highlight many of the issues we discuss in this book. They illustrate the point we wish to make in this book: crises are political at heart.

When a society or one of its key institutions encounters a major crisis, the politics of public policy making do not – as official rhetoric frequently suggests – abate. On the contrary, political rivalries about the interpretation of fast-moving events and their effects are part of the drama that crisis management entails in modern society.

Crises make and break political careers, shake bureaucratic pecking orders and shape organizational destinies. Crises fix the spotlight on those who govern. Heroes and villains emerge with a speed and intensity quite unknown to "politics as usual." Many seasoned policy makers understand this catalytic momentum in crises. They may talk about national unity and the need for consensus in the face of shared predicaments, but this reflects only part of their reasoning. Their other calculus, less visible to the public, concerns contested issues, dilemmas of responsibility and accountability, of avoiding blame and claiming credit.

This book captures our ideas about the political challenges and realities of public leadership in times of crisis. We formulate five core tasks of crisis leadership: sense making, decision making, meaning making, terminating, and learning. Rather than using this book to report and integrate the manifold research findings, we adopt an argumentative approach. In each chapter, we ask a key question and offer our central claim about the leadership task at hand.

This monograph is an exercise in theory building and policy reflection rather than in theory testing and policy design. It offers a newly integrated approach that social scientists may use to study crises. It also aims at practitioners in and beyond the public sector. We offer them – especially in the final chapter – a condensed exploration of perennial pitfalls and strategic considerations that we believe should inform crisis leadership.

This book is the result of a truly collaborative effort. Since 1993, we have worked together in research, teaching, and training on crisis management in the public sector. On the long road toward this publication we have incurred many debts. We take this opportunity to thank our mentors and colleagues; we also wish to pay our dues to those who have pioneered the various strands of crisis research upon which this book builds. Without their contributions, there would be no research-based knowledge to report upon in this book.

Uriel Rosenthal founded the Leiden University Crisis Research Center and nurtured a generic crisis approach to all types of adversity. The late Irving Janis's work on groupthink and leadership was a source of inspiration then and continues to be one today. Alexander George has been without equal as a source of intellectual and personal inspiration. His published works as well as his unselfish support of dozens of young scholars in many countries provide the standard for academics. Peg Hermann introduced us to the vast intellectual reservoirs of political psychology, where we have found great colleagues and collaborators such as Tom Preston, Bertjan Verbeek and Yaacov Vertzberger.

In the field of international relations, we have learned a great deal about crisis management from the classics by Ole Holsti, Michael Brecher and collaborators, and Richard Ned Lebow. In the field of disaster sociology, we draw heavily upon the work of Russell Dynes, Henry Quarantelli (who was kind enough to comment upon parts of this book), and their colleagues at the Disaster Research Center, University of Delaware. Our thinking about organizations and crises rests heavily on the work of Karl Weick, Charles Perrow, and the late Barry Turner. In recent years, we have enjoyed intellectual exchanges with Todd LaPorte and his colleagues of the so-called Berkeley Group of high reliability studies. We are particularly grateful to Paul Schulman for his cogent comments on an earlier version of this book. In the fields of public administration and public policy, our main beacons include the works of Yehezkel Dror, Richard Rose, and Aaron Wildavsky. Philip Selznick, Fred Greenstein, and Erwin Hargrove shaped our thinking on public leadership. We have found many kindred spirits in the emerging multidisciplinary European community of crisis studies, but we are especially grateful to Patrick Lagadec and Boris Porfiriev for enduring cooperation and friendship.

Martijn Groenleer, Sanneke Kuipers, Alan McConnell, and Mick Moran read the entire manuscript and saved us from many errors of all imaginable sorts. The anonymous reviewers provided us with constructive comments, which helped us shape our argument. Werner Overdijk advised us on the operational sides of crisis management. Noortje van Willegen and Wieteke Zwijnenberg skillfully dealt with footnotes and references.

We gratefully acknowledge the financial support we have received throughout the years. On the Dutch side, the main funders include the Dutch National Science Organization (NWO), the Royal Dutch Academy of Sciences (KNAW), and the Department of Public Administration of Leiden University. On the Swedish side, the Swedish National Defence College, the Swedish Emergency Management Agency (SEMA), and the Swedish Institute of International Affairs have been particularly supportive.

Finally, we express our gratitude to our students and colleagues. They have had to endure our peculiar fascination for understanding the inflamed politics of crisis and our periodic attempts to test our ideas on their working lives. They have offered us their analytical labours, their ideas, their patience, and often their critical comments. In the Netherlands, this goes for our close collaborators at the Department of Public Administration of Leiden University and at the Utrecht School of Governance. In Sweden, the same goes for our collaborators at the Department of Government of Uppsala University and particularly at CRISMART, the national center for crisis management research and training at the Swedish National Defence College in Stockholm. There are too many to mention here. We thank them all for their enthusiasm and skills in coping well with those minor office crises we may have induced. Finally, we thank John Haslam for his patience and professional support in seeing this book through publication.

Leiden, Utrecht, and Stockholm
Summer 2005

1   Crisis management in political systems: five leadership challenges

1.1   Crisis management and public leadership

Crises come in many shapes and forms. Conflicts, man-made accidents, and natural disasters chronically shatter the peace and order of societies. The new century has brought an upsurge of international terrorism, but also a creeping awareness of new types of contingencies – breakdowns in information and communication systems, emerging natural threats, and bio-nuclear terrorism – that lurk beyond the horizon.[1] At the same time, age-old threats (floods, earthquakes, and tsunamis) continue to expose the vulnerabilities of modern society.

In times of crisis, citizens look at their leaders: presidents and mayors, local politicians and elected administrators, public managers and top civil servants. We expect these policy makers to avert the threat or at least minimize the damage of the crisis at hand. They should lead us out of the crisis; they must explain what went wrong and convince us that it will not happen again.

This is an important set of tasks. Crisis management bears directly upon the lives of citizens and the wellbeing of societies. When emerging vulnerabilities and threats are adequately assessed and addressed, some potentially devastating contingencies simply do not happen. Misperception and negligence, however, allow crises to occur. When policy makers respond well to a crisis, the damage is limited; when they fail, the crisis impact increases. In extreme cases, crisis management makes the difference between life and death.

These are no easy tasks either. The management of a crisis is often a big, complex, and drawn-out operation, which involves many organizations, both public and private. The mass media continuously scrutinize and assess leaders and their leadership. It is in this context that policy makers must supervise operational aspects of the crisis management operation, communicate with stakeholders, discover what went wrong, account for their actions, initiate ways of improvement, and (re)establish a sense of normalcy. The notion "crisis management" as used in this book is therefore shorthand for a set of interrelated and extraordinary governance challenges. It provides an ultimate test for the resilience of political systems and their elites.

This is a book on public leadership in crisis management. It examines how public leaders deal with this essential and increasingly salient task of contemporary governance. It maps the manifold challenges they face in a crisis and identifies the pitfalls public leaders and public institutions encounter in their efforts to manage crises. To do so, we must "unpack" the notions of crisis and crisis management. In this introductory chapter, we begin this task by outlining our perspective on crisis management. First, we explain what we mean by the term "crisis." Then we argue that crises are ubiquitous phenomena that cannot be predicted with any kind of precision. Next, we outline our perspective on crisis leadership. Finally, we present five key leadership tasks in crisis management, which form the backbone of this book.

1.2   The nature of crisis

The term "crisis" frequently features in book titles, newspaper headlines, political discourse, and social conversation. It refers to an undesirable and unexpected situation: when we talk about crisis, we usually mean that something bad is to befall a person, group, organization, culture, society, or, when we think really big, the world at large. Something must be done, urgently, to make sure that this threat will not materialize.

In academic discourse, a crisis marks a phase of disorder in the seemingly normal development of a system.[2] An economic crisis, for instance, refers to an interval of decline in a long period of steady growth and development. A personal crisis denotes a period of turmoil, preceded and followed by mental stability. A revolution pertains to the abyss between dictatorial order and democratic order. Crises are transitional phases, during which the normal ways of operating no longer work.[3]

Most people experience such transitions as an urgent threat, which policy makers must address.[4] Our definition of crisis reflects its subjective nature as a construed threat: we speak of a crisis when policy makers experience "a serious threat to the basic structures or the fundamental values and norms of a system, which under time pressure and highly uncertain circumstances necessitates making vital decisions."[5]

Let us consider the three key components – threat, uncertainty, urgency – of this crisis definition in somewhat more detail. Crises occur when core values or life-sustaining systems of a community come under *threat*. Think of widely shared values such as safety and security, welfare and health, integrity and fairness, which become shaky or even meaningless as a result of (looming) violence, destruction, damage, or other forms of adversity. The more lives are governed by the value(s) under threat, the deeper the crisis goes. That explains why a looming natural disaster (flood, earthquake, hurricane, extreme heat or cold) never fails to evoke a deep sense of crisis: the threat of death, damage, destruction, or bodily mutilation clearly violates the deeply embedded values of safety and security for oneself and one's loved ones.

The threat of mass destruction is, of course, but one path to crisis.[6] A financial scandal in a large corporation may touch off a crisis in a society if it threatens the job security of many and undermines the trust in the economic system. In public organizations, a routine incident can trigger a crisis when media and elected leaders frame the incident as an indication of inherent flaws and threaten to withdraw their support for the organization. The anthrax scare and the Washington Beltway snipers caused the deaths of relatively few people, but these crises caused widespread fear among the public, which – in the context of the 9/11 events – was enough to virtually paralyze parts of the United States for weeks in a row.[7] In other words, a crisis does not automatically entail victims or damages.[8]

Crises typically and understandably induce a sense of *urgency*. Serious threats that do not pose immediate problems – think of climate change or future pension deficits – do not induce a widespread sense of crisis.[9] Some experts may be worried (and rightly so), but most policy makers do not lose sleep over problems with a horizon that exceeds their political life expectancy. Time compression is a defining element of crisis: the threat is here, it is real, and it must be dealt with as soon as possible (at least that's the way it is perceived).

Time compression is especially relevant for understanding leadership at the operational level, where decisions on matters of life and death must sometimes be made within a few hours, minutes, or even a split second. Think of the commander of the US cruiser *Vincennes* who had only a few minutes to decide whether the incoming aircraft was an enemy (Iranian) fighter or a non-responsive passenger plane – it tragically turned out to be the latter.[10] Leaders at the strategic level rarely experience this sense of extreme urgency, but their time horizon does become much shorter during crises.

In a crisis, the perception of threat is accompanied by a high degree of *uncertainty*. This uncertainty pertains both to the nature and the potential consequences of the threat: what is happening and how did it happen? What's next? How bad will it be? More importantly, uncertainty clouds the search for solutions: what can we do? What happens if we select this option? Uncertainty typically applies to other factors in the crisis process as well, such as people's initial and emergent responses to the crisis.

This definition of crisis enables us to study a wide variety of adversity: hurricanes and floods; earthquakes and tsunamis; financial meltdowns and surprise attacks; terrorist attacks and hostage takings; environmental threats and exploding factories; infrastructural dramas and organizational decline – there are many unimaginable threats that can turn leaders into crisis managers. What all these dramatic events have in common is the impossible conditions they create for leaders: managing the response operation and making urgent decisions while essential information about causes and consequences remains unavailable.

This is, of course, an academic shortcut on the way toward understanding crisis management. We know that in real life it is not always clear when exactly policy makers (who are they anyway?) experience a situation in terms of crisis. Some situations seem crystal clear, some are surely debatable. This fits our notion of crisis development: the definition of a situation in terms of crisis is the outcome of a political process. Certain situations "become" crises; they travel the continuum from the "no problem" pole to the "deep crisis" end (and back). In our choice of literature and examples, we have tried to err on the safe side: we have selected crisis cases that most informed readers would probably categorize (if they were asked to) as situations of combined societal threat, urgency, and uncertainty.

We are also aware that the management of crisis may depend on the type of threat. A traditional distinction is the one between natural and man-made disasters. Managing the impact of a tsunami (killing tens of thousands) or the explosion of a fireworks factory (killing ten) involves different activities as most of us can undoubtedly imagine. However, we claim that the strategic – as opposed to the tactical and operational – challenges for leaders in dealing with these threats are essentially the same: trying to prevent or at least minimize the impact of adversity, deal with the social and political consequences, and restore public faith in the future. In fact, we take our argument one step further: leaders can prepare for crises of the future – always different from past events – only if they learn from the variety of experiences they themselves and other leaders have had in other types of crisis.

1.3   The ubiquity of crisis

Disruptions of societal and political order are as old as life itself.[11] The Bible can be read as an introductory exposé of the frightening crises that have beset mankind. Western societies may have rooted out many of these adverse events, but most of the world still confronts these "old" crises on a daily basis. The costs of natural and man-made disasters continue to grow, while scenarios of future crises promise more mayhem.[12]

Crises will continue to challenge leaders for a simple reason: the disruptions that cause crises in our systems cannot be prevented. This bold assertion arises from recent thinking about the causes of crises. It is now clear to most people that crises are not due to bad luck or God's punishment.[13] Linear thinking ("big events must have big causes") has given way to a more subtle perspective that emphasizes the unintended consequences of increased complexity.[14] Crises, then, are the result of multiple causes, which interact over time to produce a threat with devastating potential.

This perspective is somewhat counterintuitive, as it defies the traditional logic of "triggers" and underlying causes. A common belief is that some set of factors "causes" a crisis. We then make a distinction between "external" and "internal" triggers. While this certainly facilitates conversation (both colloquial and academic), it would be more precise to speak of escalatory processes that undermine a social system's capacity to cope with disturbances. The agents of disturbance may come from anywhere – ranging from earthquakes to human errors – but the cause of the crisis lies in the inability of a system to deal with the disturbance.

An oft-debated question is whether modern systems have become increasingly vulnerable to breakdown. Contemporary systems typically experience fewer breakdowns, one might argue, as they have become much better equipped to deal with routine failures. Several "modern" features of society – hospitals, computers and telephones, fire trucks and universities, regulation and funds – have made some types of crisis that once were rather ubiquitous relatively rare. Others argue that the resilience of modern society has deteriorated: when a threat does materialize (say an electrical power outage), modern societies suffer disproportionally. The point is often made by students of natural disasters: modern society increases its vulnerability to disaster by building in places where history warns not to build.

The causes of crises thus seem to reside within the system: the causes typically remain unnoticed, or key policy makers fail to attend to them.[15] In the process leading up to a crisis, seemingly innocent factors combine and transform into disruptive forces that come to represent an undeniable threat to the system. These factors are sometimes referred to as pathogens, as they are typically present long before the crisis becomes manifest.[16]

The notion that crises are an unwanted by-product of complex systems has been popularized by Charles Perrow's (1984) analysis of the nuclear power incident at Three Mile Island and other disasters in technological systems.[17] Perrow describes how a relatively minor glitch in the plant was misunderstood in the control room. The plant operators initially thought they understood the problem and applied the required technical response. As they had misinterpreted the warning signal, the response worsened the problem. The increased threat baffled the operators (they could not understand why the problem persisted) and invited an urgent response. By again applying the "right" response to the wrong problem, the operators continued to exacerbate the problem. Only after a freshly arrived operator suggested the correct source of the problem did the crisis team manage – just barely – to stave off a disaster.

The very qualities of complex systems that drive progress lie at the heart of most if not all technological crises. As socio-technical systems become more complex and increasingly connected (tightly coupled) to other (sub)systems, their vulnerability for disturbances increases exponentially.[18] The more complex a system becomes, the harder it is for anyone to understand it in its entirety. Tight coupling between a system's component parts and with those of other systems allows for the rapid proliferation of interactions (and errors) throughout the system.

Complexity and lengthy chains of accident causation do not remain confined to the world of high-risk technology. Consider the world of global finance and the financial crises that have rattled it in recent years.[19] Globalization and ICT have tightly connected most world markets and financial systems. As a result, a minor problem in a seemingly isolated market can trigger a financial meltdown in markets on the other side of the globe. Structural vulnerabilities in relatively weak economies such as Russia, Argentina, or Turkey may suddenly "explode" on Wall Street and cause worldwide economic decline.

The same characteristics can be found in crises that beset low-tech environments such as prisons or sports stadiums. Urban riots, prison disturbances, and sports crowd disasters seem to start off with relatively minor incidents.[20] Upon closer inspection, however, it becomes clear that it is a similar mix of interrelated causes that produces major outbursts of this kind. In the case of prison disturbances, the interaction between guards and inmates is of particular relevance. Consider the 1990 riot that all but destroyed the Strangeways prison in Manchester (UK).[21] In the incubation period leading up to the riot, prison guards had to adapt their way of working in the face of budgetary pressure. This change in staff behavior was negatively interpreted by inmates, who began to challenge staff authority, which, in turn, generated anxiety and stress among staff. As staff began to act in an increasingly defensive and inconsistent manner, prisoners became more frustrated with staff behavior. A reiterative, self-reinforcing pattern of changing behavior and staff–prisoner conflict set the stage for a riot. A small incident started the riot, which in turn touched off a string of disturbances in other prisons.[22] Many civil disturbances between protestors and police unfold according to the same pattern.[23]

Non-linear dynamics and complexity make a crisis hard to detect. As complex systems cannot be simply understood, it is hard to qualify the manifold activities and processes that take place in these systems.[24] Growing vulnerabilities go unrecognized and ineffective attempts to deal with seemingly minor disturbances continue. The system thus "fuels" the lurking crisis.[25] Only a minor "trigger" is needed to initiate a destructive cycle of escalation, which may then rapidly spread throughout the system. Crises may have their roots far away (in a geographical sense) but rapidly snowball through the global networks, jumping from one system to another, gathering destructive potential along the way.

Is it really impossible to predict crises? Generally speaking, yes. There is no clear "moment X" and "factor Y" that can be pinpointed as *the* root of the problem. Quite sophisticated early-warning systems exist in certain areas, such as hurricane and flood prediction, and some pioneering efforts are under way to develop early-warning models for ethnic and international conflict.[26] These systems may constitute the best available shot at crisis prediction, but they are far from flawless. They cannot predict exactly when and where a hurricane or flash flood will emerge. In fact, the systems in place can be dangerously wrong.

All this explains why some of the most notorious crises of our times were completely missed by those in charge. As the crisis process begins to unfold, policy makers often do not see anything out of the ordinary. Everything is still in place, even though hidden interactions eat away at the pillars of the system. It is only when the crisis is in full swing and becomes manifest that policy makers can recognize it for what it is. There are many reasons for this apparent lack of foresight, which we will discuss in Chapter 2.

1.4 Crisis management: leadership perspectives

Crises that beset the public domain – this may happen at the local, regional, national, or transnational level – are occasions for public leadership. Citizens whose lives are affected by critical contingencies expect governments and public agencies to do their utmost to keep them out of harm's way. They expect the people in charge to make critical decisions and provide direction even in the most difficult circumstances. So do the journalists who produce the stories that help to shape the crisis in the minds of the public. And so do members of parliament, public interest groups, institutional watchdogs, and other voices on the political stage that monitor and influence the behavior of leaders.

However misplaced, unfair, or illusory these expectations may be, it hardly matters. These expectations are real in their political consequences. When events or episodes are widely experienced as a crisis, leadership is expected. If incumbent elites fail to step forward, others might well seize the opportunity to fill the gap.

In this book, we confine ourselves to crisis management in democratic settings. The embedded norms and institutional characteristics of liberal democracies markedly constrain the range of responses that public leaders can consider and implement. Many crises could be terminated relatively quickly when governments can simply "write off" certain people, groups, or territories, or when they can deal with threats regardless of the human costs or moral implications of their actions. In countries with a free press, a rule of law, political opposition, and a solid accountability structure this is not possible.

In a liberal democracy, public leaders must manage a crisis in the context of a delicate political, legal, and moral order that forces them to trade off considerations of effectiveness and efficiency against other embedded values – something leaders of non-democracies do not have to worry about as much.[27]

If crisis management was hard, it is only getting harder. The democratic context has changed over the past decades. Analysts agree, for instance, that citizens and politicians alike have become at once more fearful and less tolerant of major hazards to public health, safety, and prosperity. The modern Western citizen has little patience for imperfections; he has come to fear glitches and has learned to see more of what he fears. In this culture of fear – sometimes referred to as the "risk society" – the role of the modern mass media is crucial.[28]

A crisis sets in motion extensive follow-up reporting, investigations by political forums, as well as civil and criminal juridical proceedings. It is not uncommon for public officials and agencies to be singled out as the responsible actors for prevention, preparedness, and response in the crisis at hand. The crisis aftermath then turns into a morality play. Leaders must defend themselves against seemingly incontrovertible evidence of their incompetence, ignorance, or insensitivity. When their strategies fail, they come under severe pressure to atone for past sins. If they refuse to bow, the crisis will not end (at least not any time soon).

This study aims to capture what leadership in crises entails. We are interested to learn how public leaders seek to protect their society from adversity, how they prepare for and cope with crises. To organize our inquiry, we define leadership as a set of strategic tasks that encompasses all activities associated with the stages of crisis management.[29]

This perspective does not presume that these tasks are exclusively reserved for leaders only. On the contrary: these tasks are often performed throughout the crisis response network. In fact, during a crisis one may find situational leadership, which diverges from regular, formal leadership arrangements. We do believe, however, that the formal leaders carry a special responsibility for making sure that these tasks – which we specify in the following section – are properly addressed and executed (if not by the leaders then by others).

We do not wish to suggest that the performance of a set of tasks will provide fool-proof relief from crises (of whatever kind). This would be both a presumptuous claim and one-sidedly instrumental. It would deny the pivotal, yet highly volatile and complex political dimension of crises and crisis management.[30] In all fairness, one could criticize the field of crisis management studies for its overtly instrumental orientation. There is a large and fast-growing pile of self-help, how-to books that promise to make organizations crisis free.

Our book is an attempt to redress this imbalance. We view crisis management not just in terms of the coping capacity of governmental institutions and public policies but first and foremost as a deeply controversial and intensely political activity. We want to find out what crises "do" to established political and organizational orders; we seek to understand how crisis leadership contributes to defending, destroying, or renovating these orders. The distinctive contribution we seek to make is to highlight the political dimensions of crisis leadership: issues of conflict, power, and legitimacy.[31]

We thus use a more task-related than person-related perspective on crisis leadership. In general discourse, leaders are often seen as the personification of leadership. This is the myth of the "great" leader, which pervades so many efforts to understand both great accomplishments and massive failures. In this book we talk loosely of policy makers and leaders, but we concentrate on the efforts of all those holding high offices and strategic positions from which public leadership functions can be performed. Hence our "sample" of leaders includes presidents, prime ministers, cabinet ministers, senior civil servants, and public managers. We agree that charismatic bonds between leaders and followers, and personal idiosyncracies of policy makers may be important to explain how certain leadership tasks are fulfilled, but we are more interested to see how the performance of these tasks relates to the crisis outcome.[32]

The adjective "strategic" is important here: we study the overall direction of crisis responses and the political process surrounding these responses. This book is not about operational commanders and their leadership predicaments, however important these have proven to be in resolving various types of crisis. Moreover, we only touch upon the more technical activities of the comprehensive crisis management continuum (such as risk assessment or the use of tort law).[33] Let us now turn to the key challenges of crisis leadership.

1.5   Leadership in crisis: five critical tasks

The normative assumption underlying our approach is that public leaders have a special responsibility to help safeguard society from the adverse consequences of crisis. Leaders who take this responsibility seriously would have to concern themselves with all crisis phases: the incubation stage, the onset, and the aftermath. In practice, policy makers have defined the activities of crisis management in accordance with these stages – they talk about prevention, mitigation, critical decision making, and a return to normalcy. We stick closely to this phase model of crisis management, but we have slightly adapted it to account for the political perspective used in this book.

Crisis leadership then involves five critical tasks: sense making, decision making, meaning making, terminating, and learning. We devote one chapter to each of these tasks. We present our reading of the relevant literature, including some of our own research, on each of these areas of crisis management. Each chapter is organized to illustrate a central claim that we hope to defend persuasively, sometimes defying conventional wisdom and common practice.

Sense making

The acute crisis phase seems to pose a straightforward challenge: once a crisis becomes manifest, public leadership must take measures to deal with the consequences. Reality is much more complex, however. Most crises do not materialize with a big bang; they are the product of escalation. Policy makers must recognize from vague, ambivalent, and contradictory signals that something out of the ordinary is developing. The critical nature of these developments is not self-evident; policy makers have to "make sense" of them.[34]

Leaders must appraise the threat and decide what the crisis is about. However penetrating the events that trigger a crisis – jet planes hitting skyscrapers, thousands of people found dead in mass graves – a uniform picture of the events rarely emerges: do they constitute a tragedy, an outrage, perhaps a punishment, or, inconceivably, a blessing in disguise? Leaders will have to determine how threatening the events are, to what or whom, what their operational and strategic parameters are, and how the situation will develop in the period to come. Signals come from all kinds of sources: some loud, some soft, some accurate, some widely off the mark. But how to tell which is which? How to distill cogent signals from the noise of crisis?

In Chapter 2 we describe and analyze the sense making process in crises. We explain that crises are hard to detect in their early phases. Once they have become manifest, however, it is possible for policy makers and their organizations to construct reliable representations of crisis realities.

Decision making

Crises leave governments and public agencies with pressing issues to be addressed. These can be of many kinds. The needs and problems triggered by the onset of crisis may be so great that the scarce resources available will have to be prioritized. This is much like politics as usual except that in crisis circumstances the disparities between demand and supply of public resources are much bigger, the situation remains un-clear and volatile, and the time to think, consult, and gain acceptance for decisions is highly restricted. Crises force governments and leaders to confront issues they do not face on a daily basis, for example concerning the deployment of the military, the use of lethal force, or the radical restriction of civil liberties.

The classic example of crisis decision making was the Cuba Missile Crisis (1963), during which United States President John F. Kennedy was presented with pictures of Soviet missile installations under construction in Cuba. The photos conveyed a geostrategic reality in the making that Kennedy considered unacceptable, and it was up to him to decide what to do about it. Whatever his choice from the options presented to him by his advisers – an air strike, an invasion of Cuba, a naval blockade – and however hard it was to predict the exact consequences, one thing seemed certain: the final decision would have a momentous impact on Soviet-American relations and possibly on world peace. Crisis decision making is making hard calls, which involve tough value tradeoffs and major political risks.[35]

An effective response also requires interagency and intergovernmental coordination. After all, each decision must be implemented by a set of organizations; only when these organizations work together is there a chance that effective implementation will happen. Getting public bureaucracies to adapt to crisis circumstances is a daunting – some say impossible – task in itself. Most public organizations have been designed to conduct routine business that answers to values such as fairness, lawfulness, and efficiency. The management of crisis, however, requires flexibility, improvisation, redundancy, and the breaking of rules.

Effective crisis responses also require coordination of the many different groups or agencies involved in the implementation of crisis decisions; these organizations are all under pressure to adapt rapidly and effectively. Coordination is pivotal to prevent miscommunication, unnecessary overlap, and conflicts between agencies and actors involved in crisis operations. Coordination is not a self-evident feature of crisis management operations. The question of who is in charge typically arouses great passions. In disaster studies, the "battle of the Samaritans" is a well-documented phenomenon: agencies representing different technologies of crisis coping find it difficult to align their actions. Moreover, a crisis does not make the public suddenly "forget" the sensitivities and conflicts that governed the daily relations between authorities and others in fairly recent times.

In Chapter 3 we argue that time and again crisis leaders experience how difficult it is to retain control over the course of events. We show that the crisis response is not determined only by crucial leadership decisions but, to a considerable extent, also by the institutional context in which crisis decision making and implementation take place.

Meaning making

A crisis generates a strong demand from citizens to know what is going on and to ascertain what they can do to protect their interests. Authorities often cannot provide correct information right away. They struggle with the mountains of raw data (reports, rumors, pictures) that quickly amass when something extraordinary happens. Turning them into a coherent picture of the situation is a major challenge by itself. Getting it out to the public in the form of accurate, clear, and actionable information requires a major communication effort. This effort is often hindered by the aroused state of the audience: people whose lives are deeply affected are anxious if not stressed. Moreover, they do not necessarily see the government as their ally. And pre-existing distrust of government does not evaporate in times of crisis.

In a crisis, leaders are expected to reduce uncertainty and provide an authoritative account of what is going on, why it is happening, and what needs to be done. When they have made sense of the events and have arrived at some sort of situational appraisal and made strategic policy choices, leaders must get others to accept their definition of the situation. They must impute "meaning" to the unfolding crisis in such a way that their efforts to manage it are enhanced. If they don't, or if they do not succeed at it, their decisions will not be understood or respected. If other actors in the crisis succeed in dominating the meaning-making process, the ability of incumbent leaders to decide and maneuver is severely constrained.

To this end, leaders are challenged to present a compelling story that describes what the crisis is about: what is at stake, what are its causes, what can be done. Whatever one might think about his subsequent policies, there is no disputing that President George W. Bush was effective in framing the meaning of the September 11 attacks to the American public and to the world. This appears all the more true when we compare Bush with his Spanish counterpart José María Aznar who, after the March 2004 attack in Madrid, hastily tried to pin it down as yet another ETA atrocity. He failed miserably – a few days after the attack an outraged electorate voted his party out of power.

Leaders are not the only ones trying to frame the crisis. News organizations use many different sources and angles in their frenetic attempts at fact-finding and interpretation. Among this cacophony of voices and sentiments, leaders seek to achieve and maintain some degree of control over the images of the crisis that circulate in the public domain. Their messages coincide and compete with those of other parties, who hold other positions and interests, who are likely to espouse various alternative definitions of the situation and advocate different courses of action. Censoring them is hardly a viable option in a democracy.

In Chapter 4 we examine the meaning-making process. We argue that leadership credibility enhances the quality of the crisis response and increases the chances of political survival in the post-crisis phase. But leaders cannot depend on their credibility. They must excel in crisis communication if they want to reduce the public and political uncertainty that crises cause.

Terminating

Governments – at least democratic ones – cannot afford to stay in crisis mode for ever. A sense of normalcy will have to return sooner or later. It is a critical leadership task to make sure that this happens in a timely and expedient fashion.

Crisis termination is two-fold. It is about shifting back from emergency to routine. This requires some form of downsizing of crisis operations. At the strategic level, it also requires rendering account for what has happened and gaining acceptance for this account. These two aspects of crisis termination are distinct, but in practice often closely intertwined. The system of governance – its rules, its organizations, its power-holders – has to be (re)stabilized; it must regain the necessary legitimacy to perform its usual functions. Leaders cannot bring this about by unilateral decree, even if they may possess the formal mandate to initiate and terminate crises in a legal sense (by declaring a state of disaster or by evoking martial law). Formal termination gestures can follow but never lead the mood of a community. Premature closure may even backfire: allegations of underestimation and cover-up are quick to emerge in an opinion climate that is still on edge.

Political accountability is a key institutional practice in the crisis-termination game. The burden of proof in accountability discussions lies with leaders: they must establish beyond doubt that they cannot be held responsible for the occurrence or escalation of a crisis. These accountability debates can easily degenerate into "blame games" with a focus on identifying and punishing "culprits" rather than discursive reflection about the full range of causes and consequences.[36] The challenge for leaders is to cope with the politics of crisis accountability without resorting to undignified and potentially self-defeating defensive tactics of blame avoidance that serve only to prolong the crisis by transforming it into a political confrontation at knife's edge.

In Chapter 5, we argue that crisis termination depends on the way leaders deal with these accountability processes. We also show that in these accountability processes leaders are at best only partially in control of their political fate, let alone over the evolution of the crisis as a whole.

Learning

A final strategic leadership task in crisis management is political and organizational lesson drawing. The crisis experience offers a reservoir of potential lessons for contingency planning and training for future crises. We would expect all those involved to study these lessons and feed them back into organizational practices, policies, and laws.

Again, reality is a bit messier. In fact, it turns out that lesson drawing is one of the most underdeveloped aspects of crisis management. In addition to cognitive and institutional barriers to learning, lesson drawing is constrained by the role of these lessons in determining the impact that crises have on a society. Crises become part of collective memory, a source of historical analogies for future leaders. The political depiction of crisis as a product of prevention and foresight failures would force people to rethink the assumptions on which pre-existing policies and rule systems rested. Other stakeholders in the game of crisis-induced lesson-drawing might seize upon the lessons to advocate measures and policy reforms that incumbent leaders reject. Leaders thus have a big stake in steering the lesson-drawing process in the political and bureaucratic arenas. The crucial challenge here is to achieve a dominant influence on the feedback stream that crises generate into pre-existing policy networks and public organizations.

The documentation of these inhibiting complexities has done nothing to dispel the near-utopian belief in crisis *opportunities* that is found not only in academic literature but also in popular wisdom. A crisis is seen as a good time to clean up and start anew. Crises then represent discontinuities that must be seized upon – a true test of leadership, the experts claim. So most people are not surprised to see sweeping reforms in the wake of crisis: that will never happen again! They intuitively distrust leaders who claim bad luck and point out that their organizations and policies have a great track record.

In Chapter 6, we reject the thesis that prescribes structural reforms in the wake of crisis. In fact, we posit the claim that crisis response, lesson-drawing, and reform craft (the repertoire of skills and strategies that leaders use to make reform work) typically imply orientations and strategies that are fundamentally at odds with each other.

Toward policy advice

At the end of this study, in Chapter 7, we move from our primarily descriptive and interpretive aims and discourse into a more prescriptive mode. We present lessons for crisis leadership conveying the practical implications of our central claims. Together these lessons constitute an agenda for improving public leadership in crises that we hope will reach, inspire, and provoke those who govern us.

Notes

1 See, for instance, Rosenthal, Boin, and Comfort (2001); OECD (2003); Sundelius and Grönvall (2004).
2 See, for instance, Almond, Flanagan, and Mundt (1973); Linz and Stepan (1978); Tilly and Stinchcombe (1997).

3 The core idea of the interdisciplinary subfield of crisis studies is that in a crisis the modus operandi of a political system or community differs markedly from the functioning in normal times. This assumption is, of course, more tenable in highly stable systems (Rosenthal, 1978).

4 A brief period of spectacular growth may be a transition, but it is usually considered a boon rather than a crisis.

5 Rosenthal, Charles, and t' Hart (1989: 10). See also Stern (2003).

6 A threat does not have to materialize before it becomes widely seen as one. The often-cited Thomas Theorem teaches us that it is the perception that makes a threat real in its consequences (Thomas and Thomas, 1928).

7 See Kettl (2004) for an analysis of this period.

8 The use of the term "disaster" usually does presuppose damage, death, and destruction (see Boin, 2005; Smith, 2005).

9 So-called creeping crises, notably long-term environmental crises such as desertification and deforestation, soil salination and fertilizer use, global warming and the rise of the sea level, constitute a particularly interesting category of complex problems with a high crisis potential.

10 See Flin (1996) and Flin and Arbuthnot (2002) for informed treatises on operational leadership.

11 For an overview of natural disasters see Keys (1999).

12 Recent scenarios feature radical weather changes, biological terrorism, and asteroid collisions. See Pentagon weather scenarios (Schwartz and Randall, 2003); OECD crisis scenarios (2003); for a clear overview of climate contingencies, see Bryson (2003).

13 See Bovens and 't Hart (1996); Quarantelli (1998); Rosenthal (1998); Steinberg (2000). This understanding has become widespread even outside the academic community. See, for instance, the introduction to the Report of the Columbia Accident Investigation Board (2003).

14 See Buchanan (2000). Not all academic fields show this development. It is interesting to note that the long-standing adherence to linear thinking in the international relations (IR) field correlates with a long history of failed early-warning systems (Jervis, 1997; Bernstein et al., 2000).

15 Turner and Pidgeon (1997).

16 Reason (1990).

17 Perrow (1984).

18 See Turner (1978) and Perrow (1994).

19 For an excellent introduction, see Eichengreen (2002).

20 Useem and Kimball (1989).

21 This example is taken from Boin and Rattray (2004). For an application of Perrow's theory to a stadium crowd disaster, see Jacobs and 't Hart (1992).

22 Similar dynamics of destructive escalation have marked the incubation phases of corporate and organizational crises. Examples in 2004–5 included the troubles at Shell and the BBC.

23 For a classic statement, see Smelser (1962). More recent contributions include Waddington (1992) and Goldstone and Useem (1999).

24 The laws of complex systems are still largely unknown. And the more we learn about the behavior of complex systems, the less we seem to understand. Complexity theorists are busy uncovering the hidden patterns that they say

underlie this process, but practical insights (for our purposes at least) have yet to emerge. For an introduction see Buchanan (2000).

25 See f.i. Rijpma (1997) who argues that redundancy – an often-prescribed tool to help prevent incidents – may actually help cause them.

26 The internet is a great resource for tracing the many systems that are now in operation, partly run by non-government organizations (NGOs), partly by specialized academics, partly by commercial organizations catering to business investor audiences. See www.reliefweb.int/resources/ewarn.html, which is a pivotal portal in this regard.

27 One may, of course, ask whether some of the crisis responses in Western democracies – counterterrorism policies in the 1970s and in the wake of the 9/11 events come to mind – do not amount to what Juan Linz (1978) once called "an abdication of democratic authenticity" (e.g. an expansion of feasibility boundaries at the price of sacrificing values of democratic rule).

28 Beck (1992).

29 Pioneering works in this tradition include Barnard (1938), Selznick (1957), and Wilson (1989).

30 The dangers of a functional approach in studying society, politics, and their crises have been discussed extensively. Binder et al. (1971) and Almond, Flanagan, Mundt (1973) are key examples of the tradition. For a recent revivalist interpretation of functionalism, see Wilson (2002).

31 Developed further in 't Hart (1993). See also Habermas (1975); Edelman (1977); Linz and Stepan (1978); Turner (1978).

32 There is a large field of leadership studies in which the relation between personal characteristics and task fulfillment receives ample attention. A classic account is MacGregor Burns (1978). A good introduction to the entire literature is Northouse (2001).

33 For strategic leadership issues in risk assessment and crisis prevention, see among others Wildavsky (1988); Wildavsky (1995); and Meltsner (1990).

34 A classic point made by Edelman (1977).

35 Brecher (1980); Janis (1989).

36 Although much more pronounced today, the tendency to search for culprits following the occurrence of disaster and crisis is age-old – see Drabek and Quarantelli (1967) as well as Douglas (1992).

2   Sense making: grasping crises as they unfold

2.1   What the hell is going on?

The 9/11 terrorist strike took America (and the rest of the world) by complete surprise. As the drama unfolded live on television screens across the globe, people found themselves watching in disbelief: "This cannot be happening." This sense of collective stress soon gave rise to a pressing question, one that lingers on as we write this: how could this have happened?[1]

In hindsight, this question is less baffling than it seemed at the time. Commentators across the world were quick to point out that the United States had finally experienced on its own soil what many other countries had been forced to deal with for many years – terrorism. Outside the United States one would read and hear that American foreign policy had bred anti-Americanism; terrorist actions therefore were more or less to be expected. In the American media, Pearl Harbor analogies gave way to retrospectives of the 1993 World Trade Center bombing and the foiled plots involving exploding airliners and airport attacks. The 9/11 crisis events were shown to have roots.[2]

Americans then learned how the 19 terrorists had pulled it off: how they had entered the country and outlived visa requirements, took flight lessons, convened with other terrorists around the globe, walked through airport security armed with knives, and how they navigated their hijacked planes unhindered toward the unguarded core institutions of the country. Americans learned that foreign intelligence services had provided their American sister organizations with ominous and rather specific warnings. They learned that FBI agents had developed a keen interest in the flight activities of at least a few prospective terrorists, apparently failing to grasp the urgency of the situation. They learned in graphic and ever more forthcoming detail how their intelligence services had refused to share crucial information with sister agencies – as they had done before in other trying cases – thus failing to piece together the puzzle of this crisis to come. The revelations gave birth to a painful question: could the 9/11 strikes have been prevented through early recognition of the impending threat?

This question is asked after every crisis. Whether it is a prison riot or a terrorist act, a natural disaster or an international conflict, an environmental contingency or an economic crisis – hindsight knowledge always seems to reveal strong signals of the impending crisis. If this is true, and this is our *key question*, why do policy makers generally fail to see crises coming?

To understand why crises continue to surprise us, think of them in terms of disease.[3] It begins with a vulnerable state of the body, which may be induced by hereditary factors or the result of unhealthy behavior. The incubation phase sets in when pathogens proliferate and make themselves at home. When they reach a certain threshold, the pathogens overtake the body's defense system and make the patient feel sick. The disease is now manifest and the battle for recovery, or survival, can begin. A crisis follows a similar pattern of development.

This analogy helps us argue our *core claim*, which consists of two major points. First, it is virtually impossible to predict with any sort of precision when and where a crisis will strike. Occasional "check-ups" may help to spot emerging vulnerabilities before it is too late. It would be much better, of course, to do more systematic check-ups, but these tend to be quite expensive. Most policy makers are either unable or unwilling to pay these costs. Incubation processes thus remain latent and undiscovered.

Second, we argue that it is possible to grasp the dynamics of a crisis once it becomes manifest and unfolds. It is also easy to get it wrong. Policy makers are easily caught in a cross-fire between conflicting proverbs: "look before you leap" versus "he who hesitates is lost." The difference between triumph and tragedy hinges upon the ability to produce and revise adequate (i.e., plausible, reasonable, coherent, actionable, justifiable) assessments of highly unusual, ambiguous, and dynamic situations.[4] Sections 2.3, 2.4, and 2.5 explain why some crisis leaders quickly understand what is going on, whereas others experience great difficulties in "reading" a crisis as it develops.

2.2   Barriers to crisis recognition: organizational limitations

The driving mechanisms of crisis are often concealed behind (and embedded within) the complexities of our modern systems. Timely crisis recognition, then, depends crucially on both the capacity of individuals operating (parts of) these systems (we call them operators) and the organizational "designs" for early crisis detection. The research findings are quite sobering: most individuals and organizations are ill equipped to detect impending crises. Many public organizations lack so-called "reliability experts": professionals with a well-developed antenna for detecting and coping intelligently with latent safety and security threats.[5]

Operators often fail to observe that their system is failing. This is partly due to system characteristics, as Perrow has shown.[6] Destructive interactions between components are shielded by the complex technology of these systems. The tight coupling between components allows for a rapid proliferation of destructive interactions throughout the system. However, problems of inadequate error detection are also due to pervasive human tendencies in dealing with ill-structured problems. It turns out that humans have developed a surprising ability to explain aberrations in such a way that they conform to their established way of thinking (see further below). Most people have great trouble thinking "out of the box," yet this is precisely what is needed to detect impending crises.

To a large extent, what goes for individuals also goes for the organizations and institutions in which they tend to be embedded. Research shows that even in the most simple incubation processes with few factors, interacting according to standard patterns and taking a long lead time, the organizations involved were unable to detect the impending disaster. Below we discuss the three main reasons why organizations (and, by implication, governments) often fail to generate, interpret, and share information that is essential for effective crisis recognition.

Many organizations are not designed to look for trouble

Many organizations – public and private – do not spend a great deal of time and resources on the detection of potential crises. The reason is simple: they were never designed to detect crises in the making.[7] Aside from the relatively limited number of highly specialized safety and security organizations, most public agencies define effectiveness in terms of conditions to be sought rather than in terms of conditions to be avoided. These organizations seek to achieve certain politically articulated goals (make the trains run on time; provide housing for the poor; bring literacy up to 100 percent; strengthen industrial competitiveness; put a man on the moon). They are generally less well primed and evaluated to prevent certain things from happening, other than the procedural (moral, legal, financial) constraints under which they operate. This preoccupation with achievement rather than avoidance has implications for the capacity to detect crises.

Organizations engage in "problemistic search."[8] This means that they scan their environment and seek feedback only on the goals they must achieve and the day-to-day risks they have learned to recognize. But they rarely look for information that may suggest that the world is about to take a state they wish to avoid. They are simply not equipped to collect data that require them to look beyond the confines of their mandates. Their information systems are designed to provide standardized feedback on goal achievement. Clearly, to generate the desired feedback is quite a challenge in itself. By all accounts, many public and quite a few private organizations (as recent scandals in the corporate world have revealed) have a hard time producing the most basic financial data and feedback on their performance.[9] Moreover, many public organizations find it exceedingly difficult to translate their vague and complex goals into quantifiable output measures. As a result, it is hard to obtain an adequate picture of their routine performance, let alone the capacity to detect performance gaps and problems before they become critical.[10]

The detection of crisis would require the collection of data on aberrant, hitherto unknown events and patterns that may develop into a threat. However, most modern organizations do not collect this type of data. They subscribe to rational methods of data collection that tell managers about goal achievement. In the formal world of organizational decision making there is little room for the kind of intuition and "gut feeling" that may facilitate coincidental detection of emerging threats.[11] Expensive decision-support systems drive the search for data and reify the preferred self-image of the organization as a rational entity.[12] There is no room for seemingly intuitive or randomized scans of the environment to see whether there is "something out there." To compound the problem, in their drive to become efficient, public organizations have increasingly adopted "business solutions" and eliminated the seemingly redundant boundary-spanning agents that once were the informal antennas of government.[13]

Variable disjunction of information and the politics of organization

Paradoxically, research suggests that many of the clues needed to detect a crisis in the making are usually available somewhere within the organizations that are responsible for preventing the disasters they encounter.[14] But the policy makers at the top of these organizations just cannot put together the pieces of the crisis puzzle before it is too late. This happens, for example, because the signals come into very different corners of the system that do not share information or, when they do, speak different languages. Even if a more composite threat picture emerges in the organization, this does not always make it to the top-level policy makers. Nor are these policy makers always interested in listening to and acting upon warnings that lack certainty and specificity. The inquiry into the 9/11 attacks provides a textbook example of these vulnerabilities. It now appears that various field agents and regional offices of the FBI were sitting on information that by itself did not reveal anything, but, when pieced together with CIA information, could have alerted the authorities in time.

Investigations of other crises and disasters tell similar tales.[15] Time and again organizations are shown to have failed in turning the available data into usable information. This problem of collective negligence flows from the normal characteristics of complex organizations.[16] The sheer size of modern organizations and the number of people they employ means it requires a concerted effort to bring data together. At the same time, the very circumstances that necessitate these efforts conspire against them being successful.

High-quality intelligence – data about the environment that have been integrated into a coherent story – is a scarce resource in complex organizations for a variety of well-known reasons.[17] Two stand out. The primary reason is that the people in these organizations rarely agree on what the data are telling them and what they mean for the organization or domain(s) for which they bear responsibility. A timely assessment demands a certain critical mass of competent people who share cogent ideas about what is important and what is not. Many large-scale organizations – certainly in the public sector – lack a common frame that specifies vulnerabilities and prescribes a way of recognizing their development. There are good reasons why complex organizations harbor different subcultures, but the result is the collective blind spots that post-crisis inquiries so often unearth.

The obvious result of this particular organizational characteristic is that the interpretation of data becomes the subject of a political process. Interpreting the data and weighing the evidence is informed by bureaucratic pulling and hauling within and between public agencies: different values and a variety of group interests come into play. Where one stands depends on where one sits. A certain degree of bureaucratic politics is usually quite healthy for an organization. It is, after all, excessive homogeneity and conformity among policy makers that make it hard to interpret data in a new light, which is often necessary if one is to realistically detect and appraise newly emerging threats.[18] However, unrestrained intra-organizational strife and too little meaningful communication ultimately produce a similarly debilitating effect: information and analysis are no longer treated as representations of some external reality but primarily become seen as bargaining levers and weapons in ongoing intra-governmental struggles. As a result, information gets filtered, watered down, distorted, polished, or squeezed under the table for reasons wholly unrelated to the situation at hand.[19]

This brings us to the second reason that explains the scarcity of high-quality intelligence on impending crises: the absence of mechanisms that facilitate rapid sense making within governments. Whether or not such mechanisms emerge spontaneously or require intelligent design remains unclear. Yet it is clearly a leadership responsibility to bring about such mechanisms.[20] It appears that few organizations – public or private – have these mechanisms for collective sense making in place. As a consequence, policy makers may get bogged down in internal warfare over the nature and scope of the impending threat, thus creating an image of paralysis and ineffectiveness.

All this becomes infinitely more complex when multiple organizations are involved in the sense-making process. This is, of course, the rule rather than the exception. If there are data that can be interpreted as a warning of a crisis to come, those data are usually scattered across various organizations (such as the FBI and the CIA). Inter-organizational politics and rivalry flow naturally from organizational interests, which in turn are based on values, missions, considerations of turf and autonomy, political masters – to list but a few factors.[21] These factors tax the interaction and cooperation on routine issues; the high-stakes context of potential crisis does not necessarily improve things. Some organizations may elect to divorce themselves from any impending threat, as they fear that their actions will invite blame and will make the organization vulnerable to long-dragging accountability processes. Other organizations may seek to define the problem at hand in such a way that the organization will actually benefit from the crisis. The chances of a collectively shared assessment thus remain rather low.

Cognitive blinders and the perversity of intelligent design

Some organizations suffer from what we call here the perverse effects of rational design. Modern organizations in Western society are to a large extent informed by considerations of rational design. The more rational and efficient these organizations become, the better they are at translating executive orders into administrative output. But technical glitches and individual mistakes travel just as fast through the streamlined organization.[22] Just as viruses thrive on healthy hosts, the destructive interaction between common pathogens is enhanced by the rational, "lean" organization.

It is precisely the most modern organizations that deal with high technology and have a sense of vulnerability that are most likely to design early-warning mechanisms for crises. They typically do so in rational-scientific ways. Risks are calculated, possible pathways of failure are mapped, and elaborate procedures are developed to detect deviant patterns that could lead to failure and crises. But however elaborate these scenarios and mechanisms may turn out to be, two factors are likely to thwart these efforts.

First, a rational-scientific approach to identifying contingencies inevitably leads to what may be termed the "normalization of risk." Organizations create a false sense of security by describing the possible causes of crises, mapping the pathways toward failure, and assigning a quantified risk factor to each scenario. If the risk is small enough, it becomes acceptable. It also becomes neglected, as people tend to forget that risks – however small – can and do materialize. It is often true that much must go wrong before a crisis occurs, but sometimes it does.[23] The normalization of risk may lead to the often-found notion that "it won't happen around here."

Regulatory public agencies, which are supposedly designed to look for risks and vulnerabilities in the industries they oversee, may reinforce this normalization tendency in several ways. They tend to uncover shortcomings in the rational-scientific approach to risks, thus furthering an organizational investment in the methodology. Some regulatory agencies are "captured" by commercially expedient, reassuring myths concerning the state of risk prevention and mitigation in particular systems.[24] Sometimes they simply act incredulously when the worst-case scenario does materialize after all. For example, when the American airline ValuJet had one of its planes crash in the Florida Everglades, the Department of Transportation Secretary went on television saying, "I have flown Valu-Jet. ValuJet is a safe airline, as is our entire aviation system." And then, tellingly, he added: "If ValuJet was unsafe, we would have grounded it." (Meanwhile the department's Inspector General, an independent official, flatly contradicted the Secretary by disclosing statistics from the Federal Aviation Authority that ValuJet's safety record was 14 times as poor as that of other discount airlines and added, "I would not fly ValuJet.")[25]

This normalization tendency assumes absurd proportions in some of the plans that prepare American organizations for nuclear holocaust. In what Lee Clarke has dubbed "fantasy documents," authorities promise that all will be well, come Armageddon.[26] The plan of the US postal service to ensure mail delivery is especially instructive in this regard: it demonstrates that risks can be normalized to a point where they become irrelevant. This unbridled optimism may actually escalate risk by giving policy makers a false sense of their coping capacities.

Second, the very procedures of deductive reasoning and bureaucratic interaction that may help to detect the development of known risks may also create blinders for recognizing unknown risks. By creating a strongly developed framework that facilitates the rapid interpretation of certain types of crises, the unforeseen and unimagined crises are "left" to chance detections. But a rational-scientific way of sense making for chance detections does not allow for "unscientific" reasoning with regard to crisis recognition. In an organization that works hard to detect crises before they cause trouble, early signals of impending crises may be simply put aside. Efforts of crisis detection may thus become part of an escalatory process that spins the crisis wheel.

Both factors feature prominently in the analysis of NASA and the explosion of the *Challenger* (1986).[27] NASA had developed an elaborate safety system that ran on engineering logic: every decision with regard to every aspect of space shuttle safety was based on facts, rational thinking, tests, experience, and engineering science.[28] When engineers of subcontractor Thiokol feared that the forecasted cold in the night before the January 29, 1986 launch would undermine the resilience of a crucial part (the O-rings), they recommended a delay. Knowing that NASA required hard proof rather than gut feeling, the Thiokol engineers hastily put together a rationale for delay, stating that no launch should take place as long as the temperature did not rise above 53F. The NASA counterparts not only found the rationale flimsily argued (Thiokol engineers agreed), but they pointed out that the rationale contradicted earlier rationales (a cardinal sin in engineering). NASA administrators were "appalled" by the Thiokol recommendation and decided to press ahead with the launch. The O-rings failed and the *Challenger* disintegrated within 90 seconds after take-off.

The social and political construction of threat perception

We have thus far treated crises as if they were ontological "threat entities" lurking in the background that must be recognized before they can be eliminated. But crises are to a considerable degree – some say entirely – subjectively construed threats: before we can speak of a crisis, a considerable number of players must agree that a threat exists and must be dealt with urgently.[29] The process by which a group, organization, or society develops a consensus on crisis is quite mysterious. Some seemingly obvious (certainly in hindsight) threats are completely ignored, whereas other relatively minor threats can hold a society in a tight grip for a surprisingly long period of time.

On the eve of the German invasion of Holland, in the spring of 1940, Dutch politicians reassured their anxious people that the Netherlands would escape the war threat. Dutch neutrality had protected the country from the ravages of the Great War and so it would happen again as Germany prepared for war against France. When the German army powered over the border, the unprepared army was taken by surprise and capitulated within five days. The Dutch queen and her government barely managed to escape to London. The five-year occupation had begun. The Dutch belief in a neutral position may now seem preposterous, given Hitler's intentions and the strategic geographic location of the Netherlands separating the German homeland from the North Sea coastline. Moreover, the Dutch defense attaché in Berlin, Major Sas, had developed excellent connections within German defense circles, which allowed him to accurately predict the actions of the German army. Major Sas relayed his findings to his superiors back home, but was proved wrong as German invasion plans were frequently altered at the last minute. As his warnings failed to materialize, Major Sas became the tragic "cry wolf" figure in the months leading up to the invasion. The Dutch government refused to recognize the impending threat to their sovereignty.

This example illustrates a prime reason why governments fail to act upon warnings: most warnings do not speak for themselves. In the absence of hindsight, governments must consider the signals and weigh the evidence. Only when governmental leaders define a situation as a crisis will remedial action be undertaken. A large number of examples tell us that this process of recognition may take (too much) time: some threats never get recognized at all. For instance, it took the United States federal government years before it appreciated the magnitude of the AIDS epidemic, but it was rather quick in defining Iraq as a security threat in the wake of the 9/11 disaster.[30]

Research on public policy making and the paucity of reform offers a convincing explanation: many issues (including warnings of impending crises) never make it to the decision-making agenda of political and bureaucratic leaders.[31] One of the most important factors working against crisis recognition is the limited time available to policy makers and public leaders for considering, debating, and deciding upon policy issues. The policy agenda is overcrowded with issues that await decision making. All of these issues have fought a hard battle to make it to the top of the agenda; they have all acquired the status of urgency. The list usually includes deficiencies with regard to roads, schools, hospitals, criminal justice agencies, or anti-terrorist units – all of which can be framed in terms of crisis (past or future). But politicians cannot consider or act upon all of them. It is easy to see how short-term considerations keep long-term threats such as the looming pension crisis or the coming greenhouse effects from the policy agenda. Everyone may agree that these are crises in the making, but many also tend to believe that tomorrow's worries should be solved before next year's threats.

In other cases it may be hard-ball politics that keeps future crises off the agenda. Opposing interests may form a coalition, which effectively blocks an issue from discussion. If those in power do not require coalitions to govern and more or less control the policy agenda, they may simply refuse to award urgency status to a certain topic. For instance, President George Bush announced that the United States would not sign the Kyoto treaty, which effectively "killed" the treaty. When the oil tanker *Prestige* sank in 2003, the Spanish government initially denied that something terrible had happened and subsequently refused to allocate national resources to deal with the crisis.

Some crises are not acted upon because the stakeholders involved cannot attract attention to their plight. They fail to frame the issue of their concern in such terms that others understand and share the nature of the threat, sense the urgency, and act accordingly. In October 2003, the UN Food and Agriculture Organization (FAO) warned that abnormal rains had created ideal breeding grounds for locusts in the Atlas mountain ridge of Northern Africa. Nothing happened and the crisis unfolded as predicted. In the summer of 2004, the locust swarms invaded the African north-west, destroying the livelihood of small farmers. In spite of clearly communicated and accurate warnings, a preventable crisis was allowed to wreak havoc in the region. Similarly, it wasn't until the December 2004 tsunami had triggered the greatest natural disaster in recorded history that policy makers in the Indian Ocean region decided to set up an early-warning system similar to the one already operating in the Pacific, which presumably would have saved many thousands of lives.

The political career of risk issues apparently requires resourceful "claim makers" who can influence the political processing of pivotal studies or occasional incidents.[32] This explains why some "non-events" – the Y2K crisis comes to mind – skyrocket to the top of the agenda: skillful "framers" manage to translate their issue in a language everyone understands.[33]

A final barrier to crisis recognition may be the institutional setting in which the crisis must become recognized. Certain practices, indeed some parts of the modern way of life, have become so ingrained and taken for granted that they effectively blind us to recognizing certain threats and make it virtually impossible to deal with them. In a society that depends on fossil fuel, it is surprisingly difficult to gain attention for the rapid depletion of resources. Should leaders be surprised when our economies run into crisis as a result of high oil prices? Or when two passenger planes collide in the choked airways above our mega cities? Can policy makers claim ignorance when a fireworks factory explodes in the middle of a city?

Much must happen before a significant number of people agree on the status of a problem; much more must happen before they agree that a certain event warrants the crisis label. Whether it is a coalition of the unwilling or the blind, many real threats are simply ignored. This depressing fact becomes most obvious when we consider the range of permanent crises that have actually happened; they are "out there" for all to see: small communities battling pollution and mass unemployment; crime-ridden no-go areas; sloppy management of high-risk technologies; the world-wide AIDS epidemic – the list of "unrecognized" crises is long.[34]

It appears that warnings of impending crises stand a chance only if they are understood as direct threats to the way of living that is protected and serviced by the political-administrative elites. In democracies, this means that voters must be mobilized. It appears that only radical primers – preferably packaged in media-friendly symbols – can impress upon a significant majority of people that a threat exists to their way of life.[35] Events must be linked to core values by what researchers then call entrepreneurs; overwhelming numbers rarely succeed to make a case of their own. In the absence of such "packaging," public leaders and their organizations will find it hard to recognize growing threats and impending crisis before it is too late. When a crisis has materialized and has become acute, the nature of the sense-making challenge changes dramatically. But the predicament for leaders does not become any easier, as the analysis below reveals.

2.3   Psychological dimensions of sense making: stress and performance

On the morning of September 11, 2001, President Bush was listening to a group of children reading at a Sarasota elementary school when he learned about the second plane crashing into the World Trade Center. This was not a warning; it was the real thing. As the cameras captured the look of shock on his face, the President of the United States considered what to do next as leader of a country under attack.[36]

The pace of events sets the acute phase of crisis apart from the incubation phase. In a dynamic and volatile situation, windows of opportunity to intervene are often fleeting. Decisions as to whether and how to act or not must be made rapidly, or the possibility to affect the course of events may be lost. Furthermore, there are fundamental uncertainties about the nature of the threat, contextual parameters, and the efficacy of alternative courses of action.

Politicians and bureaucrats in many countries, however hectic their everyday life may be, rarely have to gauge unfamiliar situations under these extreme pressures. Their normal modes of situation assessment and policy deliberation are thus sometimes overwhelmed by the bewildering pace, ambiguity, and complexity of crisis. Routines for coping with the torrent of information – overload is a common feature of crises – are usually not in place. As a result, policy makers easily become distressed and distracted. Crucial bits of intelligence get lost in the steady stream of briefings, phone calls, faxes, emails, wire service reports, cables, and rumors.

Since crises tend to generate high levels of pressure on key policy makers and operational staff, the literature on information processing under stress is particularly relevant to the study of problem framing and sense making under crisis conditions. Stress entails a relationship between a task load and the coping capacity of an individual or collective.[37] Stress need not necessarily degrade performance – cognitive and otherwise – if the task load is balanced by a high degree of coping capacity. Experience appears to be a key factor: seasoned experts are usually far more effective at maintaining performance under pressure than novices.[38]

The relationship between stress and most people's performance takes the form of an inverted "U." Absence of stress is associated with lower motivation and performance, moderate stress with high performance (due to heightened vigilance and motivation), and excessive stress with declining performance once leaving the optimum zone of the curve.[39] We should also know that different kinds of stress may have rather different psychological consequences for policy makers. Stress deriving from overload and lack of time has different psychological consequences than stress deriving from value tradeoffs, fear of loss, internal dissent, or external conflict. The latter four are likely to be more emotionally charged – adding to the emotional component of stress dynamics.[40] A combination of these stress types – likely in crisis – will thus have serious consequences for the performance of decision makers.

Clearly, coping with several crises at once (or with the coincidence of a crisis and other demanding official pursuits such as election campaigns and summit meetings) is particularly tough. Stress is likely to be cumulative, in the sense that an individual's ability to cope may be impaired by lingering effects of previous stress loads (a "stress hangover"). Stress associated with other professional tasks or from someone's personal life adds to the total load during a crisis episode.[41]

Some do better than others at compartmentalizing stress: they isolate stress arising in one domain and prevent it from contaminating others.[42] President Clinton, for example, demonstrated a remarkable capacity to compartmentalize stress and maintain composure and focus during the Monica Lewinsky scandal, at least in his public performances. President Nixon, however, was unable to cope with the stress when he found himself confronted simultaneously with a critical phase in the Watergate scandal and the 1973 Middle East war. He consumed large quantities of alcohol and behaved in such an erratic manner that his aides took steps to limit his ability to launch a nuclear strike.[43]

Based on experimental, historical, and field studies, researchers have identified a wide range of specific stress effects. For example, under heavy stress, individuals are thought to:

- focus on the short term, to the neglect of longer-term considerations;
- fall back on and rigidly cling to old and deeply rooted behavioral patterns (often forgetting more recent ones);
- narrow and deepen their span of attention, scrutinizing "central" issues while neglecting "peripheral" ones;
- be more likely to rely on stereotypes or lapse into fantasies;
- be more easily irritable.[44]

The literature on the relationship between stress and decision making, while not entirely pessimistic regarding the possibility of effective coping, tends to emphasize the many ways that stress effects can distort situational assessments. Accordingly, the next section will assess some of the impediments to sense making in crises that may arise from psychological and organizational factors. The news from applied psychology is not all bad, however. Therefore, Section 2.5 depicts what this and related research tells us about the possibilities and antecedents of high-quality sense making in volatile, unstructured situations such as emerging crises.

2.4   Precarious reality-testing: constraints

Virtually all crises generate an energetic search for information among all the actors involved.[45] Once the vast intelligence and expert resources of modern government have been brought to bear on the crisis, a huge quantity of raw data and processed "intelligence" is generated. Without mechanisms for coping with this flow of data, policy makers may become paralyzed or indiscriminately attentive to particular items of information, which may unduly affect their judgments. How do policy makers make sense of the bewildering flow of data and the debilitating lack of critical information?

Individual constraints

A half century of cognitive research supports the view that experience – mentally coded into what psychologists call a system of stored representations – is the basis for human sense making, in everyday life as well as in extreme situations. In addition to their memory, people's expectations are highly significant. Under conditions of ambiguity humans tend to "see" what they expect to occur.[46] For example, in the absence of hard information, some decision makers and observers of the Oklahoma City bombing (in April 1995) initially operated from the assumption that Islamic Fundamentalist terrorists were responsible. Why was this the case? First of all, the first World Trade Center bombing in 1993, which was the work of such a group, was still fresh in the mind. Second, domestic groups were not expected to conduct operations on this scale on US soil. As it turned out, these assumptions and expectations proved incorrect – the culprits were American citizens associated with an extremist "militia" organization.[47]

This example suggests how people use encoded experience: they take a scrap of information (a cue, as cognitive psychologists call it) and weave a scenario around it, using encoded experience as mental yarn. Sometimes this kind of cue enlargement points policy makers in the right direction. Yet it may just as easily lead them down the proverbial garden path to misperception.[48] The tendency to focus on circumstantial cues or merely cosmetic similarities between current events and previous ones can be particularly pernicious, especially if a person is overconfident that his or her interpretation is accurate.

Psychologists now recognize the fundamental limitations of the human ability to acquire and process information.[49] Individuals tend to be attentive to a certain "set" of issues while ignoring others. What is on one's mind, the content of the cognitive "agenda" at any given time, heavily affects the way a person monitors and sorts signals from the environment, and how he interprets them.

While the human mind is capable of great intellectual feats, it is beset with limitations when it comes to monitoring and analyzing complex and volatile situations.[50] Individuals are constantly bombarded with stimuli to such an extent that the stream threatens to overwhelm their capacity to absorb it all. As a result, it is necessary to selectively monitor the environment and "tune out" much of the incoming data in order to reserve the capacity to attend to the most pressing issues at any given time. Of course, even the most skillful experts are liable to miss important information from time to time. Even when an issue is identified as important and attention is devoted to it, crucial information may be missing or uncertain, and it is necessary to "go beyond the information given" in making sense of the world.[51]

Human brains collect, organize, store, and recall information by making use of packaging and organizing devices, which are generically called cognitive structures. These cognitive structures – alternatively referred to by researchers as schemas, scripts, analogies, metaphors, or stories – enable people to draw upon encoded and selectively recalled experience to interpret the present and prepare for the future. In the face of numerous, complex, and mutually contradictory cues, people also use mental "tricks" to facilitate classification, interpretation, and judgment. These "heuristic" short cuts in processing information introduce biases in our assessment of situations. Sometimes these short cuts point us in the right direction; often they lead us astray. Decades of meticulous laboratory research have detailed many different patterns by which people overemphasize some bits of information, and ignore or underestimate others.

Irving Janis summed up much of this literature by distinguishing between cognitive, affiliative, and egocentric rules of thumb that decision makers resort to under high levels of stress.[52] Cognitive heuristics and biases amount to parsimonious but dangerously simplistic ways of "making sense" of complex situations in such a way as to facilitate the making of quick, straightforward choices. Once made, these choices will be "bolstered" by a highly selective treatment of any subsequent information that reaches decision makers. In extreme cases, they will actively seek out information that seems to corroborate their choices, and ignore or obfuscate information that contains negative feedback about these choices.

One of the most frequently used short cuts is the reliance on historical analogies to make sense of the challenges posed by a contemporary crisis.[53] Use of analogies may be a more or less spontaneous cognitive attempt to make sense of highly uncertain situations. It may also spring from calculated moves to "frame" crises publicly in politically convenient ways. In both these circumstances, there is a clear pitfall associated with applying the presumed "lessons" of one crisis to another: crises might *look* similar, but they are unique by definition (see also Chapter 6).[54]

Affiliative rules refer to modes of sense making where "policy makers are likely to seek a solution that will avert threats to important values in a way that will not adversely affect their relationships with any 'important people' within the organization, especially those to whom they are accountable, and that will not be opposed by subordinates who are expected to implement the new policy decision."[55] Behavioral tendencies of this kind include the "avoid punishment rule," which is a propensity to favor conservative options that don't rock the boat, and the "preserve harmony rule" that may give rise to the rigid concurrence-seeking in group-level sense making that has become known as groupthink.

Egocentric rules include both self-serving rules that are invoked to satisfy strong personal motives, and emotive rules that are directed toward satisfying strong emotional needs. Such motives include the need for power and control, or a desire for personal aggrandizement. In many instances these motives are essentially efforts to compensate for deep-seated feelings of insecurity and incompetence. Leaders with a very high need for power and control are likely to harden under stress, and take hawkish positions in conflicts.

The affiliative and egocentric rules of thumb are highly relevant to sense making in crises. Under normal circumstances, a senior policy maker should be seen "not as a cold fish, but as a warm-blooded mammal, not as a rational calculator always ready to work out the best solution but as a reluctant decision maker – beset by conflict, doubts, and worry, struggling with incongruous longings, antipathies, and loyalties." This is all the more true during crisis episodes.[56] As urgent threats to key societal values and interests appear to be on the rise, so do the stakes for the responsible political leaders, up to the point of affecting their personal self-esteem and sense of identity.[57]

When he first saw the pictures of Soviet missile installations under construction in Cuba, John F. Kennedy took it personally and exclaimed: "He [Kruschev] can't do that to ME!" Kennedy's anger at what he saw as betrayal by the Soviet leader was so strong that it impaired his ability to speak and reason dispassionately for several hours.[58] Leaders may also identify strongly with the plight of victims. After meeting with their families, Ronald Reagan repeatedly insisted in staff meetings that the American hostages in Lebanon should be freed. He gave the impression that he would condone any means to achieve that end short of overt surrender to the hostage-takers' political demands. He created a climate in which National Security Council staffers felt sanctioned to trade arms for hostages, thus setting up the Reagan administration for the Iran-Contra affair.[59]

Organizational constraints

One may expect these individual vulnerabilities and errors in crisis sense making to be corrected by someone else's vigilant processing of information in the organizations in which all these individuals are embedded. Unfortunately, the problems of organizational information processing sketched above for the pre-crisis stage do not evaporate once a crisis has become manifest. On the contrary, they are often aggravated.

People within organizations tend to perceive the world differently. This is an inevitable by-product of differences in tasks, jurisdictions, education, geographical location, and experience. Moreover, various organizations are often drawn into the crisis at different moments in its development: some have mandates to be the first responders, whereas others may not come into play until much later.[60] The various participating actors tend to focus on different aspects of the situation, and assess conflicting situation reports differently. They draw upon different analogies and metaphors, make different inferences and prognoses, and see different interests at stake – each from their own organizational vantage points. Not unimportantly, they are well aware that information is a critical resource in the ongoing jockeying for position that goes on within and between public organizations. To put it euphemistically, sharing information with others is not necessarily their first concern or reflex when something extraordinary has happened (see section 2.2).

Furthermore, since information is a key currency of power in governmental and other political settings, officials typically receive information in a relatively arbitrary fashion. Sometimes it is provided as a reward or sign of favor; other times it is withheld as punishment or to neutralize a potential adversary.[61] Such practices may result in distorted sense making in crisis situations, sometimes with tragic consequences.

Poor information sharing in crisis situations is not necessarily a result of organizational dysfunctions or deficient information technology. Often, it is the result of deliberate policy such as compartmentalizing information for security reasons. Sensitive issues are often handled on a so-called need-to-know basis. This makes good sense from a security perspective – the fewer people who are in the know, the fewer who can leak to the press, to political (or bureaucratic) rivals, or to foreign governments. In practice, however, it is often difficult to figure out who "needs to know" what.

2.5   Conditions for reliable reality-testing

Thus far we have painted a pretty bleak picture of the prospects for making sense of crises. There is, however, another side to the crisis sense making story. To begin with, some categories of people are known for their ability to remain cool and to stay clear-headed under pressure – take veteran military officers, journalists, and fire and police commanders, for instance. Senior politicians and bureaucrats are generally veterans too – veterans of countless political and bureaucratic battles during their rise to power. Those who make it all the way to the top of the hill in competitive political-administrative systems tend to have relatively well-developed mechanisms for coping with stress. Some researchers also point to organizations that have a proactive culture of "looking for problems" in their environment. These so-called high-reliability organizations have somehow developed a capacity for thorough yet fast-paced information processing under stressful conditions.

Mental slides

Aspiring to adequate, if not always instantly accurate, understanding of the problems triggered by a crisis is not unrealistic. A growing body of research in the so-called naturalistic decision-making tradition has transformed our thinking about how operational decisions are made in crises and other critical incidents.[62] Experienced incident commanders rarely arrive at situational assessments through an explicit conscious process of deliberation, as researchers of many stripes and colors were long wont to assume.

Professional commanders of this kind have developed a rich store of experience and a repertoire of tactics upon which they draw when confronting a critical incident. The minds of these crisis commanders work like a mental slide carousel containing snapshots of a wide variety of contingencies that they have encountered or learned about. When they find themselves in a new situation, this is immediately compared with their stored experiences. This mental slide carousel quickly revolves until an adequate match is found. Each slide contains not only an image of the situation but also a recipe for action. In order to double check that the tactic in question is appropriate for this situation, the commander may perform a mental simulation to make sure that there isn't some contextual factor that might prevent the tactic from producing the desired outcome. If not, it is time to issue orders and begin implementing the tactic. Thus once the specific type of situation is identified, the commander *knows* what to do.

This mode of information processing, though not infallible, enables competent performance under difficult, dynamic conditions and peak work loads. Clearly, this tactic works best when the new contingency closely resembles at least one of the experiences captured on the commander's mental slides. If the situation is radically different from those stored in memory, a somewhat different kind of sense-making process will be necessary. But even then, stored experience is a resource that can be used to develop a fairly accurate assessment.[63]

A key question is to what extent one can transfer these ideas from the realm of "uniforms" and operational agencies to the world of high-level policy making. One possible difference between these two types of leadership settings is the time frames involved.[64] While politicians and bureaucrats are sometimes called upon to make crucial decisions with a few moments' notice, like the incident commanders we just discussed, they usually have much more time than the latter for consultation. Situational assessments in crises often arise over a period of hours or days rather than seconds and minutes. This creates a somewhat greater potential for leaders to interact with advisers and draw upon a wider range of organizational information resources than field commanders typically have at their disposal.

However, critical-incident commanders probably have more opportunities than policy makers to practice sense making under extreme conditions. Big-city fire commanders, for example, have a chance to practice their diagnostic skills relatively frequently.[65] By contrast, top-level policy makers – though carrying a heavy everyday stress load – do not see major crises all that often, yet the potential variety of crises they might have to deal with is much larger than that of the average operational services commander. We would expect most senior policy makers to be able to count their personal experience of full-blown crises on the fingers of one hand – or in the case of those with long and turbulent careers, both hands. Most leaders enter office as comparative amateurs in the realm of crisis management and may well remain so unless they experience a major crisis during their tenure.

Resilient organizations

Some organizations develop an impressive capacity to grasp crisis dynamics. These organizations often work in extremely fast-paced and potentially deadly environments – think of military, police, and rescue service organizations – but they also exist in high-technology environments (nuclear power and chemical plants). These organizations have routines for using provisional information to create a provisional situational assessment and remember that it is just that: provisional. They resist tendencies to adopt and cling to an interpretation based on limited information and hasty analysis. They force themselves to continuously probe their situational assessments – identifying indicators that can be monitored or "tests" devised to provide warning bells to go off should the initial assessment be off the mark. As new information becomes available, assessments are updated or even abandoned if the balance of available evidence begins pointing in a different direction.[66]

The secret of their success lies in three characteristics: safety awareness, decentralization, and training.[67] Resilient organizations have created a culture of awareness: all employees consider safety the overriding concern in everything they do. They expect crises to happen. They look for them because employees know they are expected to do that – even when it comes at the cost of task efficiency. A high degree of decentralization empowers employees to act upon their intuition: when they suspect "something is brewing," they can take it "upstairs" in the knowledge that their surveillance will be noted and appreciated. These organizations do not expect employees to rely on their intuition alone (even though leaders of these organizations understand the importance of expert intuition); employees are constantly trained to look for glitches and troubling signs of escalation. All this suggests that organizational blind spots should not be seen as inherent defaults of organization but rather as the outcome of suboptimal leadership efforts.

2.6   Conclusion

A close reading of many crisis cases reveals what in hindsight look suspiciously like flashing warning lights which should have alerted authorities of things to come. Pearl Harbor, the Falklands, Chernobyl, the *Challenger* explosion, Waco, 9/11, and the French 2003 heat wave – these are but a handful of crucial events that in hindsight appeared not so inevitable as they were felt to be at the moment of arrival. Investigative reporters and blue-ribbon commissions have unearthed an abundance of lavishly detailed pre-warnings, fuelling a thriving industry of conspiracy theories.[68]

Paradoxically, it is the characteristics of modernization that prevent organizations from detecting impending crises. The characteristics of complex organizations – combined with the psychology of organizational elites – make the occurrence of critical incidents and major failures quite normal.[69] The hidden interaction between incidents and failed or late interventions drives the crisis toward critical threshold levels. This line of argument thus takes us to a rather pessimistic assessment when it comes to crisis prediction. Detecting crises before they strike seems to be an impossible task.

Policy makers at the top of public organizations and governments do not have the luxury of forming impressions about crises after the fact, as commentators and academics do. They live in a world full of uncertainty and ambiguity where at any given time numerous contingencies can materialize and have a profound effect on their domain of responsibility. They must recognize real impending crises from the sea of possible contingencies.

Once a crisis becomes manifest, policy makers must make sense of the unfolding events in order to limit the damage they may cause. Policy makers do not have perfect, complete, and uncontested information about the potentially escalating challenges facing them. Rather, they begin with a preliminary and provisional picture of what is happening, and, equally importantly, what it means. Any actions taken or foregone will derive in large measure from the nature and quality of the situational assessments that emerge from the flow of activity prior to the recognition of the crisis.[70]

They need to decide which signals to heed, which to ignore, and how to make sense of a threat that has already materialized and that calls for an immediate response. They make these decisions on the basis of incomplete, often contradictory information and advice from sources within and outside their own organizations. In this chapter, we have demonstrated how delicate and vulnerable this process is. We have shown how many organizational features and practices unwittingly obscure rather than detect threats, and how this accelerates rather than mitigates the development of crises. But the news is not all bad. We have also shown that policy makers and organizations can be successful in maintaining a fungible capacity for reality-testing in even the most difficult circumstances. In the concluding chapter we shall return to this issue, and provide some advice to leaders who want to avoid becoming the victim of information pathologies. Now we turn to the challenges of crisis response.

Notes

1 In its final report, the National Commission on Terrorist Attacks (in the remainder of this book we will refer to this as the 9/11 Commission) (2004: xv) phrased the question slightly differently ("How did this happen?") and added the equally pressing question: "and how can we avoid such tragedy again?" We will return to the latter question in Chapter 6.

2 For a discussion of these roots, see Chapter 2 of the 9/11 Commission report (2004).

3 This analogy is developed in the work of Turner (1978) and Reason (1990).

4 Compare Weick (1995: 61).

5 Some theories of safety (known under the label of high-reliability theory) see these reliability experts as pivotal safeguards against accidents and crises (Paul Schulman, personal communication).

6 Perrow (1984).

7 Leveson (1995); Weick, Sutcliffe, and Obstfeld (1999); Weick and Sutcliffe (2002).

8 Simon (1976); Cyert et al. (1963).

9 We refer here to the financial crises experienced by Enron, WorldCom, Shell, Ahold, and Parmalat.

10 See, for example, DiIulio et al. (1993); Gormley and Weimer (1999).

11 Vaughan (1996).

12 Feldman and March (1981; 1988).

13 This drive for efficiency is documented and discussed in the literature on new public management. See, for example, Pollitt (1993); Hood et al. (2004).

14 Turner and Pidgeon (1997).

15 See, for example, the case studies of the Hercules plane disaster (Rijpma and van Duin, 2001), the Rwanda tragedy (Reyntjens, 2001), and the LA riots (Miller, 2001).

16 Turner (1978).

17 Compare Wilensky (1967); Kam (1988); March (1988). For instance, communicating within and across organizations is often a problem in itself. Presenting information in such a way that the receiving party understands it, agrees with the content, and appreciates the urgency is difficult (especially when the receiving end is outside the organization). See Parker and Stern (2002) for additional factors and perspectives.

18 On groupthink, see Janis (1982); 't Hart (1994). In 2004, both American and British reports evaluating the run-up to the Anglo-American invasion of Iraq mentioned groupthink within the relevant intelligence agencies and inner-circle policymaking groups to be a major contributing cause of the distorted threat assessment regarding Iraq's possession of weapons of mass destruction. See report of the Committee of Privy Counselors (14 July 2004); report of the Senate Intelligence Committee (7 July 2004).

19 See Preston and 't Hart (1999: 54–8).

20 This builds on our leadership perspective as outlined in Chapter 1. For a classic source of inspiration, see Selznick (1957). See the work of Weick and Sutcliffe (2002) for advice on building this type of communication mechanism into an organization.

21 A good discussion of these factors can be found in Wilson (1989).

22 Barry Turner (1978) talks about "anti-tasks," which further efficiency but also take errors for a ride through the system.

23 Perrow (1999).

24 Vaughan (1996).

25 See Henry (2000: 116–19).

26 See Clarke (1999). We thank Allan McConnell for pointing this out to us.

27 We rely here on Vaughan's (1996) extensive analysis.

28 For an enlightening discussion on the engineering mind, see Petroski (1992).

29 Edelman (1964; 1971); Bovens and 't Hart (1996).
30 On the AIDS crisis, see Perrow and Guillen (1990); Shilts (1987); on the framing of Iraq as a crisis to come, see Clarke (2004).
31 In this field of studies, several "schools" exist (see Sabatier, 1999 for an overview). Here we selectively describe a set of common factors that work against high agenda status. Cf. Parker and Stern (2002).
32 Stallings (1995); Cobb and Primo (2003).
33 See Goode and Ben-Yehuda (1994) on the similar dynamics of moral panics.
34 The work of Erikson (1976; 1994) is of special relevance.
35 Think of My Lai and the recent emergence of film material exposing torture in the American-run prisons in Iraq.
36 A scene immortalized and ridiculed in Moore's movie *Fahrenheit 911*.
37 Stress has been conceptualized in a number of ways. We adopt this definition, which originates in the influential work of Lazarus (1966) and Janis and Mann (1977).
38 Klein (2001) has clearly demonstrated the capacity of experienced and well-trained practitioners to cope with extreme situations.
39 Individuals are thought to have somewhat differently shaped stress curves, in keeping with the notion that some individuals cope better with stress than others.
40 Janis and Mann (1977); Lebow and Stein (1994: 331–8).
41 Weick (1995: 103–4).
42 It is therefore important to establish empirically to what extent crisis pressures affect the various actors, and what level of stress this actually generates in each of them, as far as can be judged from their recorded behavior. This research strategy was advocated (but not always adhered to) by Brecher (1979c). The best checklist of stress indicators in policy makers dealing with crises can be found in Hermann (1979). An exemplary effort along the lines suggested here is Lindgren (2003).
43 Haldeman and Ambrose (1994).
44 Hermann (1979); Holsti (1979); Post (1991); Weick (1995); Flin (1996: 97–139). Some researchers argue that the early stress literature has systematically misunderstood the relationship between stress and performance errors. Klein (2001), for example, has argued that the more important effects of stressors such as extreme time pressure, noise, and ambiguity are that stressors (a) interfere with information gathering, and (b) disrupt the ability to recall necessary information and distract decision makers' attention from critical tasks.
45 For example, see Brecher (1993).
46 Bruner (1957); Jervis (1976: 144–54); Weick (1995).
47 Nacos (2002).
48 Weick (1995).
49 Bruner (1957); Jervis (1976: 203–5).
50 Nisbett and Ross (1980: 15–16); Devine, Hamilton, and Ostrom (1994: 3–4).
51 Lombardi et al. (1987); Khong (1992: 28).
52 Janis (1989).
53 Neustadt and May (1986).

54 Early yet still authoritative statements in this regard include Hermann (1972); Brecher (1979b).

55 Janis (1989: 45).

56 Janis and Mann (1977: 15). The most recent findings on the dual functions of historical analogies (e.g. sense making and meaning making) are reported in Brändström, Bynander, and 't Hart (2004); Dyson and Preston (2003).

57 Several decades of research have taught us much about the ways in which various types of behaviour driven by motivated biases – such as denial, wishful thinking, betrayal, and value conflict – can influence problem framing and decision making. Cf. Jervis (1976); Lebow (1981: 101–19); David (1993: 23); Vandenbroucke (1993: 164–6); Lebow and Stein (1994: 115–17); Parker and Stern (2002).

58 McCauley (1989).

59 David (1993); 't Hart (1994).

60 Rosenthal et al. (1989: 437).

61 Vertzberger (1990).

62 Psychologists' understanding of decision making under stress has changed greatly during the last decade. Social and organizational psychologists have increasingly left the laboratory behind to engage in close observation, interviewing, and case reconstructions of the behavior of skilled practitioners acting in real-world settings. The ways in which commanders at the operational level – fire, police, military – make life-and-death decisions under pressure have come under particular scrutiny. Flin (1996); Klein (2001).

63 For a case study application, see Flin (2001).

64 Compare with Simon's (1981) discussion on the importance of time.

65 Of course, incident commanders can and do run into incidents that are qualitatively and quantitatively different from those for which they have trained and prepared. The experience of the New York City Fire and Police Departments on September 11, 2001 is a case in point. The results of the McKinsey and Company studies commissioned after the attacks show that these organizations were not prepared for a contingency of this magnitude and had great difficulty in organizing an effective response. By contrast, the Mayor's office of emergency management and the Mayor himself adapted quickly and effectively to this challenging situation; Wachtendorf (2004).

66 Weick, Sutcliffe, and Obstfeld (1999).

67 We derive these factors from the research on high-reliability organizations. See Rochlin (1996) and Weick and Sutcliffe (2002).

68 The heat waves in Chicago (1995) and France (2003) provide telling examples of the stealth nature of many crises. See Klinenberg (2002) and Lagadec (2004) for analyses of these cases.

69 See also Mitroff and Pauchant (1990); Pauchant and Mitroff (1992); Seeger et al. (2003).

70 This observation does not rule out the possibility of serendipity – sometimes a shot in the dark hits the mark. Once in a while, action based on inaccurate understanding turns out to have beneficial consequences in crisis as in everyday life. Unlike ordinary people, public policy makers can ill afford to bet on luck.

3 Decision making: critical choices and their implementation

3.1 The myth of chief executive choice

On July 14, 1958, US President Eisenhower woke up to the news of a coup in Iraq, overthrowing one of the few pro-Western leaders in the Middle East. In the light of the increasing Soviet dominance and the recent merger between Syria and Egypt into the United Arab Republic, with the strident Nasser as its president, the Iraqi coup meant a blow to the United States' position in the Middle East. The sense of crisis in Washington, DC was heightened when the Lebanese president called for immediate US intervention, fearing that his country would be next. It was 9 am. After consulting with his advisers and his political counterparts on the Hill, President Eisenhower announced the decision to send in the Sixth Fleet at 2.30 pm.[1]

This long-forgotten example of presidential crisis decision making illustrates a classic notion of crisis leadership: making the critical call when it matters most. Both successes and failures of crisis management are often related to such monumental decisions. This notion of crisis as "occasions for decision making" is a dominant one in the scholarly literature on crisis management.[2] The image of the command room, the tragic dilemma, and the decisive leader not only informs academics and Hollywood movies but also plays to a widespread expectation in times of crisis: leaders must govern.

Many studies of crisis management report an "upward" shift in decision making: the scale of response is adjusted to the scale of the impact. When a crisis strikes areas that extend over multiple administrative jurisdictions, responsibility for coordinating government responses will often shift to regional, national, or, for some types of crises in Europe, transnational levels of authority.[3] The same goes for crises that are local in geographical terms but whose depth and complexity exceed the coping capacity of local authorities. This upscaling may occur spontaneously, but it is often foreseen and prescribed in contingency plans.[4]

The importance of top-level policy makers in crisis response operations is easily overstated. Public leaders do, of course, make highly consequential decisions during a crisis, but so do other officials and pivotal people outside government. Moreover, crisis responses are shaped not just by decisions but also by the implementation of those decisions. Numerous organizations and groups are typically involved in the implementation of crisis decisions. Our *key question* is why some crisis response operations seem to run very successfully whereas others end in failure.

Executive-level crisis decision making is an important factor in the answer to this question, but not as important as most people are wont to think. In most crises, the key tenets of crisis responses are shaped by many more players within the government system than just its top policy makers. Our *core claim* is that successful crisis management depends not so much on critical decision making but on the facilitation of crisis implementation and coordination throughout the response network.

3.2   Leaders as crisis decision makers

In most if not all crises, the moment arrives when a single man or woman must make faithful choices about the government's course of action.[5] They may seek and obtain counsel from others, such as professional advisers, political associates, spouses, friends, and academic experts. But in the end, the leader must decide. How do leaders cope with this role and the pressures it entails?

It is important here to recapitulate the distinctive nature of the decisional challenges that crises entail for leaders. Regardless of whether they are inherent in the situation or subjectively perceived as such by the person in charge, crises present leaders with choice opportunities that combine a number of characteristics:

- they are highly consequential: they affect core values and interests of communities and the price of both "right" and "wrong" choices is high – socially, politically, economically, and in human terms;
- they are more likely than non-crisis situations to contain genuine dilemmas that can be resolved only through trade-off choices, or "tragic choices," where all the options open to the decision maker entail net losses;
- they are baffling in that they present leaders with major uncertainties about the nature of the issues, the likelihood of future developments, and the possible impact of various policy options;
- choices have to be made relatively quickly: there is time pressure – regardless of whether it is real, perceived, or self-imposed – which

means that some of the tried-and-tested methods of preparing, delaying, and politically anchoring difficult decisions cannot be applied.

This combination of characteristics puts leaders in a difficult spot: everybody is looking to them for direction, yet a crisis makes it very difficult and painful to provide just that. In choosing, leaders have to somehow discount the uncertainties, overcome any anxieties they may feel, control their impulses, and commit the government's resources to a course of action that they can only hope is both effective and appropriate in the political context they are in.

Leaders vary greatly in this respect, as a brief comparison of US presidents shows. Some leaders tell themselves that making tough calls is part of their job. They accept that they can get it wrong sometimes, but they feel that office-holding amounts to more than retaining one's popularity. Harry Truman was a clear example of this. Preston observes that "Truman's decisiveness of decision has become legendary, as has his willingness to make tough policy decisions regardless of the political consequences . . . The sign that stood upon his desk in the Oval Office bore the inscription 'The Bucks Stops Here!' and throughout his presidency, Truman recognized this most fundamental aspect of his job."[6] Likewise, George Bush Sr., often criticized for lacking a grand policy vision, tended to grow during crisis, when critical decisions had to be made on urgent, complex matters: "Bush's style was to proceed cautiously, yet be willing to act boldly . . . Close associates describe Bush as the 'quintessential man of the moment' who rarely dealt with problems unless they are forced upon him, yet who tended to be a brilliant crisis manager."[7]

Other leaders are less comfortable with making decisions under pressure. Their personality and style may predispose them to consider all sides of a problem and therefore insist upon extensive analysis, multiple sources of advice, and extensive deliberation with and among advisers before making a decision. Yet other leaders experience crisis decision making as an excruciating predicament. This applies to leaders who dread the idea that their decisions may disappoint or even damage others, who are afraid to fail, or who become paralyzed by the need to make a choice in the face of conflicting advice.

Jimmy Carter succumbed to the cumulative pressures brought upon him by the second world oil crisis, the Soviet invasion of Afghanistan, and the Iranian hostage crisis. These complex and dynamic events shattered key components of his world view. Perhaps more importantly, the Iranian hostage crisis wore him down psychologically. A micromanager by inclination, he met with his innermost advisers almost every day at breakfast for over a year to discuss the crisis. Eventually, the frustrating lack of progress, the increasingly bitter disagreements between his state department and national security staff advisers, the failure of the military rescue operation, and the increasingly public humiliation of his presidency which the hostage crisis elicited, got to him.[8]

However eager or reluctant choosers they might be, there are occasions when leaders firmly believe that a decision simply has to be made – and fast.[9] But fast decisions are not necessarily good decisions. In one comprehensive meta-analysis of US presidential decision making during international crises, the quality of crisis decision making was low in seven, high in eight, and medium in four out of nineteen cases studied.[10] These mixed results are mirrored by many single or comparative case studies of international crisis management.

Poor presidential decision making in crisis is invariably explained by the kinds of stress-induced pathologies discussed in Chapter 2. These pivotal influences on individual information-processing capacities also seem to explain erroneous decision making.[11] Over the course of decades, a great number of scholars of international security crises using a wide range of theories and measurement techniques have all reached rather similar conclusions: the quality of decision making during foreign policy crises varies widely, but the frequent occurrence of stress-induced breakdowns of prudent leadership is a cause for special concern.[12]

3.3   Leaders and their crisis teams: group dynamics

As a rule, crisis decision making takes place in some type of small-group setting in which political and bureaucratic leaders interact and reach some sort of collective decision – whether by unanimity or majority rule. The small group appears to be an institutionally sanctioned forum for crisis leadership: most crisis contingency plans make provision for collegial bodies to gather and start coordinating the crisis response effort. These crisis teams become the critical nodes of what often are vast and highly complex multi-organizational and intergovernmental networks that come into being in response to crises.[13] Such groups may vary quite a bit in composition, size, and other relevant characteristics, even within the course of a single crisis.[14]

Small groups have virtues in crisis decision making, but they can just as easily become a liability.[15] In the high-pressure, high-consequence context of crises, the potential advantages of groups – increased intellectual and cognitive capacity (following the conventional wisdom that two know more than one) – are easily off-set by pathological group dynamics.

The main problem, borne out by historical and laboratory studies alike, is that individuals in groups often do not share and use information effectively in advising leaders or reaching collective decisions. Two extreme forms of group behavior impede the quality of group deliberation and choice: conflict and conformity. Some groups fall apart under crisis pressure. In other groups, loyalty to the leader and the preservation of unity become the name of the game: "criticism, dissent and mutual recrimination literally must wait until the crisis is over."[16]

Both extremes typically produce underperformance: too much conflict will paralyze the decision-making process, too much conformity removes useful obstacles to ill-considered actions and blunt adventurism. The possibility for extremes is enhanced by the high degree of informality that characterizes the interaction within crisis groups: procedural rules and institutional safeguards that stabilize regular modes of policy making tend to disappear. While this may stimulate innovative and creative practices, it also leaves groups fully exposed to a number of vulnerabilities. These include the following.

Newness and conformity   In many cases, the members of top-level coordination groups or crisis teams are relatively unfamiliar with what is expected of them and the rules of the game that apply. Especially in settings where crises are rare occurrences, chances are high that many top executives have little crisis experience and crisis exercises have been few and far between. Moreover, since a crisis never conforms fully to the ones foreseen in the manuals (if only because it hits at an impossible hour, or in the midst of some other hectic episode, or just after a major reshuffle of personnel and organizations), there is a high likelihood that the people gathering around the table will not always be familiar to one another, let alone have experience of working together as a group.

This likelihood is increased by the often-observed tendency for officials and agencies to "converge upon" the localities of crisis coordination centers in their effort to take part in the action. There are symbolic rewards to be reaped from being present at the core of the government response effort: participation demonstrates that one is deemed relevant. And for all the problems they cause, many also experience crises as adrenaline-enhancing breaks from the daily grind of politics and bureaucracy.[17]

These new group settings are vulnerable to what some of us in earlier work have termed "new group syndrome."[18] Particularly during the first, and often critical, stages of an acute crisis, "group members are uncertain about their roles and status and thus are concerned about the possibility of being made a scapegoat . . . Hence they are likely to avoid expressing opinions that are different from those proposed by the leader or other powerful persons in the group, to avoid conflict by failing to criticize one another's ideas, and even to agree overtly with other people's suggestions while disagreeing covertly."[19] These behaviors may partly be a product of what has been called "false cohesion," which is grounded in group member motivations to maintain their position within the inner circle of power and prestige. This renders the group process vulnerable to the kind of collective ignorance, illusory unanimity, self-censorship, and other propensities for ill-considered decision making commonly associated with groupthink (see further below).

Not all new groups develop new group syndrome. A critical factor is whether or not leaders intervene actively in order to set roles, norms, and ground rules that suspend extra-group status considerations and encourage broad and forthright participation from the very start.

Excessive cordiality and conformity Laboring under intense pressure and in relative isolation from "life as usual" in the world outside, crisis teams may easily become more to their members than functional units for deliberation or political arenas for managing intragovernmental conflict. They can become "sanctuaries" for a leader and his associates: a place of refuge from the pressures of a crisis and the dilemmas of the responsibility for dealing with the crisis. Embattled policy makers find shelter among their peers in a relatively intimate and shielded environment. This helps them to reduce the anxiety and stress that many of them experience during a crisis.

Such collective stress reduction may come at the price of a diminished capacity for reality-testing.[20] The widely cited "groupthink" tendency, which refers to excessive concurrence seeking among members of relatively closed elite groups, has been put forward in a score of case studies and experimental research as an explanation of policy fiascos and mismanaged crises. Members of groups affected by groupthink fall prey to groundless but infectious optimism about their ability to see through a crisis successfully. Members who do not share this "illusion of invulnerability," as Janis called it, will feel constrained to speak frankly about doubts and misgivings they may have about the course of action preferred by the group and/or its leaders.[21]

In more protracted crises, crisis teams of the more closed-knit kind may fall prey to "bunker syndrome," i.e. the tendency for members of the crisis group to stick together in relative isolation from their regular organizational and external constituencies, and for the group as a whole to reify its own view of the crisis even though more and more actors in the outside world are shifting perspectives and priorities.

Whether excessive conformity or destructive infighting are likely to affect a crisis team is not a matter of chance. It has, of course, to do with the nature of the interpersonal and interagency relations prior to the crisis: do they know, respect, and trust each other fully, or not at all? Is the group considered a "safe" or a "dangerous" place? Do the group members understand that they depend on each other to achieve their aims? The accountability structure under which a crisis team operates is also an important factor. When group members feel they are not accountable at all, or will be held accountable as members of the group as a whole, they are more likely to display conformity behavior in the groupthink and new group mould. When they know they have to answer individually for what they said and did during the crisis, the likelihood of more vigilant and possibly also more strident postures increases sharply.[22]

Centrifugality and politicking   Groupthink and new group syndrome produce excessive conformity and consensus seeking in crisis teams. But crises may also give rise to intense internal conflict. This should come as no surprise: the high-stakes circumstances of crises constitute a pressure cooker for pre-existing tensions between officials or the organizations they represent. Crisis groups may become political arenas, where strategic behavior is the norm. Group members will, for example, use their information and expertise as a weapon or shield in their ongoing internecine struggles rather than use their potential assets to help the group as a whole reach sensible decisions. Rumors, leaks, silences, and misrepresentations are part and parcel of this process, as are attempts to form or break up cliques within the group. There will be fierce competition for the leader's ear, and attempts to destroy the credibility of competitors for the leader's attention. And when members of these politicized crisis groups begin to lose confidence that a successful resolution of the crisis can be achieved, they will focus on saving themselves rather than keeping the group afloat.

On paper, the constitution of crisis teams is usually clear and governed by procedures and functional requirements. In reality, other considerations enter the picture, and may foster imbalances or incorporate conflict into the group process. A leader's personal needs, sentiments, and calculations typically affect who is in and who is out of the loop during a crisis. Many leaders surround themselves with trusted and liked sources of information and advice. Agencies that traditionally are low in the bureaucratic pecking order may simply be overlooked or ignored regardless of their real importance to effective crisis response. The "non-favored" and "forgotten ones" are thus precluded from airing their perspective in the top-level group.[23]

In short, leaders or other group members may deliberately attempt to reduce, widen, or otherwise "rig" the composition of the inner circle to gain acceptance for their preferred courses of action and deny proponents of competing views a platform.[24] Detailed examples of this infighting can be found in memoirs and studies concerning the Carter administration's handling of the Iranian hostage crisis. A battle for Carter's mind and soul was taking place between the National Security Adviser (Zbigniew Brzezinski) and the State Department (in particular the American ambassador in Tehran, William Sullivan, and later on Secretary of State, Cyrus Vance). Both Sullivan and Vance had to stand by and watch as slowly but surely their ability to exert influence on the deliberations of the President's crisis management group declined. They were marginalized and eventually excluded from vital moments in the decision-making process. The decision to go ahead with the ill-fated military operation to rescue the hostages was, for example, taken while Vance – an ardent critic of that plan – was on a weekend outing; his deputy was deliberately given the impression that Vance was no longer opposed to the idea.[25]

Success factors

It is good to know that crisis teams – whether they are emergency operations centers at the tactical level or inner circles and war cabinets at the senior political level – can actually work quite well, provided certain conditions are met. Admittedly, this is more the case in theory than in observed crisis practice, but at least the thrust of research is unequivocal. It shows that crisis teams are more likely to perform effectively in communities or governments where certain types of crises are recurring rather than rare phenomena. The key policy makers and agencies are thus more likely to have meaningful experience in working together.[26] Moreover, team performance is enhanced if the pre-existing interpersonal and inter-organizational relationships among the chief actors represented in the crisis group are marked by a reasonable degree of mutual trust. At the very least, entrenched competition, rivalry, and conflict among the people or organizations involved must be avoided; there needs to be a modicum of what sociologists call "domain consensus," i.e. a certain shared understanding of the purposes of the group or center, their own roles in it, and those of others.[27] Also, it helps if there is general acceptance of the different roles and responsibilities among group members: it must be clear who lead – and thus make the final choices – and who advise – and thus have a duty to "speak truth to power" to the best of their professional ability, even if this truth is unpleasant.

The institutionalization of procedures for group composition and deliberation is particularly important. These procedures help leaders of crisis groups to use their authority wisely: to create the conditions for optimal information sharing, collaboration, and frank discussion, and not succumb to the temptation of dominating or even manipulating the group process.[28]

The best-known procedure is called multiple advocacy. It directs leaders to create and maintain a courtroom-like setting where proponents of different policy proposals get an opportunity to argue their case before an as yet uncommitted "magistrate-leader." A neutral "custodian-manager" guides the process; his only objective is to ensure that all the relevant stakeholders and experts are present, that all relevant information and viewpoints are laid on the table, and that effective debate and reflection take place before decisions are made.[29] The multiple advocacy method seems eminently appropriate for the management of crisis coordination units, where so much is riding on charting a cogent policy line and dealing with decisional dilemmas in a responsible fashion.

The characteristics of crises place constraints upon the viability of this procedure. For one, the sheer pace of events during the acute stages of a crisis makes it exceedingly difficult for groups to adopt such a highly proceduralized, reflective, and time-consuming mode of collective deliberation. When faced with exogenous pressures to act fast and to be seen to take charge, leaders often feel forced to discount the requirements for optimal group deliberation and choice procedures.

Perhaps more importantly, given the high personal and political stakes that top officials have in crisis management, it may be too much to expect that they stick to the self-imposed limitations of the various roles accorded to them by the multiple advocacy model. The purely procedural role of the custodian requires an almost superhuman effort on the part of an official who is more likely than not to have been selected on the basis of substantive expertise and profile, and who will find it impossible not to get drawn into interagency pulling and hauling.[30] In crises, officials and agencies look to the top-level office holders for a clear sense of purpose and direction, but the precepts of multiple advocacy prohibit these same top officials from taking positions and expressing policy preferences until there has been ample opportunity for group discussion.

This creates a double bind for leaders: they must commit and not commit at the same time. Meltsner put it well when he argued that "there is a delicate balance between the need for the ruler to be strong-minded [in responding to a crisis, authors] and the need for openness in presenting problems and receiving advice. What is required is a ruler who appears to the external world to be in charge but who, within the inner circle, has created norms of equality to promote discussion, dissent, and multiple perspectives. . . ."[31] Even in the best of circumstances, however, the shadow of hierarchy is always present in groups with a clear authority structure: some group members will second-guess the leader's preferences and tell him what they think he will want to hear, or at least avoid telling him what they think he does not want to know.

3.4   How governmental crisis decisions "happen"[32]

Conventional wisdom dictates that government leaders make strategic decisions and coordinate government action when crises occur. They and their agencies are expected to put aside parochial interests and ongoing squabbles – they must act in concert. Under crisis conditions, concepts such as "comprehensive" or "integrated" emergency management and unifying metaphors such as "the war against terrorism" become politically salient.

It would be a mistake, however, to assume that leaders and central governments are always "in control" of the crisis response process.[33] The truth is that a great many pivotal crisis decisions are *not* taken by individual leaders or by small informal groups of senior policy makers. They emerge from various alternative loci of decision making and coordination.[34] In fact, the crisis response in modern society is best characterized in terms of a network. This is not necessarily counterproductive, as many leaders have learned, because delegation of decision making authority down the line usually enhances resilience rather than detracting from it.

Non-decision making

In concentrating upon "strategic decisions" and "responses" we may forget that the course of crises is shaped by default as well as by choice: so-called "non-decisions" determine the course of events just as much as deliberate policies. Different forms of non-decision making during crises can be discerned: (1) decisions that are not taken; (2) decisions not to decide; (3) decisions not to act; (4) strategic evasion of choice opportunities.

Consider the Heizel Stadium disaster in Brussels. The crisis began when fighting broke out between rival groups of British and Italian fans before the start of the 1985 European Soccer Cup final between Juventus and Liverpool. British hooligans attacked the Italian crowd in the adjacent section of the stands, triggering panic among the Italians locked up in their section. The death toll rose to 39; 450 spectators were wounded.[35] As the crisis unfolded, several crucial non-decisions shaped the response.

Decisions were not taken on matters of monitoring outgoing information in the wake of the disaster. No consistent strategies were devised to manage the flood of telephone calls received at the stadium from anxious friends and relatives of spectators in the Italian section, who, along with millions of viewers all over the world, had witnessed the disaster live on television. In addition, no strategy was formulated for handling the press. The informal group of authorities, assembling in the stadium's VIP lounge, never considered the idea of terminating television coverage of the match.[36]

The Belgian Minister for the Interior watched the match at his Brussels apartment. He assessed that the authorities on the ground were in a better position to judge what should be done, so chose not to involve himself and not even to go to the site of the disaster (a decision for which he was greatly criticized afterwards). This second type of non-decision making is, in essence, a meta-level response: it impacts upon the organization and process of crisis management rather than on the crisis events as such. It has the effect of (re)structuring the tasks and responsibilities of various potential decision makers and units. This subtle quality of decisions-not-to-decide can easily get lost in the turbulence surrounding crisis events, as it did in the Heizel football stadium case. Yet it may be crucial. Deliberate restraint on the part of top-level policy makers makes a significant difference at the operational level of crisis management. It may provide a recipe for chaos, but it may equally well mean a refreshing absence of the kind of political interference in operational affairs so often detested by agency leaders.

The third type of non-decision occurred when judicial authorities were summoned to the stadium immediately after the disaster. Upon arrival at the stadium, the public prosecutor and the Belgian Minister for Justice conferred with police commanders. The immediate issue was whether or not to make arrests on the spot. Given the lack of police manpower at that time and given the operational complications of apprehending individuals in an aggressive crowd, they reluctantly decided on a policy of containment rather than prosecution. This decision not to act became the center of public controversy in the days after the disaster.

Senior policy makers may sometimes seek to dissociate themselves as much as possible from managing the crisis response. Confronted with the overwhelming pressures of crisis, decision makers may question whether they and their organizations will be able to cope effectively. They may feel the chances for success are slight. This will prompt attempts on their part to escape individual responsibility for potentially fateful government choices and policies. This produces what we might call "strategic evasion": continuing to insist that the main responsibility for crisis response lies with other agencies or levels of government.

Decentralization

Well before September 11, 2001, the Federal Aviation Agency (FAA) and the North American Aerospace Defense Command (NORAD) had developed a procedure for collaboration in the event of a hijacking. Before the FAA could ask NORAD to take down a civil aircraft, "multiple levels of notification and approval at the highest levels of government" were required.[37] In the 9/11 crisis, there was no time to follow protocol, as the FAA's Boston Center – which was tracking American Flight 11 (headed for the WTC's North Tower) – realized. The Boston Center did not follow the protocol and contacted the military directly, asking for F-16s. After asking whether this was "real-world or exercise," two F-15 aircraft scrambled. As the 9/11 Commission notes: "The air defense of America began with this call."

Minutes before American Flight 11 hit the North Tower, United Flight 175 turned course toward the South Tower. This change went unnoticed, as the flight controller responsible for United 175 was still looking for American Flight 11, which had just crashed. When the controller realized he had a second problem on his hands, a colleague tried to notify the regional managers. They refused to be disturbed, as they were in a meeting discussing the first crash. Meanwhile, American 77 disappeared from the radar of the Indianapolis Center. Unaware of the other hijackings, the controller feared a crash and began to look for clues. This is what happened in the next half hour:

Indianapolis Center never saw Flight 77 turn around. By the time it reappeared in primary radar coverage, controllers had either stopped looking for the aircraft because they thought it had crashed or were looking toward the west [the flight was headed for Los Angeles, authors]. Although the Command Center learned Flight 77 was missing, neither it nor the FAA headquarters issued an all points bulletin to surrounding centers to search for primary radar targets. American 77 traveled undetected for 36 minutes on a course due east for Washington, D.C.[38]

The logic of centralization enjoys its largest appeal in times of non-crisis. Armed with knowledge of the past – the Cold War scenarios imagined threatening planes coming in from across the ocean – efficient protocols are formulated that invest crisis leaders with the means and authority to deal with the impending threat.

Betting on centralization in times of crisis can be a potential liability, however. The actual crisis always differs from the envisioned ones on which formal crisis management structures are predicated. Efficient protocols may turn out to be time consuming. Channels of centralization may lead to powerless or incapable agencies, bypassing and effectively neutralizing those that are actually capable of making a difference. As Weick observes:

> The danger in centralization and contraction of authority is that there may be a reduction in the level of competence directed at the problem [. .] The person in authority is not necessarily the most competent person to deal with a crisis, so a contraction of authority leads either to less action or more confusion.[39]

Centralization of crisis operations has been known to produce policies that are experienced by the staff "on the ground" as insufficient, ineffective, or even counter-productive.[40] Centralization may thus fuel rather than dampen a crisis. In highly centralized systems, disruption of one part of the system, let alone the system's core, can have a cumulative effect, triggering chains of component failures that are hard to stop or reverse.[41]

In some organizations and governments, awareness of these problems has led to pre-planned, formalized decentralization of authority for certain vital areas of crisis response. For example, during the Cold War era, authority to launch nuclear counter strikes in case of a "decapitating" first strike against American centers of political and military decision making was delegated to submarine commanders.[42] So-called "high-reliability organizations" (see Chapter 2) have adopted decentralization as a defining characteristic of their safety culture: operators who notice a safety hazard can (and do) call for an immediate halt of the production process.

Crisis experience tends to favor decentralization of crisis response authority: top leaders and national policy makers have learned that, particularly in highly dynamic and technically complex crises, they are usually better off relying upon and supporting local authorities and expert agencies and skillful operators rather than "taking charge" themselves. This practice is, for instance, widespread in the law enforcement communities that have done away with militarized cultures of centralization. In the modern conception of law enforcement, commanding structures for crisis are built on the premise that only those decisions that cannot be taken on the spot will rise to the top where crisis leaders reside.[43]

Improvisation

Crises have the nasty habit of rendering plans and structures irrelevant. When uncertainty leads to bewilderment, both on the ground and in the crisis center, the crisis response does not resemble a neatly delineated process of operational and strategic decision making. Situational imperatives require intense cooperation and improvisation, especially in highly volatile conditions where there is non-negotiable time pressure. Such conditions are relatively rare at the strategic level of government.

In 1970, the mission of Apollo 13 almost ended in a disaster.[44] A cumulative chain of mechanical problems caused an explosion on board the orbiting spaceship. This affected vital life-support systems, as well as the electrical power necessary to navigate the spacecraft. Carbon dioxide build-up threatened the astronauts' survival. In their efforts to solve the crisis, both the astronauts and the flight control people in Houston had to work within the hard boundaries set by oxygen and energy supply, the hostilities of space, the impossibility of determining the state of the spacecraft, and a very small window of opportunity for a safe return. To conserve water and power, engineers in Houston calculated which components could be switched off. After four days, the astronauts – dehydrated, cold, and fatigued – could barely perform the revised entry checklist and the crucial midcourse correction. By this time, many procedures and routines had been left behind. The crew had to come home. They returned home safely thanks to the vast creativity and experimentation directed at the baffling and urgent problems following the explosion.

This is not to say that improvisation always trumps structure in times of crisis. The institutional structure in which organizations are embedded both constrains and enables organizational action – structure makes certain things impossible, but it also provides something to fall back on.[45] The centrality of the NASA control room allowed engineers to see the whole picture, formulate options, and instruct the astronauts on those options.[46] But this example also shows that structure is best exploited by a healthy dose of improvisation.

Improvisation in crisis is not given: some organizational configurations and cultures conduce to it, others constrain it. One might perhaps assume that organizations will immediately suspend all standard operating procedures, routines, rules, customs, or targets that could possibly stand in the way of effective crisis management improvisation. But that is not how most public organizations operate. Large-scale bureaucracies in particular have been designed to deal in an effective and responsible way with a certain category of social problems. These organizations typically attempt to minimize uncertainty for their employees, which allows them to structure their activities and embed best practices.[47]

This creates something of a paradox: when employees realize that a crisis demands the services of their organization, the accompanying uncertainty nurtures a reliance on institutionalized response modes. However, these modes were never designed or tested with the crisis at hand in mind. Unless organizations have been trained to recognize when their available repertoire does not suffice to deal with the crisis at hand, their operational routines will become more salient during crises (which creates a potential for further escalation of the crisis).

3.5   From decisions to responses: the importance of crisis coordination

Even when leaders make well-informed decisions that define a clear course of action, they still face the challenge of seeing their decisions materialize. Leaders depend on organizations – both inside and outside their immediate jurisdiction – to execute their decisions. As most crises typically involve multiple organizations, leaders rely on some level of coordination between these organizations. The following description of New York City's immediate response to the attacks on the World Trade Center brings home both the importance and the difficulty of crisis coordination:[48]

Commanders in the lobbies of the two towers lacked reliable information about what was happening. Communications inside were sporadic. Intelligence at the lobby command centers about what was happening outside – especially about what was happening to the towers – was almost non-existent. In fact, television viewers across the world knew more about the progression of fires than the commanders, because the commanders had no access to the television reports. The New York City Police Department (NYPD) had a helicopter circling overhead, but the fire chiefs had no link to the police assessments. In fact, there were no senior NYPD personnel at the fire department's command posts – and vice versa. Desperate to help their brothers, some firefighters went directly up the stairs without waiting for orders. Department officials had a hard time keeping track of who was at the scene. The New York City Fire Department had no established process for establishing whether mutual aid was needed from surrounding communities and no formal method of requesting it. Because one half of the department's companies were dispatched to the scene, the lack of clear mutual aid agreements left the rest of the city at risk.

The characteristics of crisis, particularly the early stages of a rapidly unfolding crisis, make central coordination of operations not only highly desirable but also highly elusive.[49] Under conditions of deep uncertainty, many organizations which rarely work together under normal circumstances must suddenly try to make the crucial difference. Smooth cooperation is not easy when the cause of the crisis is unknown, the damage untold, and the potential consequences of one's actions can only be imagined. People have trouble arriving at a somewhat similar conception of what happened. Communication is impaired. Moreover, the stakes have been raised dramatically, and there is less room for experimentation and failure. The field of disaster studies has paid particular attention to this challenge.

A basic problem undermining any attempt to coordinate crisis management efforts is the *limited adequacy of the planned response*.[50] The organizations that are expected (indeed charged) to deal with a crisis all too often have trouble doing what they are supposed to do. The mobilization of organizational members may be slow, incomplete or simply impossible. In natural disasters, for instance, an organization that is part of the first response may find itself "victimized": when headquarters, essential equipment, or communication systems are ruined, mobilization will be hindered. When the towers of the World Trade Center collapsed, the New York City's Emergency Operation Center was severely damaged. A new crisis coordination center had to be set up.[51] But even if mobilization proceeds smoothly, the response of the mobilized members may be less than adequate as a result of impaired decision making. Mobilization may even be late or may not happen at all when organizational leaders do not share the sense of urgency felt by others.

An elementary problem of coordination is the *matching of place and function*.[52] Public organizations are traditionally designed to perform a specific function (e.g. garbage collection, train service, medical care, punishment, etc.). These organizations perform their function in a given geographic area, under specified conditions. Crises challenge these organizational designs. Crisis management usually entails the ad hoc formulation of function: during a crisis, the authorities in charge arrive at a definition of the situation (which changes all the time) and decide what problems must be solved first. These problems usually require the assistance of multiple organizations, each originally designed to perform part of the solution. Moreover, crises rarely correspond with jurisdictional boundaries of organizations or government. The anthrax crisis, which held the United States in its grip during the immediate aftermath of the 9/11 attacks, provides an illuminating example.[53] Many different organizations were part of the crisis management process: hospitals, intelligence organizations, police, specialized army units with knowledge of anthrax, the United States postal service, and all the organizations that received white powder letters. Yet the area of the crisis remained undefined. It never became clear who was sending these letters and for what purpose: was it a disgruntled employee, a terrorist attack, or a conspiracy? Where would the next anthrax letter strike?

The *upscaling dilemma* hinders the so-called vertical coordination that should deal with the inherent tensions between crisis centers and operations in the field. We might say that some sort of subsidiarity principle has gained ground: crises should be dealt with at the level closest to which they occur. Only when a crisis spills over the local borders or when local authorities fail to deal with the crisis in an adequate manner do higher authorities usually step in. This is technically known as upscaling.

However, it is not always clear when central authorities should step in. Nor is it clear who decides when the moment has come. Coordination efforts are usually designed at the highest levels of organization. But these designs may not be known at middle management levels and particularly at the lowest operational levels.[54] Upscaling can therefore easily create problems of its own. Moving crisis management authority up widens the gap between decision-makers and the scene. It often necessitates new relations between central authorities and local responders. It may create resentment among local authorities and victims. It is, in short, a delicate decision that comes with a dilemma: is the coordination problem that is solved really worse than the one that is being created?

An equally pressing and much-noted problem is found in the *interorganizational relations* that govern the crisis response network.[55] Horizontal cooperation between responding parties is, for instance, easily undermined by both technical and cultural communication problems. Another problem is that most organizations entertain different notions of the meaning and necessity of coordination.[56] Emergency workers, for instance, generally understand the need for cooperation but may vehemently disagree on the means by which top-level policy makers try to achieve it. Military organizations prefer hierarchical coordination, whereas medical teams are more likely to resist coordination efforts from above. The variety of interpretations concerning the nature and role of crisis coordination increases significantly with the growing complexity of the crisis.

A compounding problem of an even more serious nature is the apparent *unwillingness of some organizations to cooperate with others*, even in the wake of disaster. It would be naive to think that under crisis conditions all pre-existing bureaucratic tensions make way for a mechanistic, rationalistic mode of centralized and tightly coordinated policy making and implementation. On the contrary: interagency tensions often intensify. For some public agencies, for example, the opportunity to act during the rare real crisis as opposed to the perennial dress rehearsals constitutes a litmus test for their rationale and capability. Being invisible or looking ineffective during a major emergency can threaten the existence of specialized agencies such as civil defense organizations, special police and fire units, and medical emergency teams. Such agencies will, consequently, be bent on asserting themselves and their modus operandi to the maximum extent – with or without the cooperation of other agencies in the crisis network. In a crisis network, several officials and agencies may adopt this type of posturing. Friction increases when officials, agencies, and levels of government that are simply not used to working together are forced by circumstance to rely on each other.[57]

Interagency rivalry occurs in many domains. Intelligence agencies often refuse to share information. In war situations, military leaders experience great trouble in getting various specialized forces to work together.[58] International humanitarian efforts are plagued by conflicts between the various participating NGOs. Interorganizational tension appears to be the rule rather than the exception – a lesson that time and again comes as a surprise to politicians, public managers, and media. The December 2004 tsunami response operation appears to have been an exception: among journalists and officialdom alike there was wide and consistent praise for the coordinating efforts of the United Nations Office for the Coordination of Humanitarian Assistance (OCHA). Interorganizational relations during the first weeks were reportedly characterized by harmony and a desire for joint achievement rather than by rivalry and backstabbing.

When intergovernmental and bureaucratic politics pervade the crisis response process, the chances are slim for any central decision-making authority to impose itself upon the squabbling factions. Under these conditions, the center runs a good chance of becoming an arena in which the various stakeholders promote different approaches and priorities with regard to what should be done. The typical result is large disparities between the compromise decisions reached at crisis centers and the actual conduct of crisis operations within and between different executive agencies.[59]

Coordination of crisis management efforts is often hindered by *the actions of involved bystanders*.[60] In the disaster literature, this is known as the problem of mass convergence (or mass assault): many people try to make their way to the scene. These people may have different motives for doing so – varying from concern about the safety of loved ones and genuine altruistic instincts to plain sensationalism – but the effects are the same: roads clog up, which slows the mobilization of emergency responders; much-needed emergency responders must keep "disaster tourists" at bay; communication and physical interaction between responders is hindered. The problems of mass convergence became painfully clear during the siege of the terrorist-held school in Beslan, Russia, in September 2004. Armed locals – desperately worried about their relatives in the school – took part in storming the building, which appears to have contributed to the disastrous outcome of the operation (more than 300 children, teachers, and parents died).

Coordination may also be affected by *lessons from the past*. In the absence of useful crisis management blueprints (each crisis is, after all, unique), policy makers tend to rely on previous crisis experiences. Lessons drawn from these – what worked and what certainly did not – inform their current crisis behavior. Many different lessons exist, of course, and their impact is likely to vary considerably across the spectrum of actors. In regions or nations that are repeatedly beset by similar types of crises, interorganizational and intergovernmental crisis coordination patterns take hold in more or less formalized networks, whose composition and rules of interaction evolve as part of an emerging crisis management subculture, quite similar to the so-called "disaster subculture" that sociologists have found in communities with frequent exposure to natural disasters.

Fostering crisis coordination

The act of coordination, at heart, is a political activity: to create orderly interaction within and among organizations, delicate choices about power, responsibility, rules of conduct, and division of labor must be made and enacted.[61] The core challenge of coordination as a form of administrative politics is rather simple: public institutions tend to be recalcitrant.[62] They are not purely rational-instrumental machines, in which all employees know what to do, when to do it, and actually do what is expected of them. Neither are they devoid of parochial interests and motives, and therefore are not automatically inclined to fall in line with the pursuit of the presumably superordinate goal of a coordinated crisis response. In short, if it is hard to manage one organization toward some given goal, it becomes much harder to direct two (or more) organizations in the same direction.[63]

And yet some crisis management operations display a remarkable degree of order: crisis centers emerge, information is pooled, resources are allocated, cooperation and improvisation prevail (the 2004 tsunami emergency response operation may well become a textbook example of successful coordination).[64] This coordination is rarely imposed by leaders; it emerges almost as a natural by-product of crisis. A coordinated operation emerges, as Chisholm notes, "through a system of informal channels, behavioral norms, and agreements."[65]

This is less strange than it seems if one considers the function of crisis coordination: it helps to fill a social vacuum.[66] Crisis has a disorienting effect on people. In a sea of uncertainty, people must deal with a threat and they must do so immediately. Individuals' primary inclination in crisis situations is to reduce uncertainty.[67] But a crisis by definition deprives individuals – victims, responders, citizens, policy makers – of conceptual anchors that can guide their behavior.[68] The social system that under normal circumstances provides the means to coordinate social behavior and address uncertainty has also been "dislodged." Coordination is required to restore these crucial functions in order to reduce uncertainty.[69]

A useful way to approach crisis coordination is to see it as a by-product of the collective search for information – in order to deal with uncertainty – and the mutual adjustments in that search.[70] Some people urgently need certain pieces of information; some people possess information that is crucial to others. As people begin to seek and exchange information, so-called "information nodes" emerge. These are places where information seekers and givers interact. Once an emerging information node begins to attract additional information seekers and givers, and in fact becomes known as a place where information is to be gotten or delivered, a first and crucial step is set on the path toward effective coordination. Further development then depends on the rapid emergence of procedures and rules, which help to channel information exchanges, separate "data" from information, and "translate" this information into crisis management action. Effective crisis coordination, in other words, resembles something of a super-accelerated institutionalization process.

Such processes are governed by feedback (or the lack thereof). Each step toward increased coordination is informed by positive feedback signalling both the functionality and the legitimacy of the standing arrangement. This is not a unidirectional process. For instance, the emergence of an information node is likely to attract more information; but if this increase in information swamps the node, alternative nodes will emerge. The ill-functioning node disappears.

Coordination is most likely to emerge from crisis-induced chaos when crisis leaders nurture the right conditions. One such condition is that actors should be motivated to share their information with others in the emerging node. People must trust the "information marketplace" and the people associated with it if the node is to become the center of a coordinating network. Trust is, of course, hard to come by and easy to lose – and many factors affect the trustworthiness of existing or emerging organizational practices.[71] It suffices here to note that the *absence* of trustworthiness is a rather certain way to nip an evolving coordination process in the bud.

A second condition that fosters coordination is the availability of knowledge and capacity. To embed an information node into a physical structure (building, food, information and communication technology, supporting staff) requires resources. It would be a mistake to think that rich communities by definition enjoy better crisis coordination than poor communities. At the same time, one cannot expect highly effective coordination of a large-scale crisis response operation without phones, faxes, and internet being available.

The rapid emergence of a coordinated response can give rise to what we call the paradox of effective coordination. As the initial structuring of information, communication, and command flows is perceived as successful, the emerging coordination structure is endowed with legitimacy. This, in turn, firmly establishes the initial structuring. In no time, there is only one way to manage the crisis at hand. This "instant institutionalization" may be beneficial in the early crisis management phase, but the more beneficial it is, the more established the crisis management structure becomes. This may close the crisis decision making arena off from other actors, which, in turn, can undermine long-term coordination.

Alan Barton describes the result of this paradoxical effect, which he refers to as the "bureaucratization of altruism."[72] In time, the threat of crisis evaporates and attention is focused on a return to normalcy, damage compensation, victim assistance, and lesson drawing. These functions of crisis management typically introduce other institutional actors than the ones involved in the early crisis management phases. Yet it may be hard for these new actors to become involved in a crisis network that has built up a good track record. The shift from immediate concerns to long-term concerns then sets the stage for bureaucratic infighting, distorted information flows, and a breakdown of crisis management effectiveness.

A successful response operation can thus become redefined over time and enter collective memory as a failure. A good example is found in the aftermath of the 1992 Amsterdam air crash. The initial crisis response was widely praised. The structure of the crisis management operation was clear – both inside and outside the command center. After several weeks, new problems began to emerge. The promise issued in the immediate aftermath of the disaster that Amsterdam would act as a "caring government" and the subsequent promise not to prosecute illegal immigrants who lived in the disaster area unexpectedly led to a massive inflow of illegal immigrants who claimed that they lived in the area. They demanded shelter, new housing, and a resident status. The coordination of this crisis management phase proved much more difficult as new actors became involved who had not shared the "adrenaline rush" of the first phase. In due course, people in the area began to report (rather vague) health complaints. By this time, the crisis management operation had been bureaucratized, which solicited bitter complaints from the victims who felt left behind. Years later, a parliamentary inquiry would criticize the lack of coordination that characterized the later phase of the Amsterdam air disaster.[73]

Thus we arrive at a third condition: the formalization of the coordination process. The initial phase of crisis coordination can do without rules, but successive phases require a few key rules that facilitate the interaction between the various actors and structure information flows. In the absence of these rules, the fragile state of evolved coordination can easily collapse under the pressure of multiple actors and increased politicization (see Chapter 5).[74] Top-level leaders can play a key part in this process by making crucial decisions, keeping the decision-making process on track, guarding the quality of the decision-making process, and acting as the "external face" of the crisis management operation. Likewise, leaders of the various organizations involved in the coordination process can facilitate or hinder coordination efforts by conveying to their rank and file a cooperative versus obstructive attitude toward other organizations in the crisis response process. Leadership, in itself, does not guarantee effective coordination; its acid test comes at ground level: do organizations actually align their behavior and exchange pivotal operational information?[75]

3.6   Putting crisis leadership in its place

Most crisis response operations are characterized by a remarkable degree of improvisation, flexibility, effectiveness, and sometimes even heroism. Especially when crisis circumstances – uncertainty, threat, and urgency – are taken into account, one is bound to be impressed with the efforts of crisis responders, which, of course, may not always avert disaster. After detailing the many failures in the crisis response, the 9/11 Commission had this to say about the flight controllers and their military counterparts:

We do not believe that the true picture of that morning reflects discredit on the operational personnel at NEADS or FAA facilities. NEADS commanders and officers actively sought out information, and made the best judgments they could on the basis of what they knew. Individual FAA controllers, facility managers, and Command Center managers thought outside the box in recommending a nationwide alert, in ground-stopping local traffic, and, ultimately, in deciding to land all aircraft [4,500 airplanes, authors] and executing that unprecedented order flawlessly.[76]

The persistent myth in popular conceptions of crisis management holds that crisis leadership is the most important "driver" of crisis response. In this conception of leadership, crisis management consists of planning and control: the plan gives rise to effective coordination; leaders manage the coordinated network from their crisis centers. When the response is perceived to fail, there is a call for better coordination and stronger leadership. The result is more plans, which emphasize further centralization of authority: bureaucratic pyramids and a boss-of-the-bosses are supposed to forge coordination where it is not forthcoming spontaneously. Recent examples include the formation of the United States Department of Homeland Security and the appointment of an "anti-terrorist Czar" in the European Union.

In reality, the quality of the crisis response has less to do with planning and top-level control than these policies of centralization assume. A truly effective crisis response cannot be forced: it is to a large extent the result of a naturally evolving process. It cannot be managed in linear, step-by-step and comprehensive fashion from a single crisis center, however full of top decision makers and stacked with state-of-the-art information technology. There are simply too many hurdles that separate a leadership decision from its timely execution in the field.

In this chapter, we have attempted to put into proper perspective the role that leaders play in crisis response. Leaders are important – not as all-powerful decision makers but rather as designers, facilitators, and guardians of an institutional arrangement that produces effective decision-making and coordination processes. We do not suggest that leaders should simply rely on the innovative capacity of people and organizations to "emerge" in the wake of a crisis. Leaders must actively monitor the response. They must try to identify decisions that are critical to the quality of that response and which should be made by those who carry political responsibility. The most effective crisis leaders involve themselves quite selectively when it comes to making response decisions.

We argue that crisis leadership involves much more than only decision making about the direction and implementation of government policy. An understudied dimension of the crisis response process consists of government efforts at "meaning making": attempts to influence the public's understanding of the crisis. Such meaning making is critical because crises by definition involve a high degree of uncertainty. Their very occurrence exposes the limitations of existing institutional arrangements and the mental frameworks underpinning them. Crises threaten to undercut the legitimacy of these arrangements and frameworks, as well as the political support for the governments representing the established order. The question is how policy makers deal with this loss of "taken for grantedness." To answer this question, we introduce a symbolic-political perspective that stresses crisis governance as political meaning making. We do this in the next chapter.

Notes

1 See Eisenhower (1966); Dowty (1984).
2 Hermann (1963); Allison (1971); Janis (1989); Rosenthal et al. (1989); Brecher (1993).
3 See Larsson et al. (2005).
4 In the United States, for instance, a formal system for central government intervention operates: once the President declares a certain area officially a disaster area, the Federal Emergency Management Agency (FEMA) – now part of the Department of Homeland Security – becomes active in coordinating the disaster response. See Petak (1985); Waugh (1990); Sylves and Cumming (2004).
5 This is particularly true for political systems and policy domains in which executive office holders traditionally possess formal powers and discretionary space.
6 Preston (2001: 32).
7 Preston (2001: 199).
8 Glad (1980); Sick (1985).
9 A large amount of interdisciplinary literature has documented how they do so, and what factors influence their reasoning. Good summaries include Holsti (1979); Roberts (1988); Vertzberger (1990); Verbeek (2003).
10 Herek et al. (1987).
11 Smart and Vertinksy (1977); Roberts (1988).
12 These findings have not received much confirmation in other branches of crisis research, partly because students of disaster, disorder, and other crisis types have been much less inclined to study the behavior of top-level executives in great detail (for reasons that will become clear later in this chapter).
13 As a result, some analysts have turned toward group dynamics to explain the course and outcomes of crisis response. For example, Maoz (1990); Verbeek (2003). See also 't Hart et al. (1997); Preston (2001).
14 Studies of international crises report that critical decisions tend to be made by small numbers of chief executive officials and their most intimate advisers (Hermann, 1963; Paige, 1968; Holsti, 1972; Brecher, 1979a; Burke et al., 1989; Brecher, 1993; George, 1993). The same goes for corporate crises (Smart and Vertinsky, 1977; Slatter, 1984; Meyers, 1986; Lagadec, 1990). Nice illustrations of the variable group size and composition in crises can be found in Roberts (1988) and Verbeek (2003).

15 Janis (1982); 't Hart (1994).
16 Adomeit (1982: 39).
17 It is interesting to note how members of crisis teams sometimes get hooked on their role in the crisis response. When the crisis is finally brought to an end, they experience feelings of anxiety. It is hard to get back to normal life (see Rosenthal et al., 1994; 't Hart and Boin, 2001).
18 Stern (1997a); cf. Turner (1978).
19 Longley and Pruitt (1980: 87), cited in Stern (1997a).
20 Janis (1982).
21 For detailed accounts of groupthink, see 't Hart (1994) and 't Hart et al. (1997).
22 Kroon et al. (1991).
23 Milburn (1972); Janis (1982).
24 Hoyt and Garrison (1997). See also Glad (1980); Smith (1985).
25 Gabriel (1985); Sick (1985).
26 Wenger et al. (1986); Scanlon (1994).
27 Drabek (1985).
28 See, for example, Janis (1982); 't Hart (1994); 't Hart et al. (1997).
29 George and Stern (2002).
30 George and Stern (2002).
31 Meltsner (1990: 82).
32 This subtitle borrows from March (1994).
33 See Rosenthal et al. (1989); Rosenthal et al. (2001). In many international crises studied by Brecher and his associates, the key decisions that shaped the crisis participants' behavior during the crisis period were taken by a variety of what Brecher (1993: 223–5) calls "decisional forums." Likewise, the various country volumes on Baltic and East European post-Cold War crisis decision making produced by the CRISMART team in Stockholm document a strong variation in the composition of decision making units within and between various types of domestic and international crises (see, for example, Stern and Nohrstedt, 1999; Stern and Hansén, 2000; Stern et al., 2002; Lindgren, 2003; Brändström and Malesic, 2004).
34 See 't Hart et al. (1993); McConnell (2003).
35 This example is taken from 't Hart and Pijnenburg (1988).
36 Afterwards, the decision to continue broadcasting the match was severely criticized. The match had been left to proceed in order to allow for a mass mobilization of police forces from all over Belgium, specifically to contain the crowd upon leaving the stadium. Yet to many, the broadcast was taken simply as a manifestation of the apparent feeling among the authorities that "the show must go on."
37 The 9/11 Commission Report (2004: 17).
38 The 9/11 Commission Report (2004: 25).
39 Weick (1988: 312).
40 Schneider (1993); Larsson et al. (2005).
41 Perrow (1984).
42 Bracken (1983).
43 See Pearce and Fortune (1995).
44 This example is taken from Murray and Cox (1989).

45 Wilson (1989).
46 We are indebted to Paul Schulman for pointing this out.
47 Thompson (1967).
48 Taken from a McKinsey evaluation cited in Kettl (2003: 255–6).
49 A conceptual distinction should be made between crisis coordination as process – the acts and interactions aimed at aligning interactions between groups and organizations involved in crisis response operations – and as an outcome – the degree to which the behavior of groups and organizations involved in crisis response operations is actually aligned, so as to promote optimal implementation of the policies of a crisis coordination center or "ultimate decision unit." In the text that follows, we use coordination mostly in the former sense.
50 Barton (1969).
51 See Wachtendorf (2004) for details.
52 Schneider (1993); Kettl (2003).
53 Boin et al. (2003).
54 This point was brought to our attention by Henry Quarantelli (personal communication).
55 Barton (1969); Rosenthal et al. (1991).
56 Quarantelli (personal communication).
57 See the classic account in Dynes (1970).
58 The disjointed and fatally flawed planning and execution of the Iran rescue mission stands out as a classic horror story, but there are many others, even in what presumably is the mightiest military machine in the world. See Gabriel (1985).
59 Rosenthal et al. (1991).
60 Compare with Turner (1978).
61 Ekengren and Sundelius (2004).
62 Wilson (1989).
63 Hood (1976); Dunsire (1978).
64 See Wachtendorf's (2004) study on the emergence of effective crisis coordination in the wake of the 9/11 attack on New York City. We should note that the nature of crisis (for instance, conflict- versus consensus-type crises) is likely to constrain or enable efforts aimed at establishing coordination (Quarantelli, personal communication).
65 Chisholm (1989); Bardach (2001).
66 Barton (1969).
67 Sorokin (1943); Raphael (1986); Hodgkinson and Stewart (1991). For a sociological account, see Shibutani (1966).
68 In many cases, a crisis undermines regulatory and normative anchors as well.
69 It is interesting to note what happens when these structures do not emerge. One potential consequence, for instance, is the proliferation of unsubstantiated rumors (Shibutani, 1966).
70 "The lack of information is always the problem. In the absence of one single authority, the search for information creates coordination" (Drabek, 1985: 88). See also Dynes (1970) and Chisholm (1989: 11).
71 On trust, see Braithwaite and Levi (1998).
72 Barton (1969: 297).

73 This example is taken from Rosenthal et al. (2001).
74 Cf. Schneider (1993).
75 Many botched crisis management operations also feature "strong" leaders (or feature multiple leaders or no leaders at all). The point is that leadership is no magical solution to the challenges of crisis coordination, but that some form of leadership is needed to facilitate it.
76 National Commission on Terrorist Attacks (2004: 31).

4   Meaning making: crisis management as political communication

4.1   Crisis communication as politics

In the months leading up to the invasion of Iraq, President George W. Bush and Prime Minister Tony Blair repeatedly emphasized the clear and present danger posed by Iraqi weapons of mass destruction (WMD). As the conflict with Iraq escalated, and skeptical voices were heard in the United Nations Security Council, presidential and prime ministerial rhetoric intensified. The two leaders assured that there was virtually no doubt that Iraq possessed such weapons and that only military intervention could guarantee that these illicit programs, which had allegedly eluded UN WMD inspectors, would be found.[1] Both leaders staked their personal credibility on this claim and managed to drum up a considerable amount of political support at home for their position. However, both leaders quickly became the subject of increasingly bitter attacks from the opposition and from elements of their own parties when no evidence of ongoing WMD programs was turned up in the wake of the military intervention.

In a crisis, authorities often lose control, if only temporarily, over the dramaturgy of political communication. They are literally overtaken by events. The mass media rapidly generate powerful images and frames of the situation, well crafted for mass consumption.[2] The crisis turns into a "symbolic contest over the social meaning of an issue domain."[3] The *key question* of this chapter is why leaders succeed in some crises (George W. Bush in the months following the September 11 attacks) whereas they fail in others (Blair in the months prior to and following the invasion of Iraq) in shaping people's understanding of a crisis and thus in building public support for their policies.

We refer to these attempts as "meaning making": leaders, along with other stakeholders in a crisis, attempt to reduce the public and political uncertainty caused by crises.[4] They do so by communicating a persuasive story line (a narrative) that explains what happened, why it had to be that way, what its repercussions are, how it can be resolved, who can be relied upon to do so, and who is to blame. In this meaning-making process, which unfolds during every crisis, public leaders coalesce and compete with other political actors in shaping the public's view of the crisis. This question is especially intriguing in the context of democracies and contemporary information societies, where channels of communication abound, and many other stakeholders other than governments can transmit powerful facts and images of a crisis around the world in a matter of minutes.

Leaders must excel in this communication dimension of crisis management. Our *core claim* is that crisis communication makes a crucial difference between obtaining and losing the "permissive consensus" leaders need to effectuate their policies and bolster their reputation.[5] If they do not get their message across to the public about the causes, consequences, and cures of crises, others will. The political communication process is highly competitive: each and every detail of words, pictures, gestures, and performance matters.

Effective crisis leadership cannot be brought about by simply "doing the right thing" on the ground; it also presupposes a sure-footed manipulation of symbols that shapes the views and sentiments of the political environment in ways that enhance leadership capacity to act. In viable democracies there are, of course, legal and ethical as well as practical limits to governmental "news management" in a crisis. Barring total government control over the flow of information – as in situations of military censorship[6] – there are many ways in which news about the crisis reaches an already aroused public.

Much of the existing literature deals with crisis communication in a rather instrumental fashion. Textbook cases of communication failures give rise to detailed and hands-on prescriptions.[7] Many of these are very useful and well borne out by decades of experience; most of them are embedded in management and public relations analysis in the corporate sector.[8] What is missing, however, is a systematic understanding of the specific challenges of crisis communication in the public sector, i.e. in a political setting, which is what this chapter seeks to provide.

4.2   Crisis communication in a mediated political world

A crisis entails a breakdown of symbolic frameworks that legitimate the pre-existing socio-political order.[9] The pillars of "normal" life have come down; what remains no longer seems to work. Crises cause multiple levels of uncertainty. At the personal level, affected individuals face cognitive conflict: they still believe in the "normal" order but they confront repeated and undeniable information that things are seriously wrong. At the societal level, this cognitive conflict is emulated in the activities of multiple groups and organizations espousing different definitions of the situation – offering different claims about its causes, impact, and further development, and advocating alternative and often conflicting strategies to deal with the situation.

All this may also occur at the international level. In the wake of the accident at the Chernobyl nuclear reactor in April 1986, Soviet government spokespersons struggled to play down the scope and depth of the accident and the risk it posed to public health, as they tried to minimize the domestic political ramifications of the accident. Meanwhile, the American government viewed the disaster primarily in Cold War terms and recognized an opportunity to demonstrate the hollowness of Gorbachev's *perestroika* rhetoric, which had received a lot of positive play in Western media. The Americans sought to exploit the crisis to dramatize that Soviet technology was backward, and that the current Soviet regime was as callous and deceitful as its predecessors had been. As a result, government spokespersons from the two sides offered sharply contradictory figures and interpretations of the situation.

Even in Western societies, incidents involving controversial technologies or policies tend to exhibit this adversarial configuration – the government's account of the crisis pitted against the one put forward by environmentalist or victim groups – which exacerbates the crisis communication challenge for leaders.[10] People expect leaders to provide a believable and authoritative account, which promises a way out of the crisis. They must arbitrate the conflicting interpretations of the critical events. Leaders who understand this try to offer "believable futures." In the Chernobyl case, the Reagan government set up a presidential commission to investigate the accident and instructed US government scientists to abstain from making public statements, leaving it to the government to "speak with one voice." The strategy worked, partly helped by the haphazard Soviet information policy: American television networks and newspapers overwhelmingly prioritized American sources and the political messages they implicitly conveyed about the disaster.[11]

In the ever more densely "mediated" political context of crisis management, the capacity to capture public attention and a reputation for accuracy and trustworthiness have become fundamental political-administrative assets.[12] The buzz word here is credibility, which has been called "the most important key to political survival and influence."[13] For policy makers who possess it, risky political ventures become possible, and major political storms can be ridden out with relative ease. Without it, even the most basic tasks become difficult and subject to intense scrutiny by the media and other watchdogs. Communicative strategies of crisis management can be effective only if policy makers manage to retain the attention and confidence of the intended audiences.

Credibility, however, does not automatically lead to effective crisis communication. Many actors with their different angles clamor to make the news. In a crisis, past performance records are easily and rapidly undermined by emerging accounts of what went wrong. As a result, governments and their leaders may find themselves targets of intense criticism rather than being accepted by the public as authoritative sources of information.

The context in which policy makers communicate is best conceived of as a triangular relationship between political actors (governmental and non-governmental), the mass media (i.e. news producers: journalists and news organizations), and the citizenry (itself a pluralistic aggregate of all kinds of individuals, groups, and subcultures).[14] The bulk of the communication between governments and citizens is mediated communication, transmitted through mass media in a setting where all other political actors – parties, pressure groups, companies, trade unions, and more – try to get mass media to convey their information and opinions to the public.

Each of the constituents of this triangle sends, receives, and perceives information about the crisis at hand. Each is subject to all kinds of constraints to information processing and reality-testing. Moreover, each actor faces a particular set of behavioral incentives flowing from its position and role in the institutional context. Below we briefly discuss each corner of the triangle and touch upon some of the most distinctive features of its modus operandi in the crisis communication process.

The mass media

Mass media are a pivotal force in discovering, conveying, and (de)escalating crises. It is not uncommon for journalists to "discover" a threat before the officials responsible for dealing with that threat are even aware that something has happened. The defining example of recent history must be Woodward and Bernstein's exposure of the Watergate burglary, which created the political crisis that ended Nixon's presidency.[15]

In so far as every crisis is at least partly caused or aggravated by human and institutional flaws and failures, it provides a golden opportunity for journalists and news organizations to "score." Hot news stories sell well to aroused and captive audiences. In addition, journalists can (and do) claim to perform their civic roles as checks on public power in society.

In his classic study on social control in the news room, Breed observed that "newsmen are close to big decisions without having to make them."[16] This is accurate only to some extent. We should not overlook the fact that major crises also require tough calls on whether and how to commit scarce journalistic resources under conditions of uncertainty and time pressure. Moreover, crisis reporting involves serious risks for journalists and media organizations themselves.[17] Misreading the crisis means missing the story that the competition does get. And when the political stakes are high, blaming the messenger of bad – or badly produced – news is a strategy that all kinds of parties frequently employ. A classic illustration is the near accident with a nuclear reactor in Harrisburg, Pennsylvania:

The press were at the center of Three Mile Island. They were charged with interpreting the event for the nation. Strangely, for accepting this task, they came under the most criticism of any group involved – criticism for sensationalism, for being antinuclear, for being pronuclear and for not keeping reactor specialists on the reporting staff. While the press was searching for information, some involved agencies tried to provide it and others tried to hide it, even to the point of lying to the press and, through them, to the American people.[18]

If a given media organization's coverage is well received and widely followed, the position of that organization is strengthened. If the coverage is poorly received and generally ignored, the position of the organization is weakened. The widely watched and praised coverage of the Gulf Crisis and War following the Iraqi invasion of Kuwait in 1990 was a major breakthrough for CNN. In contrast, the BBC suffered serious reputation problems when one of its reporters, Andrew Gilligan, created a political storm with a controversial choice of words ("sexed up" intelligence) which he put in the mouths of anonymous government sources talking about the alleged presence of weapons of mass destruction in Iraq prior to the Anglo-American invasion of 2003.[19]

The central role of the media in creating and modulating crises is by no means new. In recent decades, however, television and the internet have added new layers to the media scene. The monopolies of national public service companies have been broken in many countries. Technological developments – satellite television, the internet, mobile phones – have globalized the media market. Communication, as a result, has changed fundamentally. Contemporary leaders in many countries feel the pressure of the "24/7" news cycle. The structure and culture of media markets and organizations have become more competitive, more sensationalistic, and more aggressive in their surveillance of political-administrative elites. The ideal of independent, investigative journalism as a watchdog of democracy holding elites accountable has diffused rapidly and has become firmly entrenched in many, though not all, parts of the world.[20]

There is much debate about the relative power of media and government elites in the crisis communication process. Media are sometimes portrayed as lambs, easily duped by devious political leaders and the spin doctors who serve them. When "new" and unexpected forms of crises emerge and media organizations lack specialized knowledge about the technical and political problems at stake (and especially if non-government experts are in short supply), they are temporarily disarmed by knowledge disadvantages and temporarily left at the mercy of government experts. (In today's media climate, this situation tends to be short lived.) Similarly, the prescriptive literature on communication and the (sometimes self-serving) memoirs of retired spin doctors tend to emphasize the possibilities for crisis managers to take control of the agenda and lead the media in desirable directions.

The other extreme image portrays the media as more lion than lamb, emphasizing their power in shaping public opinion. It emphasizes the predatory and nihilistic nature of modern journalism, which casts the politician or bureaucrat in the role of prey. Some analysts speak of "attack journalism" where "packs" of reporters stray around as "junkyard dogs" (as opposed to the more benign "watchdogs") looking for consumable dirt on political leaders and other actors inside and outside government. In line with this latter image, some communication scholars argue that the force of contemporary political communication imperatives – the message has to go out fast, it has to be packaged in simple catchphrases, there is no room for any doubts or weaknesses – threatens to undermine the quality of policy deliberation that goes on inside governments as it breeds a garrison mentality in their dealing with the news media.[21]

Journalists themselves appear to conceive of their roles in more benign ways: as transmitters of vital public information (a role more likely to be adopted during the acute phase of civil emergencies), as watchdog and critic of public authorities (more likely to be adopted during politically charged crises such as civil disorder, policy fiascos, and scandals), or as providers of entertainment and human interest stories (crises tend to create a public climate receptive to sensationalism and emotionalism).[22]

In practice, the tone of the mass media's crisis reporting varies widely between news organizations, from crisis to crisis, and sometimes even in the course of a single crisis: the spectrum ranges from grim "fault-finding" to uncritical echoing of government pronouncements. Aside from political ideology and editorial policy, the character of crisis reporting is also influenced by organizational factors, such as reporting styles and traditions, and news organizations' crisis response capacities.[23] Some news organizations are better equipped to mobilize quickly and massively than others; others may be better at maintaining rigorous reporting standards even in hectic circumstances. This is not just a matter of resources. It also has to do with the quality and experience of pivotal decision makers within news organizations. Some editors, for example, understand better than others the need to balance short-run and long-haul considerations – a familiar tension for policy makers in crises.

The public

Citizen responses to one and the same crisis tend to vary widely, not just according to what information about the events gets through to them but also by virtue of their demographic and social position or cultural orientation.[24] Moreover, in some types of crises – such as civil disasters or social conflicts – citizens play various roles. As spectators, they are the objects of media and political efforts to inform and influence them. As victimized actors, they search for information. As witnesses, they are irresistible sources for journalists, so much so that in the wake of major crises debates often arise as to the ethics of sensationalist "human interest" journalism.

Public authorities often rely on rather crude stereotypes and myths about citizen behavior during crises in devising their crisis responses and communication strategies. For example, one persistent myth that has proved nearly impossible to dispel is the idea that citizens panic in a disaster. This is striking because scores of studies have consistently shown that citizens tend to act quite rationally even in the most extreme circumstances. Much of the behavior that authorities – and journalists, for that matter – describe as panic is better understood as rational improvisation under conditions of very limited or contradictory knowledge about the situation at hand. Authorities who realize this and want to prevent citizens from "panicking" in case of civil emergencies, terrorist attacks, or financial crises are much more inclined to be proactive in providing citizens with information they actually need.[25]

The average citizen is no expert in the technical intricacies of the complex systems in which crises occur. But the ordinary citizen (voter) is no fool, as V. O. Key once observed.[26] Even if the public's ability to make sense of complex issues is limited, in a pluralistic democracy, authorities and journalists cannot mislead the public for a long period of time and get away with it. As Halper explains:

In crisis situations, the public's interest rises sharply, but its knowledge remains at a fairly low level. Initially, then, crises are apt to make the public even more receptive to information emanating from a legitimate government because citizens demand news, and yet are unable to evaluate it adequately. But precisely because the public *does* tend to be more interested during crises, it becomes more alert to basic discrepancies and inconsistencies contained in the official versions, particularly if these flaws are pointed out by a critical press or by well-known and respected political figures.[27]

The government

In every crisis, government actors seek to direct or influence the behavior (and opinions) of the citizenry. For example, governments tell citizens how to protect themselves during a natural or technical disaster. Such instructions might include when and how to evacuate a stricken area, how to cope with or avoid contaminated food, or how to avoid contracting an infectious disease such as SARS. Even this relatively straightforward operational crisis communication is often more difficult than it seems, if only because governments cannot communicate to their citizens directly but have to work with the mass media whose crisis behavior has its own logic.

Many public leaders and organizations are ill equipped for crisis communication, not just politically but even in the most basic operational sense. Normal communication infrastructures and mechanisms generally cannot cope and must be reinforced from other parts of the organization or with outside help. The pace and pressure are often greater than anticipated. It is, in other words, a constant struggle to keep up, and in the best case take the initiative in crisis communication. Under these conditions, policy makers can easily fall into a reactive mode of "fire-fighting," which causes them to lose track of the big picture. Three factors are particularly important in determining the effectiveness of governmental crisis communications efforts:

- *Degree of preparedness.* Lack of preparedness translates into a loss of speed and coherence in the first, critical stages of an acute crisis: authorities will be trailing the crisis story instead of shaping it. Lack of preparedness also tends to produce logistical chaos in dealing with the large army of reporters that besieges authorities in a crisis. It increases the chance that officials who emerge in the front line of the communication effort have no competence or authority to be effective in this role. A classic flaw in this vein is putting technical experts on air without proper training: they use technocratic language that many do not understand and that therefore will be wide open to misinterpretation. Information intended to reassure may thus have exactly the opposite effect. For example, following the Chernobyl nuclear accident, Finnish and Swedish government experts told citizens that measured levels were *only* a few hundred times the normal background levels – a degree of contamination that experts knew to be harmless but which sounded ominous to the uninitiated and which exacerbated public confusion.[28]

Feedback is essential if the organization is to quickly identify and correct information distortions and unsubstantiated rumors, and respond to developing public concerns. Yet our research suggests that proactive monitoring and rumor-control efforts are often lacking, particularly in organizations that have not planned in advance for performing this function.

- *Degree of coordination of outgoing information.* As we have seen in Chapter 3, multi-actor, multi-level governance is a typical characteristic of crisis response. In most crises, there are different places where authorities congregate, decide, and act, if only because of the common differentiation in strategic and operational crisis centers. Reporters will target them all. Moreover, many of these units will feel the need to communicate their part of the story to the public. Coordination among these various units is often limited. In many cases there is even rivalry between them, and there might be political and legal incentives for them to start pointing fingers at each other. In some crises, open information warfare breaks out between various parts and levels of the government, generating an escalation cycle that makes all the participants look bad.[29] Improving coordination and "message discipline" is a common mantra of public relations and political consultants. At the same time, government communication that proves ill founded or deliberately misleading is as deadly for its meaning-making efforts as internal division.[30]

- *Degree of professionalization.* Governmental communication has become the domain of public relations (PR) professionals. In times of crises, these PR professionals are put to the test: the need for a professional approach dealing with the mass media is larger than ever, but at the same time the political imperatives to keep the media at arm's length or even manipulate them may also increase. Professional spokespersons always run a risk of getting trapped between the conflicting demands of their political masters and their journalistic audiences; in crises, with the stakes of meaning making even higher than during politics as usual, these risks increase exponentially.

The operational challenge of crisis communication is hard enough: absorbing the massive onslaught of the media in odd places and at odd times in such a way as to avoid hindrance to the crisis response. The frenetic pace of deadlines-driven journalism must be met with well-timed and thoughtfully packaged pieces of information. In seeking to accomplish this, PR officials often lack the authority that others derive from their badge or their technical expertise. To reporters, PR officials form the impenetrable barriers between the crisis managers and the sound bytes they want them to produce. Contemporary reporters are easily irritated by what they see as an unprofessional communications operation, which is characterized by inadequate provision of logistic facilities for the media, PR officials who possess limited knowledge and information about the issues at hand, PR officials who do not speak proper English (let alone German, Spanish, or French), and PR officials who are more preoccupied with fencing off and protecting the policy makers than with facilitating a dialogue between the media and the authorities.

4.3   The battle for credibility

The most important factor that determines the effectiveness of governmental crisis communication efforts is, of course, the degree of credibility that governments and their spokespersons possess. If leaders want to shape public and political meanings attached to crises, they must be seen as credible, trustworthy sources of information.[31] When leaders are trusted, their actions and words are more easily perceived as sincere, competent, and signs of good faith. Where trust has broken down, all actors involved will scrutinize the words and deeds of the "untrustworthy" leader; they will be less likely to believe official announcements, let alone act upon them.

Dynamics such as these can easily become self-reinforcing – distrust breeds low credibility, which breeds fault-finding interpretations of past and current behavior, which in turn reinforces distrust. Pre-existing credibility deficits, or those which emerge early on in a crisis process, are thus likely to be particularly destructive – they make everything else that comes after more difficult.

Policy makers want to be seen to be in control of the crisis. This is quite a challenge because if they really were in control, there would presumably be no crisis. Yet they need to get across the idea that "yes, it is tough, but we are hanging in there, and will be able to deal with the problem." In dealing with the escalating oil spill on the shoreline of Prince William Sound in Alaska, which was caused by the grounding and rupture of the *Exxon Valdez* in 1987, the company (Exxon) initially ignored the mass media as much as possible. When this strategy clearly compounded Exxon's problems, it started to use dramaturgical means. One of those was creating ritualistic spectacles of a clean-up in full progress. Davidson reports:

Scores of workers were helicoptered to a remote beach on the Kenai Peninsula two hours before a *USA Today* film crew arrived to film beach cleaning. When asked if this was a made-for-TV cleanup episode, Exxon representative Dean Peeler said, "A planned media event? No way." But within an hour of the time the television crew left, three helicopter flights swooped off ten to twelve workers at a time, and another four left by skiff. Said one of the cleanup workers who had been shuttled to and from the beach, "Exxon was definitely putting on a show."[32]

When faced with indicators of potentially critical problems that run counter to their policies, leaders may be tempted to play down the gravity of the problem. This is what the British agriculture minister John Gummer tried to communicate by eating a beefburger and by feeding one to his reluctant four-year old. This spectacle was broadcast on television at the time of growing worries in the UK about Creutzfeld Jakob disease (also known as "mad cow" disease). At the time the move seemed simple, straightforward, and effective. In retrospect, knowing the cycle of escalation that was to follow, the gesture seems preposterous. And even after the escalation of the crisis, ministers continued their attempts to reassure the public and their EU partners. Gummer's successor, Douglas Hogg, for example, stated in November 1995 that "British beef has never been safer," referring to new and tougher safety measures, but completely ignoring the fact that there might already be hundreds of thousands of older infected cattle in the food chain. By simultaneously and inexplicably extending the existing offal ban to include food from the spinal cord and mechanically recovered meat, the minister heightened concerns that the existing ban had been inadequate.[33]

The inherent features of crisis put pressure on a government's meaning-making capacity: spectacles of dead bodies, mass destruction of property, people in distress, widespread violence, and stock exchange panics allow for only so much "spin." If they are lucky, the press does not immediately blame policy makers for the negative event or threat in question. This grants them a "breathing period" in which the so-called "rally around the flag" effect may prevail: political actors, the media, and the general public alike tend to suspend their disbelief and criticism, and lend their support to the government. Which factors account for these different patterns?

Sources of credibility

First, the *history and reputation of organizations and their spokespersons* shape pre-crisis images, which, in turn, affect the ways in which media representatives and the public at large interpret their credibility. Past performance weighs into these equations. Well-publicised instances of successful crisis management during similar contingencies increase personal or organizational credibility. And vice versa: spokespersons for the Swedish navy, for example, had a hard time convincing Swedish media that foreign submarines were covertly violating Swedish territory on a regular basis after a series of controversial and fruitless anti-submarine hunting operations during the 1980s and early 1990s.[34]

Second, the *initial responses* set the tone. Even when the unimaginable or the "impossible" has occurred, do policy makers sometimes continue to engage in denial or wishful thinking? They play down the crisis and mask or embellish the course of crisis response operations. While very strong reactions to signs of (imminent) trouble can be liable to charges of overreacting or attempting to escalate and exploit a contingency, the media and mass public tend to be more forgiving of overreaction than denial and innuendo. It is much easier to be in the position of saying that precautionary actions proved superfluous ("it wasn't as bad as we thought") than to have to admit that opportunities to mitigate an emerging contingency have been missed ("it was worse than we thought").

Immediately after being informed of the tsunami catastrophe in Asia involving many German holidaymakers, German chancellor Gerhard Schröder cancelled his Christmas holidays, returned to Berlin, and promised €.5 billion of aid – deferring any worries he might have had about how the already strained government budget would pay for this. This picture of compassion and decisiveness gave him much credit domestically as well as abroad. In contrast, Swedish policy makers displayed a remarkable lack of empathy and communication savvy during the first days after the tsunami. They remained publicly invisible for more than a day, continued their Christmas leisure routines, and when they finally started talking, they seemed to be understating the gravity of the crisis, which after all affected thousands of Swedish holidaymakers in Phuket, Thailand. The image of a cavalier attitude on the part of the government in the first period of the crisis was reinforced by a dramatic public statement from the Swedish king, who managed to strike the right tone of concern and compassion. The onus of negligence would not die away in the aftermath, and caused severe political problems for the prime minister and the minister for foreign affairs.

The *timing of messages* makes a tremendous difference in the way they will be perceived. If an organization that discovers embarrassing facts about its performance voluntarily discloses this information before the media do, it will at least be credited for its openness. If the same information is presented after the story has already broken in the media, the organization will be suspected of attempting to cover up or "spin."

Detailed knowledge of news cycles and typical rhythms in media behavior allows an organization to select the optimum time for sending out a particular type of information. For instance, when policy makers feel they need to disclose unflattering information "for the record," they may elect to release it at times when the news organizations are likely to be less alert or already preoccupied with other crises. When it was discovered that many alleged acoustic signals of foreign submarine activity were probably caused by swimming minks rather than foreign (read Russian) submarines in 1994, the Swedish Defense Staff released the information in the form of a tersely worded press release, given out on a Friday afternoon during the summer vacation. The press did not pick up on the story, but the organization had at least acquired an insurance policy for itself. Should the story leak eventually, defense officials could always point to the press release to prove that no cover-up had been intended. Later, when it was established beyond all doubt that the culprits were in fact minks in a large number of cases, the Swedish defense minister held a "prime-time" press conference during which he frankly disclosed the errors made.[35] This proved an effective strategy.

Credibility management in crisis communication

Leaders may fall into a so-called credibility trap – a self-created decline in one's perceived trustworthiness – through ill-advised crisis communication: this happens when they succumb to the temptation of espousing myopic, highly partisan readings of the situation; deny unwelcome, yet widely covered aspects of crisis reality; or make imprudent public commitments of government resources and results. This may work in the short run, but it is sure to erode credibility in the longer run.

One classic error is *overemphasizing rosy scenarios*. When leaders present constituents with unqualified optimistic prognoses, their future credibility becomes a hostage to the accuracy of the prognosis in question. A recent example was when George W. Bush prematurely declared the end of military hostilities in Iraq in a widely publicized, but ill-advised, public relations stunt aboard the aircraft carrier *Abraham Lincoln*. From the flight deck, under a banner proclaiming "Mission

Accomplished," the president declared that "Major combat operations in Iraq have ended." Even though Bush did caution that difficult work was still to be done, this episode left the US public ill prepared for the ensuing guerilla war, which would see many more US casualties than the initial invasion had done.

Second, there is the *temptation to appear decisive*. The media and other crisis actors pressure leaders into making strong statements about the crisis and how they will handle it. It is always tricky to "shoot from the hip" when dealing with complex, intractable issues; it is outright foolish to claim publicly that critical problems will be brought under control swiftly when no time has been made for reliable expert advice to ascertain whether such a claim can be backed up. Quick promises – to salvage a sunken ferry and recover the hundreds of bodies (following the tragic *MS Estonia* disaster in the Baltic Sea in September 1994), to capture and convict a political assassin (Olof Palme, Prime Minister of Sweden, was shot and killed in February 1986), to "crush terrorists" – often prove embarrassing and painful to actors and stakeholders alike when it turns out they are impossible to deliver.

4.4   Meaning-making strategies: symbolic crisis management

Meaning making in crises is not just a matter of following existing contingency plans or implementing strategic choices made at the outset of a crisis. It also entails intuitive and improvised public communication by leaders who are suddenly cast into the hectic pace of crisis reporting. Whether by preconceived plan or by skillful improvisation, seasoned politicians and other crisis leaders employ deliberate and concerted moves to influence public perceptions and emotions. The literature on symbolic politics and political communication identifies such recurrent strategies and the conditions under which these are successful.[36] We have selected three for discussion: engaging in *framing*, using crisis *rituals*, and *masking* dimensions of crises and crisis response operations.

Framing

Those who successfully "frame" what a crisis is all about hold the key to defining the appropriate strategies for resolution.[37] Framing typically involves the selective exploitation of data, arguments, and historical analogies; actors also seek to frame a crisis by forming "discourse coalitions" with like-minded groups.[38] Leaders typically use rhetorical and judicial languages in the open arenas of political meaning making.[39]

Strong rhetoric full of metaphors and emotive concepts is used to increase or dampen collective anxieties – the very act of labeling a particular set of social conditions a "crisis" is in itself a major communicative act with potentially far-reaching political consequences.[40] It makes quite a difference whether one labels events in terms of an "incident," an "accident," a "tragedy," a "disaster," or a "crisis." These terms convey different assessments of the situation in terms of its seriousness and the allocation of responsibility for it.[41] Labels such as these invoke "archetypical narratives" that shape people's expectations about what is to follow, who is in charge, who are the heroes, and who are the villains of the story.[42] Buzan and colleagues talk about framing events in terms of "securitization," which is aimed at increasing leaders' political room for maneuvering: "In security discourse, an issue is dramatised and presented as an issue of supreme priority; thus, by labelling it as *security*, an agent claims a need for and a right to treat it by extraordinary means."[43] Or as Edelman puts it: "Any regime that prides itself on its capacity to manage crises will find crises to manage."[44] The Bush administration, for example, was surprisingly quick and energetic in dramatizing the scope and immediacy of the dangers posed by Saddam Hussein's regime's alleged possession of weapons of mass destruction, right after its successful operation against the Taliban regime in Afghanistan.

From the perspective of power-holders, an important function of judicial language is to de-politicize the crisis by employing a non-partisan channel for defining the situation and assessing success and failure. This strategy proved quite effective in Great Britain throughout the 1980s and 1990s when the country experienced a series of inner-city riots as well as a disturbingly high frequency of man-made disasters (a plane crash, a ferry disaster, an oil-platform explosion, a boat collision on the Thames, several major railway crashes, an underground station fire, a stadium crowd disaster). In each case, official inquiries were called for by the government and performed by judges, who – whilst being tenacious and objective in their pursuit of the immediate causes and implications of these events – by the very nature of their position and terms of reference steered clear of underlying political issues and conflicts.[45] In addition to judicial language, framing critical events in terms of scientific discourse has proven to be an effective way of de-politicizing them.[46]

Once a problem is framed and politically adopted in terms of "critical choices," the hard facts and cold risks become less salient in deciding what should be done; the psycho-political imperatives weighing upon the senior policy makers win in importance. This was exemplified by the Swine Flu crisis during the Ford administration, when the decision was made to embark on a massive inoculation program designed to reach every American citizen; it was also sure to kill a few people because of side effects: "It mattered a little that the experts could not tell whether the chance of pandemic influenza was 30 percent, or 3 percent, or even less than 1 percent. What the assistant secretary for Health, the secretary of [the department of Health], the president, and Congress heard, was that there was *some* chance of pandemic flu and this was enough. No responsible politician wished to put himself in the position of opposing the program, thus running the risk that pandemic illness and death might prove him a villain."[47]

Successful crisis-framing efforts relieve policy makers of the pressure or urge to reflect upon and publicly defend the normative underpinnings of their policies. When an issue is widely defined as a struggle against an evil threat, much – though not anything – goes, including policies that harm people or interests that have been stigmatized as enemies and "outgroups," or simply have been discounted in the "big picture." In the long run, the normative simplification that framing enables may come to haunt policy makers, but in the (self-imposed) heat of the crisis response it increases their freedom to maneuver.[48]

The framing of issues in terms of crisis thus generates a self-binding dynamic. This might lead to highly ineffective and costly policies, but if carefully staged may also be put to political use. In many instances, it makes good political sense to first dramatize the seriousness of the situation, for example by personifying threats and constructing diabolical enemy images, before going on to propose bold, even extreme, courses of action that under normal conditions would never stand a chance of being accepted.[49] In doing so, stakeholders may appeal to deep-rooted "threat biases" in how people perceive their environment:

If a widely publicized event can be interpreted as confirmation that a conspicuous enemy is dangerous, a political coalition can usually be broadened. When Russia shot down a Korean airliner carrying 267 passengers in 1983, the officials of the Reagan administration who spoke in public of their anger and revulsion at the action also benefited from the occurrence of an event that could be used to mobilize public support for defeating a nuclear freeze resolution in Congress, building the MX missile, and increasing the arms budget.[50]

Rituals

Crisis responses are also shaped by rituals, defined as symbolic behavior that is socially standardized and repetitive. Rituals follow highly structured, more or less standardized sequences and are often enacted at certain places and times, which themselves are endowed with special symbolic meaning. They are an important component of social and governmental responses to many different types of crises, as indeed they are of government and politics in normal times (think of election campaigns, annual budget speeches, parliamentary debating procedures).[51] Crisis rituals both shape and conform to public perceptions of grave disturbances of the existing order.

The laying of wreaths at the site of an accident or attack, or another symbolic spot, is an obvious example. The Hillsborough Soccer stadium crowd crush in 1989 that killed more than ninety Liverpool fans sparked a symbolic mourning ritual. Starting hours after the disaster occurred in Sheffield, the Spionkop side of Liverpool's Anfield Road stadium became a shrine for the thousands of people coming in to pay their respects. More organized forms of mourning rituals followed later, with public masses in both Sheffield and Liverpool, and a one-minute pause at the start of soccer matches throughout Britain.

Official state funerals for political leaders are among the most powerful and politically significant forms of crisis-related ritual, as evidenced by analyses of the funerals of Mahatma Gandhi, John F. Kennedy, and Indira Gandhi.[52] An essential symbolic strategy for leaders in response to an acute and large-scale crisis is to inspect the relevant sites and visit victims and operational staff.[53]

The symbolic importance of publicly displayed compassion for those suffering hardship and those working under dire circumstances cannot be overstated. Failure to engage in this ritual amounts to a serious underestimation of the collective emotion that such crises generate. It is sure to bring officials instant and intense public-relations problems, and, occasionally, political embarrassment.[54] In countries with a high frequency of major incidents and emergencies, it is often well-established good practice for dignitaries to visit the site of major disasters and terrorist attacks.

The Dutch home office minister received a blaze of media and political criticism when he initially declined to travel to the tsunami-hit areas in Thailand despite being on vacation in the country at the time. He complained bitterly that his decision was sound since there was nothing he could have done to facilitate local response operations. He thus clearly misunderstood the symbolic imperatives of crisis management in the media age. A notable example of an organization that did understand what was required of it was Japanese Airlines (JAL) in its response to a big plane crash in 1985 during which 520 people perished: "The airline followed an elaborate protocol to atone. Personal apologies were made by the company's president, memorial services were held [at a cost of over $1.5 million to the company, authors] and financial reparations paid ... At the memorial service, JAL's president, Yasumoto Takagi, bowed low and long to relatives of the victims and to a plaque bearing the victims' names. He asked forgiveness, accepted responsibility and offered to resign."[55] The chief maintenance officer took it one step further, and – in keeping with a streak in Japanese culture – committed suicide. Overall, JAL's response was seen and depicted by the media to be humane, caring, and responsible. After the initial major loss, the company fully recovered its market share.

Another classic ritual in crises is to unleash an official investigation. Writing against the backdrop of the massive street protests and riots of the late 1960s in the United States, Edelman argued that such rituals – including judicial rituals resulting in the punishment of perpetrators – help reduce anxiety levels and give the impression that people can exert a certain degree of control over their lives, even though their actual influence is negligible.[56] Ritualized and seemingly dispassionate inquiries thus reinvigorate public belief in the rational procedures of government. The terminology used is appropriately evocative: a "full-scale, objective inquiry" to be conducted by "independent experts" or "wise men" where "no expense will be spared," and so on. Such attempts to salvage rationality myths from the turbulence and anxiety of crisis are further amplified by employing a language of "learning." If "the lessons" of the present crisis will be distilled, concerned citizens can at least hope that every effort is made to prevent new traumas (see further Chapter 6).

The leaders of governmental crisis response might also have to cope with rituals enacted by opponents. The burning of enemy portraits and flags is standard practice in international conflicts, whilst anti-police demonstrations, identifying police as "pigs" or "Nazis," are among the standard animosity rituals practiced by protest groups. More recently, Iraqi terrorists have harked back to ancient rituals by beheading their hostages – only today they distribute the pictures to the mass media and the worldwide web, maximizing the psychological effects in the West.

Masking

During crises, as one analyst has noted, "officials may sometimes see greater advantage in concealment than exposure."[57] Some officials self-consciously maintain that crises bestow upon governments the "right to lie."[58] If crises expose deep-rooted conflicts and vulnerabilities of the established social order, it follows that one important dimension of crisis response by status quo-oriented officials and agencies is to counteract such exposure or to dampen its impact. They will engage in a specific form of impression management called masking: not telling the full story, downplaying the seriousness of threats and damages, obscuring sensitive aspects of their own crisis response operations. Authoritarian regimes have a long history of masking – up to the point of flatly denying the occurrence of major nuclear accidents and environmental disasters. In times of crisis and war, democratic governments may also go down this path. The United States government, for example, did everything it could to prevent the media from monitoring its treatment of alleged terrorists in Guantanamo Bay.

Masking efforts may succeed and buy the official or agency time or political credit. Yet short-term success is not all that counts. If successful masking is not followed by more substantive remedial actions, it may generate severe backlashes when in the longer run the "real" problems surface (the My-Lai and Watergate "cover-ups" come to mind, as do many corporate scandals such as Enron). Again, timing is crucial. If masking does not help to alleviate short-term concerns, its very failure to convince people tends to aggravate the situation: it raises questions about incompetence and it breeds distrust. This kind of masking failure occurred in the immediate aftermath of the Three Mile Island nuclear incident. The persistent denial and innuendo in the first instance, and subsequent uncoordinated admittance of serious problems on the part of most notably the Metropolitan Edison Company that operated the plant, outraged both state and national politicians, contributed to serious collective stress among local inhabitants, infuriated the media, and precipitated a confusing parade of radiation experts who all made different claims about what was going on and what might happen. The fact that at the time of the accident a major Hollywood movie (*The China Syndrome*), which powerfully depicted concerns about the risks of nuclear plants, was screened around the nation certainly did not help any kind of masking effort.[59]

4.5   Conclusion

Crises generate a context of fundamental ambiguity, confusion, and speculation, conflicting beliefs, and collective arousal. In these circumstances, it is both essential and exceedingly difficult for policy makers to shape the societal and political meaning-making process by which crises come to be labeled, understood, and evaluated – not just in their own right but also in what they tell us about the social and institutional status quo.

The picture of crisis communication that emerges from this chapter is one of delicate, negotiated order. Policy makers and their PR professionals understand that management of media reporting is pivotal to their communications strategies, but at the same time they are often at a loss in doing just that. Journalists may be willing to swallow the treatment they get and publish what information is provided by policy makers, but only as long as they have either no time or no opportunity to do something else, or feel that the access and information given to them produces stories that are likely to satisfy their editors and audiences. When they feel this is not the case, at least some of them will start digging for context and background. By doing so, journalists shape the story, at least partly, which complicates the policy makers' ability to dominate the meaning-making process.

Even if they are able to handle the media onslaught in a professional way, policy makers should perhaps not overestimate their capacity to control the public's understanding of a crisis. In the internet age, conventional and national mass media have become just one among a plurality of information sources. There is little that leaders can do to stop people from believing what they see and read on the web, even if some of this amounts to the most outlandish conspiracy theories. Despite these clear limitations, however, leaders and their governments will continue to engage in meaning-making efforts for the simple fact that, apart from pure despotic regimes, all public power-holders need public loyalties.[60]

Notes

1 Woodward (2004: 92–3, 294, 333, 362). See also Cook (2004) and Rutherford (2004).
2 Combs (1980: 119–21). The distinction between images (general perceptions of events, actors, or conditions as malign or benign) and frames (more specific diagnostic and prognostic issue definitions) is useful here, and has been elaborated by Eriksson (2001: 8–16).
3 Schön and Rein (1994: 29).
4 Meaning making is defined here as the production of facts, images, and spectacles aimed at influencing socio-political uncertainty and conflict generated by crises.
5 The term is taken from Key (1961: 35).
6 Even that has its limits, as the story of the Abu Graib prison atrocities reveals: pictures of abused prisoners made it to the web via mobile phones from insiders.
7 See, for example, Nudell and Antokol (1988); Barton (1993); Fearn-Banks (1996); Regester and Larkin (1997); and Henry (2000).
8 An outstanding book that captures this literature is Seeger et al. (2003); another great collection is found in Millar and Heath (2004).
9 See 't Hart (1993), who bases his account on Turner (1978).

10 See Walters et al. (1989) and Wildavsky (1995).
11 Patterson (1989).
12 Bennett and Entman (2001); Meyer (2002); Seymour-Ure (2003).
13 Smith (1989: 46).
14 Graber et al. (1998: 4).
15 Woodward and Bernstein (1994).
16 Breed (1955).
17 In some types of crisis, these risks are indeed life threatening. Quite a few
    journalists die each year during war coverage around the world (in 2004, 129
    journalists perished [49 in Iraq alone] according to the International Feder-
    ation of Journalists).
18 Stephens (1980: 5).
19 See also the reputation damage suffered by *The New York Times* when one of
    its reporters (Jason Blair) was shown to have committed serial offenses of
    plagiarism and "thumb sucking."
20 Blumer and Gurevitch (1995); Bennett (1999).
21 Meyer (2002); Lloyd (2004).
22 This typology of journalistic roles was first developed in 't Hart and Rijpma
    (1997: 81).
23 Quoted and paraphrased from Nimmo and Combs (1985).
24 For a case study, see Rosenthal et al. (1994). See further Wildavsky and Dake
    (1991).
25 Quarantelli (1954); Dynes (1970); Tierney et al. (2001); Aguirre (2004).
26 Key (1966).
27 Halper (1971: 7).
28 Nohrstedt (1991); Stern (1999: 226).
29 Stephens (1980) offers the ultimate horror example.
30 Libertore (1993).
31 For a survey study of the key components of credibility, see Ohanian (1991).
32 Davidson (1990: 200).
33 Regester and Larkin (1997); Baggot (1998).
34 Bynander (1998; 2003).
35 Brändström (2000).
36 See, for example, Pfetsch (1998).
37 Reversely, for those who seek to instigate changes, it is vital to aggravate the
    sense of societal crisis in order to foster a psychological and political climate
    receptive to non-incremental changes.
38 See, among others, Lebow and Stein (1994) and Brändström et al. (2004).
39 Administrative and bargaining languages form the vehicles for behind-the-
    scenes striving for advantages and deal making (Edelman, 1964; 1977); cf.
    Entman (1993); Iyengar (1996).
40 Edelman (1977) uses the term "semantically created crisis."
41 See, for example, Wilkins (1989); Millar and Beck (2004).
42 Heath (2004).
43 Buzan et al. (1998: 26).
44 Edelman (1977).
45 Cf. Platt (1971); Lipsky and Olson (1977); Dekker (forthcoming).
46 See, for example, Snider (2004).

47 Silverstein (1981: 135), cited in Jervis (1992: 191), orig. italics.
48 Compare, for example, Turner and Giles (1981); Janis (1982).
49 Edelman (1977: 14); White (1986); Edelman (1988: 66–89).
50 Edelman (1988: 70).
51 See Bennett (1980); Nimmo and Combs (1990: 54ff).
52 Shils (1968); Combs (1980: 41–7); Kertzer (1988: 140–4).
53 Leaders who fail to do this may suffer the consequences. President Putin's continued vacation in the wake of the *Kursk* crisis in August 2000 is a casebook example. Putin was typecast in the media and by political opponents as "cold" and "indifferent." Similarly, the German contender for the chancellorship, Edmund Stoiber, lost his lead in the final stage of the 2002 election race against incumbent Gerhard Schröder when he – unlike Schröder – initially declined to visit flood-stricken areas, and seemed to want to play down the issue. Schröder won the election.
54 This is true even when it comes to observing rituals of other nations' crises: the Swedish government and the prime minister in particular faced critical media and parliamentary questions and even ridicule when it turned out that neither the prime minister himself nor any other senior politician or member of the royal family were to participate in the memorial service for the victims of the 2004 Madrid bombings, whereas all the other EU members were represented by their government leaders or top statesmen. Things got even worse when the prime minister was photographed visiting a farm in rural Sweden at the time the ceremony in Spain took place.
55 Regester and Larkin (1997: 146).
56 Edelman (1971); see also Elder and Cobb (1983: 116ff).
57 Halper (1971: 16).
58 As argued by Assistant Secretary of Defense in the Kennedy administration, Arthur Sylvester. Quoted in Halper (1971: 17).
59 Stephens (1980).
60 Robertson (2001), quoting Price (1995: 3).

5 End games: crisis termination and accountability

5.1 It ain't over till it's over

In July 1995, Bosnian-Serb forces took the town of Srebrenica, a UN safe haven, after a long siege and a brief military campaign.[1] The Dutch military contingent (Dutchbat), which acted as UN protector of the enclave, surrendered and was allowed a safe retreat. The Netherlands sighed with relief that this brush with war had not resulted in a Dutch blood bath. Upon return, the Dutch troops were welcomed as national heroes by their families, the Prime Minister, and the Crown Prince. For the Minister of Defense, who had spent several days and nights in "the bunker" where the military commanded the besieged troops, the crisis was finally over.

At least, that is what he thought. Within days, it became clear that the Serbs had committed heinous crimes after taking over the Bosnian enclave. Upon investigating the role of the Dutch men in uniform, media reporters began to assert that they had not done much to defend the enclave. Rumors began to circulate to the effect that the Dutch had condoned and even cooperated with the Serbs in their ethnic cleansing. The world learned that 7,000 men had been murdered, many of them while the Dutch battalion was anxiously awaiting its safe passage home. The Minister of Defense would spend the remainder of his political career defending the decision to surrender and leave. Many investigation reports were conducted (most of which were published), yet doubts lingered on in the public mind. Finally, an official inquiry was initiated. After the commission published its report in the spring of 2002, clearing the army of the cowardice charges, the government resigned. Seven years after Srebrenica, the political crisis was finally over, while the human drama continued.

After the worst has passed – hostilities have ceased, the fire has been extinguished, the threat averted, the wounded are in the hospital – one would expect a crisis to wind down. But crisis leaders often discover, to their bewilderment, that the worst for them is yet to come. They may have negotiated the challenges of sense making, urgent decision making and meaning making, only to encounter what may be the biggest challenge of all: ending the crisis. They discover that operational heat gives way to aftermath complexities. The early phase of 9/11 ended with an outpouring of sympathy for rescue workers, but the political aftermath continues to the day we write this. The first Gulf War "ended" with a glorious return of the troops, but it also brought home the Gulf War Syndrome from which many soldiers still suffer. This is the case even in natural disasters. The shared experience of adversity may foster solidarity and unite people behind the common cause of victim assistance and reconstruction, but these crises also provide opportunities for critics of the existing status quo to "get to the bottom of this."[2]

Some crises last for a surprisingly long time, others fade quickly into oblivion. This chapter's *key question* is: what factors make the difference? It is tempting to think that the scale of the crisis and the skills of the crisis leaders explain why the Srebrenica crisis lasted longer than the Y2K crisis, which ended effectively with the start of the new millennium.[3] However, the number of deaths and the crisis performance of leaders do not fully determine the intensity of crisis – certainly not in the long run.[4] Crisis termination depends to a considerable extent – and this is our *key claim* – on the way leaders deal with the accountability process following the operational phase of crisis.

The Srebrenica case shows that the accountability process may be a lengthy one, and that judgments about the performance of crisis actors are not cast in concrete as long as investigations and debates continue: today's heroes may be tomorrow's villains (and vice versa). Policy makers cannot take for granted that a perfect correlation exists between what actually happened prior to and during a crisis, and the political distribution of praise, blame and sanctions that follows in its wake. A deeply institutionalized system of accountability sets democratic polities apart from non-democratic ones (as argued in Chapter 1), but this in itself does not guarantee that democratic accountability works after crises in ways that are predictable, fair, or controllable.

Crisis leaders can be competent and conscientious, but that alone says little about how their performance will be evaluated when the crisis is over. Policy makers and agencies that failed to perform their duties prior to or during the critical stages need not despair, however: if they "manage" the political game of the crisis aftermath well, they may prevent losses to their reputation, autonomy, and resources. Crises have winners and losers. The political (and legal) dynamics of the accountability process determines which crisis actors end up where.

5.2 The political challenge of crisis termination

Crises are fuzzy and indeterminate; identifying and framing them is not a self-evident or unproblematic act, as we saw in Chapter 4. Neither is deciding when they are over. Some actors may find it expedient to move back to normalcy – however defined – as soon as possible, whereas others may seek to stretch the life span of an ongoing crisis as much as they can. How, may we ask, do crises in fact evolve over time? And how do they come to an end?

These questions require us to think about crises as episodes, sometimes even epochs, and not as one-shot events. Crises develop, escalate, and end in dynamic processes. Some crises smolder and flare up again. Some are like weeds: they constitute a constant threat or nuisance that is hard to eradicate, and if neglected can do much damage. Others are like bolts from the blue: they come and go in no time. Thinking about crisis termination in this processual manner opens up possibilities for discerning different types of crisis trajectories. We begin by discerning two main ideal types: the fast-burning crisis and the long-shadow crisis.

The fast-burning crisis

The key characteristic of a fast-burning crisis is that the termination of operational response efforts also marks the political end of the crisis. The natural disaster – earthquake, hurricane, tsunami – is often cited as a textbook example: it suddenly arrives and visits only briefly.[5] After the source of destruction is gone, the stricken community can bury the dead, care for the surviving victims, and repair the damages. This crisis is intense and short, even though it will certainly be remembered as a painful and time-defining calamity. It is not clear whether crises ever conformed as a rule to this paradigmatic type, but it is fairly certain that the fast-burning crisis will be the rare kind.

Other paradigmatic examples of fast-burning crises include hijackings and hostage-takings that are met with swift military intervention or a quick, negotiated solution. The conspicuous success of complex and risky raids on hijacked planes at Entebbe (1976) and Mogadishu (1977) have set some sort of standard for effective crisis management: rapid interventions through commando operations are to be preferred over long-winding, exhausting negotiation processes. If they succeed, everybody basks in glory: a victory without concessions and with minimal pain. If they don't, they may still be construed as heroic failures, especially in a crisis when leaders who try but fail tend to be more respected than those who fail to try.

Fast-burning crises have cathartic effects, as has been noted in cases of international confrontations between major and minor powers. The latter gradually up the ante by continuing to challenge the former; the major power then decides it has had enough and intervenes militarily (Libya and Grenada versus the United States in the 1980s are key examples). Some trade disputes and other major international negotiations follow this pattern: disputes build up over a long period of time, then a protracted period of back-door negotiation follows, deadlock results, tensions escalate, and the resolution has to be brought by the (self-imposed) deadline of a major summit, during which frantic last-minute negotiations take place. When these are successful, the dispute is suddenly over.[6]

Three conditions in particular seem to facilitate a rapid termination of crisis. A first condition conducive to "fast burning" is the run of the mill nature of a crisis. When the scope and impact of a crisis do not transcend widely shared notions of what can be expected and do not overtax the capacities of response services, it will quickly lose its critical properties once the operational flurry has died down. Some communities, in which certain types of crisis happen more often, develop resilient subcultures. An earthquake in Japan, a tornado in Florida, a bomb explosion in the Basque country, a rail crash in Britain – these crises are unlikely to continue very far beyond the operational crisis horizon.

A second condition for rapid closure is the absence of democratic fora required for accountability processes. This absence allows a leader to simply declare the crisis to be "over." This does not necessarily mean that the episode is erased from public memory. The emergence of democracy may create an opportunity for citizens to demand justice, as happened when the Argentinean military leaders gave way to elected leaders. In the summer of 2004, a Mexican prosecutor charged senior politicians of the opposition party PRI with manslaughter during the riots of 1971 in Mexico City. This fast-burning crisis thus became political dynamite well over three decades after it was terminated (this instructs us to be careful in using the label).

A third condition for rapid crisis termination is the emergence of something bigger or worse. After the deadly Al Qaida attack on commuter trains in Madrid (March 2004), the government's anti-terrorism policy was firmly redirected toward Muslim terrorism. The creeping crisis of the Basque independent movement ETA's terrorism was relegated to secondary status, at least temporarily.

The long-shadow crisis

Not all crises are over when the operational challenges have been met. The long-shadow crisis demarks that category of crises that remain alive in political and societal arenas, even though the threats that gave rise to the crises no longer exist.

The US and Soviet predicaments in Vietnam and Afghanistan, respectively, constitute classic illustrations. Lured by lofty ambitions yet faced with an entropic reality on the ground, American and Soviet leaders repeatedly escalated their commitment to prevail in a conflict they could not win. De-escalation in these circumstances takes time, which is needed to readjust ambitions and expectations, and to prepare mentally for embarrassment and defeat. Extricating themselves from these foreign quagmires became a major challenge in both countries, which they accomplished only slowly and with enormous human and political costs. Years after the last soldiers departed, these wars continued to cause crises at home.

Sometimes it is the other way round: operational challenges remain after political closure seems to have been achieved. Environmental crises, for instance, tend to be chronic rather than short lived. Solutions involve much trial and error, radical U-turns after political turnovers, symbolic gestures, and rearguard battles during implementation. Political attention may decrease through sheer exhaustion of the attention of mass media and political actors, as well as through the emergence of newly "discovered" crises. The global AIDS epidemic lost its crisis status in the Western world through a combination of painstaking scientific progress and a slowdown in the number of newly HIV-infected people. It remains, however, a crisis of massive proportions on the African continent, but Western attention for it is fleeting and at best erratic.

Some crises are of such large scope and significance that they retain a special place on governance agendas indefinitely. These "endemic" crises include global warming, overpopulation, deforestation, and water management. These crises are essentially "unmanageable," at least from a national, short-term perspective. Transnational in origins and impact, these crises defy existing institutional orders. Combating their origins requires draconic measures that few powerful actors are willing or able to implement. As a result, the problems do not go away and may come to haunt future leaders and policy makers.

Crises cast a long shadow when they come to be seen as indicators of deeper problems or when they "connect" with critical issues in other organizational or policy domains. They may expose flaws in existing prevention and preparedness arrangements, which trigger intense scrutiny of institutional structures. In some cases, they escalate into full-blown institutional crises, i.e. fundamental challenges to organizational structures or policy paradigms.[7] Three distinctive types of crisis have this capacity for political and institutional "endurance."

The "incomprehensible" crisis openly defies existing political-bureaucratic repertoires of crisis prevention and response. The sense of shock generated by an aberration tends to produce an unusually thorough search for the causes of the incident. In turn, the investigations undertaken typically reveal deep-rooted causes, which raise thorny issues about leadership, responsibility, and future improvement. The 1986 murder of the Swedish Prime Minister Olof Palme is a paradigmatic example. Its very occurrence in one of the most enduringly peaceful polities on earth was as baffling as it was traumatic to the Swedes. The subsequent police investigation caused yet another shock: it was unsuccessful and exposed hitherto invisible and bitter infighting within the Swedish criminal justice system.[8]

The "mismanaged" crisis When the response to an incident is widely perceived as slow and inadequate, the image of failure may continue to fuel the crisis. The filmed beating of Rodney King by a group of officers from the Los Angeles Police Department (LAPD) is a perfect example.[9] The LAPD downplayed the incident and tried to explain (in vain) that King had represented a threat to the officers, as he refused to obey direct orders. The home movie, televised over and over again, merely confirmed the dominant perception that the black population of LA held of its police force. A year later, in 1992, a jury acquitted the policemen. Los Angeles erupted in violence; the rioting lasted for days. The LA authorities had failed to deal properly with the King incident, which led to a much bigger crisis for them.

Mismanaged incidents also pertain to the many cases where victim groups feel they have not been adequately cared for, and undertake political and legal action against authorities. This gives rise to protracted legal battles and negative publicity, which may easily take a decade or more. The case of the 1984 Bhopal petrochemical explosion, which caused thousands of deaths in this Indian town, is a case in point: court battles between Union Carbide (the American mother company), Indian regional authorities, and victim organizations were finally concluded 20 years after the disaster.

The "agenda-setting" crisis has a "frame-breaking" quality. It becomes a symbol of hitherto unknown or neglected risks and vulnerabilities. It provides a major opportunity for issue advocates to shape the problem definition and salience of some issue for years to come ("see what happens if you turn a blind eye to. . ."). The accident at the Three Mile Island nuclear power station provoked a major scare even though there were no victims. The incident repoliticized the use of nuclear energy in the United States.[10] The industry never really bounced back from the episode. One cost estimate puts losses at $500 billion.[11]

When a disaster takes place in a predominantly ethnic neighborhood, it can easily expose the surprising intricacy and complexity of governing multi-racial, multi-cultural urban areas, and "boost" these as political issues. After the Amsterdam air crash in 1992, for example, the Dutch suddenly learned about the large number of illegal aliens in their country, contributing to a marked change in the political environment of immigration policy that took place during the 1990s.

To end a crisis: the delicate art of timing

The discussion of the various types of crisis dynamics suggests that the termination of crisis is "completed" only when closure has been achieved on both the operational and political dimensions of crisis management. From an operational perspective, the key challenge in crisis termination is to make an accurate and balanced assessment of the need to keep the crisis response infrastructure in place (the legal framework of emergency procedures and by-laws; centralized modes of decision making and the mobilization of resources). At some point, this state of emergency is no longer necessary. It is a leadership task to determine when that point in time has arrived.

Leaders must also assess the political expediency of crisis termination. The key challenge is to recognize when the breakdown of symbolic order has been restored. They must decide whether there is strategic or tactical mileage in extending rather than dampening the crisis mood, and in continuing rather than abolishing the crisis governance regime. This judgment depends on many considerations, including the perceived political success of the crisis management effort so far (as conveyed in the mass media and reflected in public opinion data), the positions and resources of oppositional forces and rivals, and their presumed ability to keep controlling the public perception of crisis and its policy implications.

If we juxtapose the operational and political dimensions, we can sketch various states of "closure" (see Figure 5.1). Perfect closure is achieved when operational demands cease while the political and public sense of crisis dissipates as well. This was roughly the case in several Western European countries immediately after World War II, including

Political closure

		Yes	No
	Yes	post-WWII	Waco
Operational closure			
	No	AIDS	9/11

Figure 5.1. Four ideal-typical states of crisis closure.

the Scandinavian countries and the Netherlands: after hostilities had ended, the widespread inclination in societal and political circles was to move on and rebuild. As long as operational definitions of crisis fit with political and societal perceptions, a crisis continues. This has been the case in many Western countries – not to speak of Afghanistan and Iraq – after the 9/11 events sparked a "global war on terror."

The most interesting cases are found in the mismatch between operational and political definitions of crisis. Operational closure often invites termination at the political end of the crisis spectrum, but this rarely happens without a glitch. The Waco crisis provides one of many examples. When members of the Branch Davidians Sect barricaded themselves into a house in Waco, Texas in 1993, Federal Bureau of Investigation (FBI) and Alcohol, Tobacco, and Fire-arms (ATF) agency forces fought their way into the compound, ending the operation quickly with a death toll of seventy-four men, women, and children. For the FBI, the ATF, and attorney-general Janet Reno, however, the crisis had only just begun. The botched operation (which had taken the lives of four ATF agents) provoked a political crisis complete with high-profile investigations and criminal proceedings.[12]

Sometimes, political closure is achieved while in an operational sense the crisis continues unabated. Think of the forgotten crises of food shortages and warfare – crises that continue to beset the African continent.

From this discussion, two major "timing deficits" emerge. On the one hand, leaders may terminate the crisis regime prematurely. This occurs when they underestimate the complexity and tenacity of the problems at hand, or misread the residual stress level existing in the affected community. The danger of premature revocation of the crisis regime is twofold. First, it may create vacuums in policy making and service delivery. Focused, large-scale and quick activities give way to politics and bureaucracy as usual: disjointed, incremental, slow. In other words, the effectiveness of the crisis operation may be undermined. Second, premature closure is likely to invite disbelief, disappointment, and intense criticism. Especially in a community that is still experiencing acute needs and stress, premature closure exposes policy makers to charges of being "insensitive" and opportunistic ("they forgot their promises as soon as the cameras were gone").

The alternative risk is that of overextending the crisis. Leaders may become so focused on the operational dimension of the crisis that they lose sight of the big picture. This happens, for instance, when they get caught up in the myopia of the "bunker syndrome" (see Chapter 3). They sit in a command center for weeks on end, where they "manage" the crisis and lose themselves in streams of seemingly urgent communication. The world outside moves on to other concerns, but the authorities have cut themselves off from that part of reality by continuing to allocate all their attention to a crisis that in many ways is no longer "hot."

Leaders may also elect to delay termination for purely political reasons. In the last century alone, authoritarian leaders of all stripes and colors have routinely invoked and subsequently prolonged states of emergency to consolidate their positions, and to vilify and persecute political opponents. Such leaders risk overplaying their hand when they stick to the crisis mode when most perceive that the "real issues" lie elsewhere. It leaves them open to charges that they are exploiting the crisis politically as a means to deflect attention.

5.3 Crisis termination and the challenges of accountability

Leaders cannot control the evolution and termination of crises. For one thing, they are, of course, at the mercy of the developments on the ground: when the crisis continues for all to see, leaders cannot declare on television that the situation is under control. The immediate consequence is then measured in the currency of rapidly declining trust. In an example both tragic and comical, the mayor of the Dutch town of Uithoorn was interviewed live against the backdrop of a burning factory. Just as he declared the crisis to be under control, the viewers could see black smoke bellowing from the factory in the background, instantly disqualifying the mayor as a credible crisis leader.[13]

Leaders are also constrained by institutional routines and rituals. As we saw in Chapter 4, the extraordinary and impressive character of crisis requires that leaders explain what happened, what went wrong, and where to go next. The existing procedures and codes of debriefing, investigation, and accountability provide key channels for this meaning-making process. There is a societal expectation that policy makers will account for their actions in these circumstances, and there are often political and legal pressures to do so as well.

The accountability process is not just a way of bringing closure to a crisis; it can also extend its life span, and transform it. In many cases we have studied, crisis-induced accountability processes give rise to a veritable "crisis after the crisis." They lift the original set of events from the level of operations to the levels of policy and politics. What began as an accident or a series of incidents turns into a story about power, competence, leadership, and legitimacy (or lack of it). Hence the difference between crises that end quickly and those that do not depends in large part on the peculiar dynamics of investigation and accountability. In this intensely political phase of crisis management, leaders must negotiate the challenges of accountability in order to preserve the legitimacy of governance. It is to these challenges that we now turn.

Leaders face something of an upward battle here, as successful instances of crisis prevention and mitigation draw little attention. These are, by definition, "non-events." To claim credit for things that have not happened is hard in a media environment obsessed with finding fault and a political arena that is geared to addressing problems rather than praising policy makers (as we saw in Chapter 4). In contrast, when things do go wrong they meet with a blaze of negative publicity and critical scrutiny.

The situation is compounded by the fact that success and failure are judgments, made by observers and parties with an interest in representing the story of a crisis in particular ways. Efforts to shape the public understanding of the events generally start in the very midst of the acute stage (see Chapter 4). But it is not until the immediate threats have been dealt with that impression management really becomes the most important game in town. And no professional crisis actor can afford to shun that game. For those who think that their actions speak for themselves, the accountability process may harbor unpleasant surprises.

After all, rendering account involves a delicate blend of factual reconstruction, manipulation of images, and lesson-drawing. Reconstructing and assessing complex governance episodes is hard enough in normal circumstances. In the context of major crises, it is nearly impossible to do so without encountering major political headwinds. Because of their dramatic and disruptive nature, crises give rise to tough questions that defy simple answers: why did this happen? What was done to stop it? What should happen next?

These questions are shaped in the mass media and the public mind, as well as in the political-bureaucratic arena and the legal system. The way they are dealt with is intimately connected to pre-existing public views about the role of nature, chance, control, and responsibility in social life.

Take, for example, the attribution of causes. In the twenty-first century, fatalistic ideas about natural forces and divine supremacy have lost currency in large parts of the Western world.[14] Technology has become the principal tool to tame fate. Yet technology can be applied adequately or inadequately, and sometimes the application of certain technologies itself generates new risks (nuclear energy, genetic engineering). It is now also commonly understood that the responsibility for handling this technology does not rest solely with the operators: "many companies now realize that almost every accident is due to a management failing, and they will not accept human error as the cause of an accident."[15] Nor will political investigation committees and judiciary bodies.

Characteristics of accountability

The accountability process is subject to change, as evidenced by the creeping juridification and the development of tort law in Western societies. It has essentially moved from a fatalistic no-claim to a high-accountability, high-remedy system offering more and more scope to victims of accidents to seek compensation. Modernity has, in other words, raised the stakes for public policy makers and organizations. People may still accept that public leaders cannot eradicate fate and fortune altogether, and they do not expect perfect crisis prevention, yet, the burden of the argument has shifted to the regulators and managers: they have to establish beyond doubt that they cannot be held responsible. When it comes to crisis response assessment, the margins for excusable failure are even smaller. Governments are assumed to be well prepared for critical contingencies, and to take effective measures that protect the public, limit harm, and compensate damages. Any behavior that deviates from this generalized expectation is treated with suspicion and indignation.

If a post-crisis investigation identifies "failures" of prevention or response, the situation becomes politically delicate. Two types of reaction modes compete for dominance in the public arena. The debate may highlight the need to learn from past mistakes and induce organizations and policies to improve accordingly. Or it may zoom in on questions of responsibility and guilt.

The first mode is premised on the idea that crisis management is all about optimizing societal abilities to prevent and absorb extreme circumstances. In this line of thought, accountability performs two important functions. First, it offers an opportunity for catharsis that enables all involved to demarcate the end of the crisis and prepare for an altered future. Without it, crisis-induced anxieties and tensions would continue to linger. Post-crisis debriefings and investigations provide a controlled format for professional criticism, expressions of (self-)pity, and emotional outbursts deemed odd or unacceptable at other times. Precisely because it is controlled in terms of more or less routinized organizational and political protocols, it can perform a sanitizing function. Second, the process provides crucial inputs to organizational learning. Crises in this view can be viewed as natural experiments, testing the resilience of people, organizations, and governance systems. Evaluations then provide the feedback needed to assess and improve the level of this resilience (see further Chapter 6).

The second mode treats the accountability process as an extension of crisis politics. Politically speaking, the "aftermath" should be considered a crisis in and of itself, because it is then that the tough questions about performance, leadership, and responsibility get asked. On one level, this accountability process is simply an enactment of democracy. The rule of law and the constitutional checks and balances on executive power reassert themselves after a period where the need to respond effectively to a perceived threat has dominated all other considerations. The political accountability process is always fragile, if only because parliamentarians themselves may have been supporting the very laws and policies that they need to scrutinize in exercising oversight.

Accountability is hollow when the investigation and debate that lie at its heart become ritualized. Realpolitik often dictates that majority factions in parliament support the political leaders, particularly with regard to a highly salient issue such as a crisis, irrespective of how those leaders actually performed. Leaders, in turn, may play along with the script of being called to account if they think they can mask embarrassing facts from public view, and if they are convinced their political support is secured in advance.

The accountability process, however, not only takes place in the controlled setting of parliaments. It also plays on the volatile stage of public opinion, which is potentially much more dangerous to policy makers. Publicity waves and media hypes alter the way people see and remember a crisis period.[16] Media hypes are difficult to control, perpetuated as they are by the sheer number of media and the competition between them. Aggressive media reporting about crisis management performance puts strong pressure on even the most docile legislatures to assume a more assertive and critical stance.

These different modes – learning and reflection versus accountability and blame – come with their own discourses, which tend to intertwine during the accountability process. This does not make things easier for crisis leaders:

The knowledge that responsibility brings accountability and that blame for accidents and disasters will be laid, and possible legal sanctions invoked, may be needed to motivate organizations and individuals to examine their activities and act in good faith. On the other hand, if a "culprit" has to be found whenever an error has occurred, the processes of political sense-making [in this study we use the term meaning making to denote these processes, authors] will emphasize avoidance of blame rather than critique and honesty.[17]

5.4   Blame games and the politics of meaning making

A study of post-crisis accountability processes reveals what may be called the paradox of open societies: the more "open" the accountability process to interested actors, the longer it takes for a crisis to end. Free press, political democracy, and bureaucratic pluralism may even help crisis investigations and accountability processes degenerate into blame games.

The term "blame game" refers to the interaction between actors who are out to protect their self-interests rather than to serve the common good. When efforts to investigate crises turn into blame games, truth-finding through dialogue and debate loses out against defensive rationalization ("we made no mistakes"), deliberate silences, and factual distortions. As a result, democratic accountability is perverted and institutional learning capabilities are impaired.

Many crises do give rise to political and bureaucratic blame games. This poses a dilemma. The evaluation process has to be guarded against the danger of runaway politicization, but in the context of a major crisis, who has the authority and is sufficiently motivated to play the guardian role? Brändström and Kuipers picture a crisis-induced blame game as a decision tree that consists of the strategic choices actors face in the accountability process.[18] All actors make choices on three dimensions: severity (how bad was the situation?), agency (how could it happen?), and responsibility (who is to be sanctioned?). First, they must assess the events: what values and interests are at stake and in which respect have these been violated or threatened? When they conclude that core values have been violated, or when the dominant opinion among other powerful actors suggests this has been the case, they need to position themselves by giving accounts of their own behavior and that of others.

The second key question is whether the situation should be seen as an incident – which it is when it can be argued that it was produced by ad-hoc failures at the operational level – or as a symptom of underlying policy failures. In the latter case, the crisis is usually depicted as "an accident waiting to happen" for which neither operators nor executive agencies should be blamed but rather those officials and institutions that designed the contested policy.

The third question is how central any single actor (individual but more likely organizational) was in producing the undesirable situation. Were the crucial acts or omissions produced by a single organization or an entire network of organizations?

The dominant judgment which results from the combination of choices that the various participants in the blame game make can take four forms (outcomes A–D in Figure 5.2). When the participants arrive at outcome A (scapegoating), blame is deflected toward specific sectoral or crisis-response agencies (see further below). When they collectively decide on network failure (outcome B), sanctions against an entire range of operational organizations become a possibility. This may set the stage for adjustment of policies, rules, and procedures that govern the implementation network in the policy sector at hand.

The politically most explosive outcome, at least from a blaming perspective, is C. The crisis is interpreted as a product of errors or other shortcomings that a set of clearly identifiable senior policy makers have committed. From a dispassionate researcher's position outcome D is perhaps the most salient one. This collective judgment implies that not individual human errors or misjudgments but rather flawed systems of

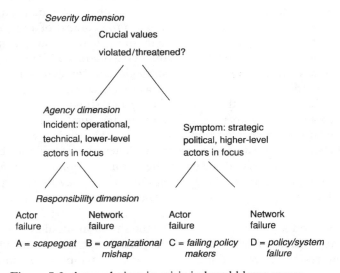

Figure 5.2. Actor choices in crisis-induced blame games.
Source: Brändström and Kuipers (2003: 302).

policy making or service delivery lie at the heart of the crisis. "When crises are defined in this manner, some sort of institutional reform or major policy change becomes hard to avoid, irrespective of the political fate of the incumbent elites."[19]

These assessments are not arrived at through a smooth process of evidence taking, polite argument, and rational decision making. Crisis-induced accountability processes are better understood as episodes of high politics where not just the careers of individual office holders but the futures of entire organizations, policies, and governance networks are at stake. Politically astute actors are acutely aware of these stakes (but not each and every group or agency involved in a crisis is necessarily politically astute) and act accordingly to try to protect their interests.

In the political arena of crisis investigation, actors apply a wide range of rhetorical tactics and arguments (see Table 5.1). The viability of any particular tactic or argument varies: when they are used (timing), where they are used (forum), by whom they are used (credibility), and how well they are presented (staging, delivery). Nor are these tactics mutually exclusive. They are used simultaneously in various fora addressing different accountability questions. They can also be used sequentially, for example when the emphasis in the blame game gradually shifts from issues of agency to issues of responsibility, or when earlier use of particular tactics has proved to be ineffective.

How likely are the various actors in a crisis to assume the various positions described above? Let us review the position of the most important stakeholders in crisis-driven accountability processes and review their relation with crisis leaders. After all, the political survival of crisis leaders depends to a considerable extent on the positioning of stakeholders in the post-crisis accountability process.

Media

The mass media are "all over" the accountability process, ready to cover new information about risks, dangers, mishaps, failures, and flaws that may sustain or transform the running story of the current crisis. Media representatives therefore play a powerful role in shaping the dominant interpretation that will emerge from accountability processes. The same rule applies here as it does for initial phases of meaning making: accountability processes do not speak for themselves; they must be interpreted. And media representatives know how to reduce a complex analysis of cause and effect to a simple, evocative story of heroes and villains.

Table 5.1. *Playing the blame game: argumentative tactics*

Accountability dimension	Tactic	Argument
Severity	Denial	Nothing bad happened
	Mitigation	Harm was negligible
		Harm was compensated
		You can't make an omelet...
	Positive spin	It was a success
Agency	Combating causation	It was not my doing
		I was only a small contributor
		Uncontrollable forces reigned
	Combating capacity	I was not informed
		Others made vital decisions
		I was under orders
	Blaming messenger	Publicity caused the harm
	Disqualifying investigators	Investigation was unfair
		Investigators are incompetent
		Report is unprofessional
Responsibility	Justification	I chose the lesser evil
		I prevented worse by others
	Preventing labeling	This was atypical behavior
	Scapegoating	I have punished the culprit(s)
	Repentance	I apologize, please forgive me
		I have learned my lesson
	Symbolic reform	I have changed policies

Source: adapted from Bovens et al. (1999)

The media comprises a wide variety of professionals. Some report in fairly objective terms, leaving their audience with the opportunity to make up their own minds. Some assume a more proactive stance and try to get to the bottom of the case. Yet others turn into crusading entrepreneurs who exploit the openness of the accountability process in order to argue their preconceived position. All media will be open to "deep throats," which are inherent to any crisis. Leaders, in other words, cannot presume that the accountability process is one of reconstruction and fact; they must expect the worst if they want to come out unscathed.

Executive organizations

Perhaps even more so than their political masters, agencies charged with day-to-day policy implementation are put to the test when they get drawn into a crisis. The immediate response phase usually requires transformation. Most agencies tend to be more or less autonomous and professional service-delivery organizations, used to processing individual clients or case files sequentially into nodes. During a crisis, these bureaucratic agencies are thrown into tightly coupled inter-organizational networks that deal with numerous cases simultaneously under time pressure.

The accountability process may bring two types of charges. When a crisis occurs on their turf, so to speak, they face charges of having failed to prevent it: why did they not foresee the crisis, and why were they unable to prevent simmering problems from escalating? Think of the criticism directed toward the US intelligence community after the September 11 attacks. Or think of the Chinese public health agencies, which stood accused of underplaying the dangers of SARS and misinforming their political superiors and international colleagues about the scale of the problem in China. But even when an agency had nothing to do with the outbreak of crisis but was called in to help combat it, it can be criticized as an ill-prepared, sluggish, and uncooperative partner in crisis response. For instance, specialized crisis response agencies such as the police or the fire brigade often complain about the disorganized or rigid "bureaucratic" nature of the non-emergency services (housing services, social work, public transport, public utilities) they must work with during major disasters.

Much depends on the formal division of labor and responsibility between policy makers and agencies. When policy implementation and service delivery have been delegated to private actors, quasi-independent agencies, or lower levels of government, it is easy for policy makers to deflect blame on them. Seen in this light, a side effect of decentralization, delegation, outsourcing, and other techniques of new public management that became *en vogue* in the 1990s is that they provide policy makers and regulators with protective coating in cases of failure and crisis. Policy makers will not hesitate to point out that they were no longer the "agent" determining the nature, level, and quality of policy implementation. They were far removed from the source of trouble; hence their causal impact on the crisis outbreak was negligible. They redirect questions to the implementing actors.

Whether this strategy of blame deflection actually works in this fashion depends on many factors.[20] But there are certainly telling examples of instances in which it did. When the British prison service faced a string of embarrassing incidents in 1994–95, Home Secretary Michael Howard argued that he could not be held responsible for incidents. Pointing to the operational responsibilities of the prison agency, the Home Secretary removed Director General Derek Lewis from his post in the Prison Service. Lewis did not go quietly, but Howard survived.[21]

Crisis response agencies

For crisis response agencies, a crisis is both a challenge and a blessing. It is a challenge in the sense that of all the actors in the crisis network they are held to the highest standards of preparedness, speed of mobilization, smooth communication and coordination, and effective service delivery. Crisis response is what they are all about, so they had better be good at it. A crisis also presents a welcome opportunity to demonstrate relevance and confirm performance capacity. Without such opportunities, these organizations risk "unlearning" the capability to perform, as organizational memory fades and the experienced crisis commanders move to other positions.

Crisis response organizations thus have much to gain from crises and the accountability processes that they entail – provided they do well, or are seen to have done well, in performing their duties. Credit-claiming behavior is to be expected in these circumstances, particularly when the agencies in question are not monopolists in their task area. They can flag their successes and boost their image among budget providers, the press, and the public. Effective agencies usually make sure their successes are appropriately marketed to captive audiences, both during and after the accountability process.

However, when their operations have experienced problems, the accountability process is not so much an opportunity as a major threat. Since being good at containing crises is at the heart of their *raison d'être*, any evidence to the contrary erodes their legitimacy. At the very least, it gives their competitors a chance to discredit them. In such circumstances, beleaguered agencies may resort to cover-up, blame-avoidance, and blame-shifting tactics during the accountability process.

Legislators

The accountability process following crises is a mixed-motive game for the members of the principal accountability fora themselves (legislators). On the opportunity side, the legislature as a whole, as well as certain groups (notably opposition parties) and individuals (ambitious political entrepreneurs) within it, welcome crises as opportunities for self-dramatization. Legislators seize upon a crisis to show their ability to monitor and control government, to demonstrate their toughness as a countervailing power, and, in partisan mode, to inflict damage upon or create dissensus within the opposing camp.

Legislators can take this proactive stance only when their hands are free – that is, when in their role as (co-)regulators they were not involved in making and approving the very policies and agency statutes they now want to criticize in light of the crisis experience. Past involvement, in other words, diminishes the opportunity for legislators to exploit the post-crisis accountability process. Sometimes the reverse happens. When today's inquisitors are seen to be conveniently forgetting that they were yesterday's lawmakers, they are open to charges of hypocrisy. These charges may come from the outside, notably the mass media, but they also become the stuff of partisan squabbles within the legislature. When these occur, the accountability process is likely to suffer in quality. The investigation efforts, the drafting of findings, and drawing political conclusions from these findings: all risk being permeated by internal bickering and power struggles.

Ad hoc commissions

Blue-ribbon commissions are often set up to provide "comprehensive" and "independent" assessments of a crisis. These commissions define the parameters for judgments on political, judicial, and financial accountability. They construct – or at least pretend to – the officially certified version of an important part of a nation's recent history. But they cannot always break the hold that the politics of partisanship and defensiveness exert on the accountability process. In fact, their potential roles as truth tellers, political conflict managers, and institutional agenda setters easily turn the composition, mandate, and modus operandi of crisis commissions into objects of political contestation. When the investigative work or the findings of commissions become controversial, the post-acute crisis stage is fueled by allegations and counter-allegations, which merely perpetuate different versions of the crisis story.[22]

These crisis commissions serve several purposes for the various stakeholders; only one of these, and not necessarily the most important one, is to contribute to governmental learning. The government's position is informed by symbolism and damage control; in some crises, the government appoints an investigative commission with considerable fanfare in the hope that the eventual report will draw much less attention. Paradoxically, the implementation of recommendations tends to be a much more arduous task involving much higher political risks than merely demonstrating commitment to "getting the facts straight." We will return to the role of commissions in Chapter 6.

Investigation boards

In various countries and in various sectors – such as transport, food safety, and public health – governments have set up permanent investigation bodies, with varying mandates and degrees of independence from the ministries involved. These bodies are staffed with experts and often command considerable budgets to conduct investigations into ongoing practices and crucial cases in their respective sectors. They can do so both on their own initiative and after government or parliamentary requests, and they report to either or both of them. Bodies like these are supposed to provide an independent, non-political, professionally sound analysis and formulate recommendations. The more they are viewed as independent, the higher the likelihood that their reports will be regarded as authoritative by all parties concerned.

The position of investigation boards after a crisis is similar to the position of response agencies. It is part of their core business to provide high-quality input to the accountability and learning process triggered by crisis, and therefore they experience pressure to perform fast, reliably, and effectively. However, speed and accuracy rarely travel well together. The situation becomes complicated when more investigative boards are involved: interagency rivalry will speed up the investigative process, which, we must assume, does not further the quality of the investigation.[23]

The board may want to move swiftly, but it will have to behave cautiously at the same time. This could be named the Hans Blix dilemma, after the chairman of the UN weapons inspection team in the 2002–3 Iraq crisis.[24] Like Blix and his team, investigation boards are dependent upon all other actors to give them the necessary information. They may have the means to enforce cooperation, but they still depend on voluntary compliance to unearth all information needed for a considered assessment. When they push too hard, they may provoke countermeasures, including efforts to hinder their performance, detract from their credibility, and question their independence – which is exactly what Blix experienced.

Citizens, victims, and interest groups

The role of ordinary citizens and interest groups in post-crisis accountability processes seems to have increased over time.[25] In the not so distant past, accountability processes were less prominent and citizens had little access to them. Enduring harm suffered by individuals, groups, and communities tended to be dealt with in a rather low-key, bureaucratized manner, if at all. It was not easy to get public recognition, better compensation, and a more intensive reconstruction support. Communities had to muster inner strength because they were more often than not left to their own devices after the initial flurry of activity had died down and the camera lights had been shut off.[26] Those who wanted more had a good chance of being bogged down in protracted legal battles or simply being ignored by their political leaders.[27]

Today, citizens have stronger voices. They can quickly organize themselves into pressure groups. And they are more likely to use their voices and organizational resources when the treatment received from private and public actors involved in crisis response does not meet their standards. During floods, for example, political decisions to conduct preventative evacuations of endangered areas have become the topic of intense controversy in various countries. Not only have governments had a hard time persuading citizens to leave their houses, during the aftermath they have experienced difficulties answering convincingly to charges that they acted overly cautiously at the expense of citizens and businesses.[28]

Citizens have learned to organize, mobilize media attention, and forge coalitions with other segments of civil society as well as individual political entrepreneurs seeking to call policy makers and politicians to account for and to "re-open" the crisis, or create a new one. Journalists, opposition politicians, interest group activists, and lawyers have plenty of incentives as well as opportunities to empower citizens.[29] The contemporary political climate favors restorative justice, which gives victims a better chance of placing their suffering and traumas high on the public agenda. They do not have to wait for the dust to settle and for formal investigation and compensation procedures to run their course. Instead, they appear on television instantly to make their claims or take their case to court: from citizen to victim to claimant in a matter of hours.

5.5   Accountability, blame games, and democracy

Moral entrepreneurs, political ambulance chasers, spin doctors, cover-up artists, bureaucratic zealots, and media guerrillas: the crisis accountability arena harbors a colorful cast of characters. Their interaction provides for a dynamic process, which in and of itself is not guaranteed to result in outcomes that pass the test of fairness, efficiency, lawfulness, or citizen well-being. Crises put not just the response capabilities of

authorities to the test but also the democratic authenticity of the governance systems in which crises occur. To what extent does the accountability process become a truth-finding dialogue, and to what extent does
it escalate into inquisition and blame games?

This chapter has documented a tension between the characteristics of
the accountability process and the "smoothness" of crisis termination.
Democracy requires both, but the practice of crisis accountability is
marked by trade-offs. To be open and transparent may be impossible
when it comes to accounting for the deeds and omissions with regard to
crises, greatly upsetting and therefore controversial episodes as they are.
A crisis tests the strength of the institutional mechanisms for calling
elites to account, certainly when they themselves prefer not to dwell on
what has passed.[30]

The latent tensions that exist in any polity between public, the opposition's, and government interests do not melt away during crises. On the
contrary, since the visibility and political stakes of crises are so high,
these tensions will be even more pronounced than usual. Crises induce
or amplify divisions not just among and between (segments of) society
and the government but also between officials, groups, and organizations
within government. One of the most obvious potential rifts is between operational units, their managerial bosses at headquarters, and
their political or bureaucratic bosses at the peak of the government
hierarchy.[31] The same leaders who seek to centralize authority and
decision-making powers during the crisis are quick to point out that they
cannot be held responsible for policies whose implementation they
themselves have delegated to agencies or local governments. These, in
turn, will seek to reverse blame by arguing that they might have been
given the tasks and the formal authority to deal with certain matters, but
they never obtained the necessary (financial) means or the *de facto*
freedom to maneuver. The big risk is that both parties end up sharing
blame and public embarrassment in a game where everybody loses.

To be sure, it is not all politics in the accountability phase of crisis.
Parallel to the bureau-political domain is the professional domain of
specialists in many different disciplines who look back on a crisis and
consider the possible lessons these events may harbor for the future. As
will be explained in the next chapter, learning requires a safe environment, where the drive for improvement and not the desire to score points
or avoid losses dominates. This is hard to accomplish when the professional accountability process is engulfed by the political domain, where
different rules apply. To complicate matters even further, both the
professional and the political domains of accountability may be "held
hostage" by the legal domain. When the crisis is taken to court, different

rules, risks, and odds enter the picture. Of course, justice must be served when people get hurt, but an unmitigated desire for justice may exact a high price: the inability to learn for the next crisis.

There is no single, self-evident institutional design solution readily available to overcome these tensions. Even independent investigation boards cannot always fully escape the dangers of agency capture. Nor can their reports substitute for parliamentary dialogue and legal judgment. Ultimately, the quality of crisis accountability depends upon the extent to which key actors display a sense of proportionality and self-restraint in playing the game of meaning making.[32] Political scientists have argued that democratic accountability is not just a way of putting structures of checks and balances in place; it is also about developing and maintaining a culture in which transparency is the norm, and political debate about past performance is not completely overshadowed by politicking. This is particularly true in the context of political crisis management. Only those who have the wisdom and the courage to prioritize the effectiveness and legitimacy of the system as a whole rather than their short-term personal and organizational interests can hope to escape self-defeating blame games.

Notes

1 Honig and Both (1997); Honig (2001).
2 The standard work is Cuny's (1983), who noted that natural disasters often undermine the legitimacy of government in third world countries. As a tragic sideline, we note that Cuny disappeared in Chechnya while doing research on that protracted crisis.
3 Who remembers Y2K? This crisis was terminated without so much as a whisper (and certainly without evaluations). An amazing episode of global crisis, which still awaits thorough, systematic analysis.
4 See Bovens and 't Hart (1996); Quarantelli (1998); Quarantelli and Perry (2005).
5 Quarantelli (1998).
6 Multilateral trade and environmental disputes seem to follow this pattern (Zartman, 1994).
7 On the topic of institutional crisis, see Boin and 't Hart (2000); Alink et al. (2001); Jacobs and Boin (2001).
8 See further Hansén and Stern (2001) who analyze the case as a national trauma.
9 This example is taken from Miller (2001).
10 Baumgartner and Jones (1993).
11 See Quarantelli (1996).
12 Vizzard (1997).
13 Crisis Onderzoek Team (1994).

14 An odd exception might be (parts of) Iceland. See Bernardsdottir and Svedin (2004).
15 Kletz (1994: 240).
16 Vasterman (2004).
17 Pidgeon (1997: 9).
18 Brändström and Kuipers (2003).
19 Brändström and Kuipers (2003: 303).
20 For a more detailed analysis, see Hood (2002).
21 This example is taken from Resodihardjo (forthcoming). See Lewis (1997) for an inside account of this crisis.
22 See Dekker (forthcoming).
23 See Charles (2001) for a detailed account of the investigation into the crash of TWA flight 800.
24 Blix (2004).
25 We have to be careful here. Some authors claim that in the past, organized efforts to manage crises were terminated relatively soon after the acute threat had abated. Both the public and the elites are portrayed as "eager" to return to business as usual (see, for example, Rosenthal, 1998). This may be more an academic bias than historical fact, however. See, for example, Brandt (2003) on Chicago's Iroquois theatre fire of 1903 in which citizens played a very active role.
26 Erikson (1976; 1994).
27 Shrivastava (1987); Jasanoff (1994); Sarangi (2002).
28 Perry and Lindell (1997); see Steinberg (2000) for an historical perspective.
29 A fairly new tool for citizens is to create survivor websites. See, for example, the Paddington Survivors Group (www.paddingtonsg.org.uk).
30 Douglas and Wildavsky (1982); Douglas (1992).
31 Another rift is between agencies or departments involved in ongoing juris-dictional and budgetary struggles.
32 The 9/11 Commission serves as an intriguing example. In a politically divided climate (to use an understatement), the bipartisan commission wrote a report that was heralded by politicians and media as high-quality and non-partisan writing. For a dissenting voice, see Posner (2004).

6   Learning from crises and the politics of reform

6.1   Never again!

The post-9/11 era has seen new policies, legal changes, and major institutional innovations that were pushed through the legislative processes at unprecedented speed – in the United States, the European Union, and many other countries. In the US, the so-called Patriot Act was adopted in near unanimity, enacting policy changes in the judicial system, in the handling of immigrants and resident aliens, and in the allocation of government funds for national security and public safety. In a major administrative reorganization effort, various security-related agencies were merged at the stroke of a pen into the vast Department of Homeland Security. The department harbors 170,000 employees and has wide responsibilities in preparing for and dealing with different crisis contingencies.[1]

The European Union learned and changed as well: the scope and depth of cooperation in the field of justice and home affairs have deepened markedly since 9/11 and Madrid. A uniform definition of terrorism has been accepted; extradition rules for potentially terrorism-related crimes have been extended. Police units can track suspected criminals across national borders and, if necessary, act with full authority on foreign soil. Europol, the European agency for police cooperation, has been strengthened, and Eurojust, a similar agency designed to foster cooperation in public prosecution, is in the making. The EU has also accorded higher priority to the protection of its external borders; the new member states receive strong support to upgrade their border-control capabilities. A solidarity clause for mutual assistance in terror attacks has been formulated for inclusion in the new, now elusive, EU Constitution.

Conventional wisdom has it that progress requires learning from failure. Crises provide clear-cut opportunities for learning and adapting, so it is generally assumed. In a perfect world, the right lessons emerge and policy makers adapt their organizations and policies accordingly.

The real world does not always live up to conventional wisdom, however. It is, to begin with, not so easy to determine what went wrong and what should be adapted to prevent similar crises from happening again. Many different and sometimes contradictory lessons are often distilled from one and the same crisis experience. Moreover, it is not easy to have stakeholders agree on what the right lessons are. As we have seen in the previous chapter, the post-crisis period is not necessarily one of unity and open inquiry. The adversarial politics of the aftermath will affect the identification and selection of the lessons to be learned from crisis. Even when there is agreement on certain measures to be taken, there is no guarantee that lessons learned will actually be implemented.

Yet it is clear that governments can and do learn from crises. The *key question* of this chapter is what explains the capability to learn appropriate lessons and implement the lessons learned. There are two sides to this question: "puzzling" and "powering."[2] The "puzzling side" refers to the capacity to learn: what went wrong, why, and what needs to be changed so that it will not happen again? The "powering side" pertains to the capacity to reform: can policy makers instigate substantive changes in the wake of a crisis?

Strong leadership during crisis does not necessarily translate in the effective management of post-crisis learning and reform processes. Learning is an incredibly complex process, all the more so in the post-crisis context of public organizations and high politics. The implementation of lessons learned poses entirely different challenges: research on policy and administrative reforms shows how hard it is to break the hold of incrementalist politics as usual and enact more far-reaching changes.[3] Our *core claim* is that the capacity of governments to learn and change following crises is constrained by the fundamental tensions that exist between the imperatives of political crisis management and those of effective lesson-drawing and reform craft.

Our argument unfolds in four steps. We begin by analyzing the opportunities and constraints that crises entail for governmental learning. We then explain how the politics of crisis aftermath creates opportunities for stakeholders to push drastic policy changes that may have little to do with any lessons learned. We also explain why many leaders – contrary to conventional wisdom – shy away from exploiting reform opportunities (and why that may be a wise strategy for them). The final part of our argument takes us to what perhaps is a somewhat pessimistic conclusion, as we posit our claim that crisis leadership, learning, and reform craft typically demand skills and strategies that are at odds with each other.

6.2   Learning from crisis

Crises are often thought to stimulate learning. This is especially true in the conception of crises as commonly experienced, exogenously induced threats to a jointly valued status quo. In such situations – where no thorny political and institutional issues arise and all parties concerned are motivated to ensure that never again can such adversity reoccur – "learning is a golden concept: everybody is for it."[4]

Students of government have defined learning in many different ways, but most would agree that it involves purposeful efforts to (re)examine, (re)assess, and (re)calibrate existing and proposed beliefs, policies, and institutional arrangements. The distinguishing feature of learning from other forms of governmental activity is that it involves "puzzling": gathering new information and ideas, and applying them to policy issues, and creating the conditions under which all this can take place.[5] In order to learn, governments need to have not only some institutional capacity for lesson-drawing but also a (sustained) motivation to use this capacity and work with its products.[6]

A well-developed learning capacity combines at least three types of learning.[7] The first type is *experience based*. Direct exposure to a crisis is a powerful, to some literally unforgettable, experience. Vivid memories may allow an individual or organization to develop insights with regard to the causes of crisis and the effects of the coping operation. Experiential learning presupposes memory: organized recording, recollection, and retrieval of past events and actions. In addition, it requires some sort of mechanism to translate memories into lessons.[8] This type of learning occurs most naturally within professions that more or less routinely deal with certain types of crises through standardized procedures for recording and re-examining past experience.

Yet relatively few public leaders deal with more than one or two crises in their careers, and hence their personal experience is often limited. Crisis exercises give them some vicarious impressions, as do stories and reports about how their peers handled recent and past crises. These are, of course, nothing but supplements to the real thing.

A complementary form of learning is *explanation based*. Learning then becomes a rational-scientific search for the causes of failure and the effects of the response. This type of learning requires a critical mass of people qualified to tease out cause-and-effect relations and determine their validity. It also assumes a considerable level of autonomy to protect these "crisis auditors" from political interference. Moreover, it requires time and resources to allow them to do their job in an unhurried and meticulous manner. Some inquiry committees actually manage to do all this. Some organizations have set up their own machinery to generate explanation-based learning. For instance, NASA has an institutionalized capacity to study and explain causes of even minor failures.[9]

A third type of learning is *competence* or *skill based*. When a crisis exposes a deficit between a threat and the governmental capacity to deal with it – crises almost by definition do exactly that – new skills and competences may be in order. Emerging epidemics – AIDS, Ebola, SARS – typically require that doctors and health workers learn new techniques (the general approach to epidemics is well established). Technology-driven crises – think of computer viruses or software glitches such as Y2K – also demand fresh skills.

If one looks at the mechanisms by which crisis-induced learning in the public sector takes place, several stand out. Learning is often pursued through ad hoc commissions and the use of consulting firms or academic research.[10] In some sectors, institutionalized learning mechanisms are well developed. For instance, in many countries some type of safety board is set up for the transport sector. The US National Transportation Safety Board is probably the best known: it leads post-crisis investigations into the causes of disaster, with the explicit aim of learning lessons that will help to prevent similar disasters from re-occurring. How successful are such efforts, and what factors enable learning to take place? Here, as in other domains of crisis studies, optimists and pessimists disagree.

Pessimists: constrained and perverse learning

Pessimists hold that despite the many ways in which crises induce public leaders and their organizations to learn, the result is often disappointing. This is due to a wide variety of constraints that operate on both individual and organizational learning capacity.[11]

Social-psychological researchers are especially pessimistic when it comes to the capacity of small groups to learn about crises. The so-called "threat-rigidity hypothesis" – borne out by an impressive body of experimental research – predicts that the conditions of crisis make it hard if not impossible to learn.[12] People tend to respond in a rigid and inflexible manner to threats and uncertainty. They can no longer process information in an adequate manner, which throws them back to learned routines and instilled reflexes. It is easy to see how, during a crisis, fear may impede one's intellectual performance. We can imagine the impact of crisis on the direct aftermath: leaders who fear for their position are unlikely to encourage others to investigate thoroughly what exactly went wrong before and during the crisis.[13]

The research on organizational learning is equally pessimistic.[14] In Chapter 2, we introduced Barry Turner's work, which details the collective failure within many organizations to heed signals of impending danger.[15] His work, like the work of many other organization theorists, explains the underlying problem: organizations cannot properly communicate and understand information.[16] They fail to collect sufficient relevant data. They find it hard to distil cause-and-effect relations from their limited and flawed pool of data (and even if they do, they have no way of testing their n=1 findings).[17] They rarely possess a systematically organized "institutional memory."[18] Moreover, they generally do not have "uncommitted resources" that can be used to deal with these shortcomings and improve their information-handling capacity.[19] This body of literature suggests that there is no such thing as "crisis-induced learning" – or, if organizations do try to learn, that the results are likely to be sub-optimal at best.

A particularly subversive type of learning has been observed in organizations that have *successfully* dealt with a crisis. When leaders feel that they and the system as a whole have done well during the last crisis, this assumption will lead them to repeat their strategies and actions. In their eagerness to preserve these lessons, the leaders of these organizations make sure that the crisis experience is ingrained in the rules and routines that guide employees. The crisis is embraced as a formative experience and is carefully nurtured into an instructive legend. The crisis becomes the bedrock of organizational stamina and perseverance. The lessons thus translate into sanctified management principles. The perverse effect, however, is noted only in the long run. As crises never return in the same shape or form, lessons from the past are likely to become tomorrow's blind corners. Hence the saying "nothing fails like success."[20]

Likewise, recent failures may stimulate drastic alterations of existing organizational repertoires and policies pursued before the crisis. Widely visible and costly errors prior to or during crises invite sweeping policy revisions and reversals. This strategy has the virtue of simplicity and cognitive parsimony, but it is fundamentally risky. No causal links have been established between cause and effect; the strategy draws on a presumed analogy with the most immediate past. This is likely to be self-defeating in the long run, when the future turns out to be not the past repeated.[21]

The politics of accountability, discussed in the previous chapter, further undermines the capacity to learn. The escalation of blame games has a particularly debilitating effect. In the extreme case, many people and institutions gather comprehensive and minute information about everything that went on prior to, during, and after the crisis episode. The entire government apparatus, from lower-level bureaucrats up to the most senior political officials in charge, spends at least an equal amount of energy on gaining command of the facts, but primarily in order to deflect blame as much as possible. Information is tailored to be used as ammunition. Data are selected and moulded to construct winning arguments in a battle for personal and institutional survival. Individuals and organizations tailor their memories: when it is opportune to remember, they will; if needed, they "forget" – unless and until other players in the blame game force them out of their strategic amnesia.

Crisis-induced learning thus appears quite paradoxical. When the need to learn is at its peak, the institutional capacity of public leaders and their organizations may be disappointingly low.[22] Moreover, the more intensive the post-crisis information-gathering efforts are, the lower the chances that effective learning from crisis takes place, because "politics" undermines their motivation: the "powering" required to survive crises politically overtakes the drive to engage in the "puzzling" that lesson-drawing presupposes.[23]

In the pessimistic perspective, crises might simply be too big an experience for organizations and polities to absorb in a reflective and even-handed way. We may then expect "over-learning": premature, one-sided, and rigid application of hastily drawn inferences supported by the dominant coalition, at the price of a more open, inquisitive, and contingent approach to lesson-drawing.[24]

Optimists: enhanced and purposeful learning is possible

These pessimistic conclusions about crisis-induced learning are by no means universally supported by the entire body of available evidence. Quite a few studies report instances of ambitious and successful learning efforts in the wake of crises. Many crises not only create a politically charged atmosphere, they also induce a strong motivation in people at all layers of the organizations involved not to be caught unaware or incapable in the future. For example, the fear of a nuclear holocaust is said to have pushed US and Soviet leaders to deterrence rather than escalation after the Cuba Missile Crisis had come dangerously close to all-out war.[25]

When leaders share this motivation, they can act as pivotal forces in making sure that widespread desire to learn is translated into organizational or system-wide policy changes.[26] A classic and useful distinction here is that between single-loop and double-learning made by Argyris and Schön.[27]

Single-loop learning refers to the correction of practices within the existing policy paths and organizational frameworks. It is learning to deal with manifest problems without having to change core beliefs and fundamental rules of the game. This type of learning is common after crises: most crisis commissions' and investigation bodies' reports contain large numbers of recommendations for minor rule adjustments, innovations in equipment and training, improved communication routines, and so on.[28]

Single-loop learning is a necessary but in many cases not sufficient component of crisis-induced lesson-drawing, since many crises have a "paradigm-shattering" quality to them. Their very occurrence or the haphazard response to them exposes more fundamental limitations, weaknesses, and contradictions in existing policies and institutional arrangements. To deal with these, double-loop learning is required, which refers to types of "organizational inquiry which resolve incompatible organizational norms by setting new priorities and weightings of norms, or by restructuring the norms themselves together with associated strategies and assumptions."[29] The term "double-loop" refers to the fact that in learning processes of this kind the detection of error is not only being connected to "the strategies and assumptions for effective performance [as in single-loop learning, authors] but to the very norms which define effective performance."[30]

Double-loop learning initiatives are likely to touch sensitive nerves because they call into question fundamental tenets of the status quo, including the core beliefs that policy makers hold about the nature of the world around them. But some crises give rise to what we may call enabling factors: external pressure to improve performance; a persuasive diagnosis of existing problems coupled with feasible proposals for change; a coalition of motivated advocates of learning and change who are influential in both the political arena and the civil society; a motivated, capable, and patient bureaucratic machine. These factors seem to be required to produce radical, yet widely supported and effectively implemented departures from past policies.[31]

Time management appears to be an especially crucial factor. The necessary political support and scarce resources to adopt and implement crisis-induced lessons are more likely when the initiative to make changes follows quickly on the heels of the crisis. The sense of urgency that lesson-drawing enjoys in the wake of a crisis evaporates quickly. A crisis investigation that takes years to produce its findings should not expect an army of eager political entrepreneurs waiting to run with the ball. Nor is it realistic to expect that pending such long investigations, major financial resources are being kept in reserve to cover the often considerable costs of major policy changes.

The research on so-called high-reliability organizations (HROs) supports these conclusions. It suggests that learning is highly contingent upon the right mix of factors and actors. It also shows – this would be the good news – that organizational leaders can build and maintain safety cultures in organizations that facilitate effective learning.[32] When a safety culture takes hold, Argyris and Schön would say that deutero learning has occurred: the organization has learned to learn. It has, in other words, acquired an institutional capacity for lesson-drawing.

Policy change based on double-loop learning is possible, but it is precious and vulnerable: if one or several of the enabling factors are absent, efforts to discover, adopt, and implement intelligent policy changes after crises are easily aborted or subverted.[33] This explains why we can learn without seeing any change.

Sometimes we see change without learning. In fact, more than a few crises are followed by speedy reform proposals that hardly build upon the type of analytical underpinnings discussed above. Political logic rather than learning requirements dictate the pace of the action: creating a public appearance of responsible and forceful action *now* is given priority over launching more highly informed proposals later.

6.3   Change without learning: crisis as opportunity for reform

Crises do not create only cognitive puzzles and political problems for leaders: some of them are sure to view the crisis as an opportunity to instigate major policy and institutional changes (as will other stakeholders inside and outside government). Crises signal that pre-existing plans, policies, or organizational practices have failed. Institutional renewal becomes a possibility. Crises create opportunities for breakthroughs that in normal times are simply unthinkable or politically infeasible. They make possible the rotation of elites, the revision of policies, and the redesigning of institutions. They represent a window of opportunity for reform.[34]

The relation between crises and reform is often noted in both academic theorizing and popular wisdom.[35] In political science, for instance, students of democratization have posited that crisis is a necessary condition for change.[36] Students of government argue that governance unfolds as a pattern of "punctuated equilibria" – long eras of stability alternated with short-lived periods of uncertainty and conflict.[37] They point to critical junctures during which existing polity settings, policy goals, and institutional arrangements for policy-making come under pressure. This pressure may jeopardize their self-evident legitimacy and de-institutionalize governance. These notions suggest the reform potential of crises, which can be fully exploited by leaders acting upon these critical junctures.

This belief finds rich and easy support in practice. Many crises, after all, give birth to ambitious efforts to reform the policies and institutions of government.[38] They become viewed as symptoms of underlying societal vulnerabilities and governance problems. The critical problems are framed as endogenous to government. Government is no longer seen as part of the solution of social problems but has become part of the problem (to paraphrase a famous Ronald Reagan dictum). Reform is in order and seems to follow as a matter of course. Media reports rarely fail to recast crises and disaster in terms of new beginnings.

Upon closer scrutiny, however, the relation between crisis and reform is less straightforward than commonly assumed. In many crises, elites desperately struggle to preserve rather than to reform the status quo. Many policy changes announced with fanfare during or in the wake of crises are reforms in name only and are better described as efforts to preserve pre-crisis structures and practices. Even when reform proposals are truly intended to bring about double-loop lessons and structural changes, they rarely materialize in the long run. The belief that crisis and reform make a happy couple is, therefore, in need of qualification. Hence, crises do create opportunities for reform, but incumbent leaders tend to shy away from seizing upon them. Let us now elaborate on both parts of this thesis.

Why crises make reform possible

Under normal circumstances, reform of public policy and organizations appears to be nearly impossible. Scholars of government have filled libraries with their catalogues of reform failures.[39] In order for a reform proposal to become successful, it must survive bureau-political infighting in its conception phase, political debate in its birth stage, and entrenched opposition in its early years. Every now and then crisis lessons or change proposals do survive and "stick." Explanations of such rare successes are usually couched in terms of leadership and crisis.[40]

A crisis creates an opportunity for reform when it highlights a performance deficit. This happens when a government agency or policy either is shown to have contributed to the development of that crisis or has proven evidently incapable of responding adequately to it.[41] This performance deficit, which becomes manifest at a time when good governance is needed most, becomes a source of contention. The effectiveness, efficiency, and appropriateness of existing policy-making procedures, organizational routines, and traditional modes of public service delivery are subjected to intense criticism.[42] It is clear that the "old way of doing things" is no longer feasible. Tried-and-trusted routines are suddenly weighed against promising yet wholly uncertain alternatives. In other words, political and public support for the pre-crisis policy or organization is disappearing swiftly.

In 2004, this happened to one of the most venerable British institutions: the BBC. The crisis found its roots in the Iraq dossier put together by the British government in the early fall of 2002. The Blair government used the dossier to convince the British public of the threat posed by Saddam Hussein's regime. The claim that Iraq needed only 45 minutes to send rockets to the UK proved a convincing argument in winning over the House of Commons. Shortly after British and American forces had invaded Iraq in the spring of 2003, BBC reporter Andrew Gilligan accused the Blair government of exaggerating the Iraqi threat. The "45 minutes claim" did not emerge from solid intelligence, Gilligan asserted, but out of the spin-doctoring pen of adviser Alistair Campbell. A public row ensued between the BBC and the government, with representatives of both institutions accusing the other of lying. The crisis tragically escalated when the source of Gilligan's reporting was exposed by government leaks: weapons expert and government employee Dr. David Kelly committed suicide several days later.

The BBC, supported by its long-standing and internationally reputation for fair and accurate reporting, was winning the battle for public sympathy. The Blair government stumbled. The decisive turn in the crisis came when the spotlight shifted to Gilligan. Other reporters began to question the accuracy of his reporting. Gilligan refused to show the notes of his conversation with Dr. Kelly. Then his record of rather "creative" reporting was unearthed. When the Hutton inquiry into the affair concluded that Gilligan had violated the standards of quality reporting, the BBC came under fire. Its director resigned and its reputation was tarnished.[43]

Consider another example of an institution in crisis.[44] After the fall of the Berlin Wall in 1989, article 16 of the West German constitution came under siege. This article specified that all refugees would be entitled to asylum in the German republic. It symbolized the German transformation after World War II into a democratic state and communicated the intention on the part of the West Germans to assist their German brothers and sisters under communist rule. When the gates opened, however, the influx of asylum seekers soon became too much. In addition to pressing humanitarian concerns (decent housing), immigrants began to meet with outright aggression and violence. In December 1992, all political parties agreed after an acrimonious decision making process that article 16 had served its purpose and had to go.

In these examples the very institutional make-up of the BBC and West Germany's constitutional framework was at stake. These crises challenged the core beliefs that guided the formulation and implementation of policies and practices within a particular area of government.[45] Moreover, the organization of the policy process is challenged: authority relations, rules, routines, and technology that structure processes of policy making and implementation.

These institutional frameworks are usually the long-term product of trust, successful performance, and coherence between policy ideas and organizational forms. A solid institutional framework is important because it determines to a considerable degree how policies are made and how they are administered. It brings certain stability to government behavior, provided it stays in tune with the dominant societal and political conceptions of what is appropriate. It helps to create "believable futures": we know what to expect from a stable policy sector.[46]

There are three reasons why a "deep," highly politicized crisis suspends this equilibrium. First, and perhaps most important, a crisis relaxes the structural constraints that tend to keep institutions in place.[47] It focuses attention on their previously unnoticed vulnerabilities. Instead of devoting periodic, diluted attention to many different problems, policy makers, media, and mass publics alike are consumed by one single set of issues for some time. The sheer force of physical events or political representations of their meaning raises public anxiety to such levels that there is an increased willingness to follow leaders who claim to be able to cope and an equal readiness to support unconventional and risky policy options. Far-reaching mandates may be delegated to centralized authorities and the number of potential veto points in the policy process is temporarily reduced to "let the government govern." Some crises give rise to the "rally around the flag effect": substantive conflicts over issues, entrenched modes of adversarial behavior, and ongoing institutional battles between different players in the policy arena are temporarily suspended.

Second, as the routine way of working and thinking becomes discredited in the eyes of outsiders, room for alternatives suddenly emerges. The chief characteristic of a stable public institution is that its modus operandi remains unexamined and is taken for granted. A crisis invites everybody to take a close look; it prompts the question whether this institution and the way in which it operates are effective and beneficial to all. In short, the loosening of institutionalized structure makes it possible for new structures to be considered.

Third, a crisis "unfreezes" entrenched ways of thinking not only at the top but throughout the policy sector in which a crisis has occurred. As we know from the research on policy implementation, it is ultimately the way that middle-level and street-level bureaucrats "walk the walk and talk the talk" that determines the success and failure of public policies.[48] A crisis tends to shatter their confidence in those trusted routines because of the very fact that they have proven unreliable in the face of pressure.

Combined, these factors allow for a radical break in the chains of historical legacies. A window of opportunity opens for implementing lessons learned and making the system more robust. Much, however, depends on what happens during the crisis and its immediate aftermath. Crisis management is a crucial factor in explaining why, how, and how deeply a crisis-stricken organization, network, or polity learns from crisis.[49]

Why reform does not always follow crisis

Whether lessons learned are actually implemented depends to a considerable extent on the management strategy that is adopted to deal with the crisis. The continuum of possible positions is marked by two extreme ends: the conservative approach and the reformist approach.[50]

When leaders adopt a *reformist approach*, they aim to change policies or redesign the institutional features of a public organization in order to ensure a new fit with the changed environment. This strategy attempts to bridge the exposed performance gap and restore faith in the sector by breaking with past practices and adopting lessons learned. It usually requires bold, risk-taking forms of leadership, as crisis lessons tend to move away from (rather than back to) the status quo. Policy makers adopting this approach amplify rather than dampen the crisis mood; they must "sell" the new alternatives for the pre-crisis status quo in both political and bureaucratic arenas.[51]

A *conservative approach* aims to defend and maintain the pre-existing institutional essence in the face of pressures to change it. The core idea is that incremental improvement rather than radical redesign will close the performance gap and restore legitimacy. This leadership strategy amounts to a form of "dynamic conservatism": adapting policy instruments and recalibrating organizational structures and routines to accommodate external pressures for change, as a means to preserve the institutional core, for example the prevailing policy paradigm and organizational mission.[52]

Most leaders do not automatically embark on the path of reform when confronted with a crisis. In fact, they appear to be rather inclined toward a conservative strategy. To understand why this is so, one must recall the essence of crisis: it constitutes a threat to valued ways of working and thinking. The political-administrative elite that deals with this threat will prefer to curb it before trying to change organizations or policies. The centralization reflex of most government crisis-response systems endows them with special authority, with the unstated aim to preserve what exists: as a rule, hierarchies do not funnel authority to those who seek to change their very modus operandi.

This appears to be especially true for incumbent authorities who must deal with a crisis that is framed in terms of *internal* causes. To start with the latter, internal problems are typically addressed first in terms of repair. A glitch in the institutional machinery requires a competent mechanic, not new machinery. It is not until this perception changes that crisis managers will contemplate the necessity of reform. Whereas incumbent authorities tend to see it as their job to maintain and protect the values they have been socialized into as well as the achievement record of their own administration, newly appointed elites are much more inclined to view their task as one of renewal. It is only under these special circumstances that policy elites may perceive crises to be a window of opportunity.[53]

The political calculus usually advises against reform-oriented strategies. Consider the four most likely futures that leaders can expect, depending on their choice of strategy (reform or repair) and the way the crisis outcome will be perceived (see Figure 6.1). A conservative approach is relatively low risk. If a state of order returns, leaders can claim credit. If things change for the better, leaders can still claim credit. Reform is the risky road to choose. Leaders may win big when they

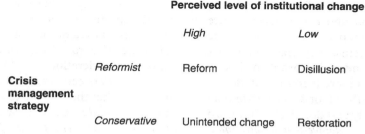

Figure 6.1. Alternative post-crisis futures.

promise and accomplish long-overdue reforms, but they also run the risk of disillusion and deep credibility losses.

Our first maxim of post-crisis reform politics can thus be summarized as follows: *in response to crisis, incumbent policy elites are more likely to aim at conservation than reform*. This thesis is firmly rooted in the psychological literature on decision making and commitment. It also fits the dominant view of public policy making in established democracies, which suggests that public policy normally evolves in a slow, incremental fashion.[54]

If this claim is accurate, it follows that there must be one or more special factors at play when a double-loop learning, reform-oriented approach comes to prevail in a crisis. After all, reform *does* occur – if only sporadically – in the wake of crises. Policy makers must, in other words, either be induced or enabled by specific circumstances to adopt a reformist approach. Four factors seem especially relevant.

Perceived inevitability   Crisis leaders may consider reform inevitable, indeed the only way to deal with the crisis. This is most likely to happen when a crisis is seen as the outcome of shifts in the external environment. External shifts such as war, climate changes, economic depressions, and energy shortages can acutely threaten the very existence of a policy sector. Repair is not an option, as the threats cannot be managed; nothing short of all-out reform will save the day. This perception of inevitability may be self-evident or it may grow in the wake of ineffective restoration efforts. Our second maxim is therefore: *leaders will be more likely to adopt double-loop lessons and a reformist crisis management strategy if they attribute the cause of the crisis to external factors.*

Annoyance   Leaders are, obviously, more likely to adopt far-reaching changes the more annoyed they are with the existing institutional make-up (and the less politically committed they are to uphold it). As argued before in this book, we should never forget that crises put people under immense pressure and provoke emotional reactions. When leaders perceive the crisis as a result of previously noted or long-standing problems, they may be tempted to exploit the crisis to rid the sector of the underlying problem. Even when rational considerations would suggest a more incremental, deliberative course, leaders can get so annoyed with the "foot dragging" of policy organizations that they decide to move swiftly and decisively. Our third maxim is: *policy makers will be more likely to adopt double-loop lessons and a reformist crisis management strategy if they are convinced that the crisis makes it possible to solve long-standing irritations and nagging problems.*

Political survival   Under routine circumstances, policy plans tend to be informed by an assessment of what is politically and technically feasible. What is feasible during a crisis, however, is determined more by the desire to survive politically than by technical feasibility. If a sufficient number of powerful actors in the political arena favor reform initiatives over conservation efforts, a reformist strategy is more likely to be adopted. Having presided over the development of the crisis and at risk of being blamed for its occurrence, incumbent elites will be especially sensitive to political moods and majority preferences. It becomes nearly impossible for them to argue against reform on the basis of technical arguments only. This becomes more plausible when the crisis is more severe, or when the autonomous rhythms of the political process (ranging from election time to imponderables such as Zeitgeist) favor trailblazing over maintaining trodden paths. Our fourth maxim is: *leaders will be more likely to adopt double-loop lessons and a reformist crisis management strategy if they perceive that there is (at least) a minimum winning coalition favoring reform in the political venues that are essential to their own survival in office.*

Structural opportunities   It becomes much easier to contemplate more unorthodox policy alternatives for dealing with a crisis when a leader experiences few checks and balances. In some types of emergencies, most notably natural disasters, civil disturbances, or near-war situations, authorities can invoke formal powers and create bylaws that amount to a significant centralization of authority. This allows them to temporarily bypass routine bureaucratic and parliamentary procedures, curb media activity, or even relax legal constraints on state actions. The more veto power is removed from the scene, the higher the chances that a reform coalition may triumph. Our fifth maxim is: *leaders are more likely to adopt double-loop lessons and a reformist crisis management strategy when they can operate within the framework of an ad hoc centralization of initiative and authority.*

Conditions for reform success

Whichever strategy crisis leaders select (reform or restoration), the question is whether they can effectuate it. Their strategy must gain political ascendance and acceptance, it must be implemented, and finally it must restore trust in the problem-solving capacity of a public policy or organization. Three preconditions are required to make this happen.

A first condition is that the chosen strategy corresponds with political and societal conceptions of the future. Conservation efforts can be effective only when the core values and beliefs underpinning the pre-crisis institutional regime have survived the crisis. Likewise, reform efforts stand a chance only when the underlying opinion bias goes the other way: a widespread feeling has escalated into existence that status-quo actors and institutions have lost their prominent position in the system.

A second condition is that crisis leaders manage to seize and retain the initiative in the crisis process. They must demonstrate that they have recognized the impending crisis and have begun to address it well before their own actions become portrayed by others as part of the problem. Early recognition (and acceptance, which is not self-evident) of a widening performance gap and decreasing legitimacy increases the probability that crisis management strategies will be effective when the situation has escalated.

A final condition is simply that leaders are adept at playing the game of post-crisis reform politics. There is no such thing as the "ten golden rules" that will help to play this game. Leaders must, of course, avoid the obvious mistakes, such as sacrificing their public credibility in pursuit of short-term relief from media pressure. They should avoid the temptation of heroism: adopting a leadership style of "going at it alone" is likely to prove quixotic at a time when their political stature is weak and they need allies more than ever.[55] However, the challenges of post-crisis politics may require skills that are fundamentally at odds with all those other challenges outlined in this book. This brings us to the paradox of crisis leadership.

6.4   Implementing lessons of crisis: an impossible task?

One would be justified in asking how policy makers can be expected to learn the right lessons and smoothly implement them, making use of the opportunity window that crises tend to open. Consider what we expect from them. While they are still busy coordinating all sorts of operational challenges that directly relate to the crisis at hand, they must exercise reform leadership. They need to articulate that the status quo is unten-able, propose a coherent set of radical and politically sanctioned reforms, and guard their integrity during reform implementation. They must embrace novel policy ideas, sell them to diverse audiences, and wield power to see them enacted.[56] Reform leaders must exercise their gusto in an environment of inherent uncertainty and considerable resistance in societal, political, and bureaucratic arenas.

Hence, a compounding tension for crisis leadership comes to the fore: the imperatives of effective crisis containment conflict with the imperatives of "puzzling" and "powering." It suggests, at the very least, that crisis management and reform leadership cannot be the province of the same executives. Two sets of tension seem especially relevant in this discussion.

Repair or reform?

Reform leadership is an exercise in "creative destruction."[57] Old structures must be destroyed before new ones can be implemented. In order to be effective reformers, leaders will want to seize upon the damage done. They dramatize the seriousness of the situation, yet at the same time "externalize" its causes. Leaders can use the language of crisis only if they themselves are not at risk of being blamed for the crisis at hand (newly incumbent leaders are, ceteris paribus, in a much better position to do so than veteran leaders).

But in the thick of crisis, learning and reform are not always priorities for crisis leaders. They are under tremendous pressure to restore a sense of normalcy. Core values and proven methods then become anchors in stormy seas; crisis is not a time for critical self-reflection and exploring new options that pay off in the long run only. The use of reform rhetoric at this time of turbulence may compound rather than alleviate the collective stress that has been generated by crisis. It will surely evoke resistance among those who have a stake in the status quo ex ante. Even new leaders who have emerged on a platform of change prior to the occurrence of crisis may be forced to suspend their reform ambitions. Attractive as it may seem, seizing the crisis opportunity for the sake of gaining momentum for reform amounts to taking a huge gamble with history. Many leaders avoid it.

Persuasion or muscle?

Reform leadership is about persuasion. Commands and intimidation do not work in pluralistic polities. Reform leaders, in particular, have much persuading to do because their plans differ markedly from what exists. They have to convince multiple audiences that what they want is good, realistic, and inevitable. Moreover, they must convince stakeholders that the benefits of the proposed double-loop lessons outweigh the sunk costs of existing structures and policies. This requires not only effective command and selection of facts, and the rhetorical skills to present them; it also touches upon the socio-emotional bond between leaders and citizens. Leaders need to reassure followers that they know a way out.

Effective reform leaders also anticipate implementation obstacles. They display an awareness of implementation structures, identify key players, and build sufficient support among them. They know that blueprints made in the ivory tower will not materialize. Organizational heterogeneity, powerful clienteles, and professional autonomy are but a few factors that make consultation with implementing actors a prime condition for effective reform.

During a crisis, policy makers tend to use a top-down, command-and-control style. Short-circuiting the decision-making process speeds up the government's response capacity in the face of urgent threats. But the fiction of control continues once they are organized into small and coherent crisis centers and special committees. Gone are the endless negotiations with many stakeholders. Instead of brokering painstaking compromises, leaders actually make decisions and issue orders. Even considerate policy makers who do not become addicted to top-down governance will be forced in a crisis to make crucial and controversial decisions without engaging in the normal procedures of consulting all involved.

These centralization tendencies are most likely understood and temporarily accepted by many stakeholders. In the early phases of crisis, political support is granted near-automatically. It usually begins to wane, however, as soon as the first shock has been absorbed and the first revelations of causes surface. Leaders who seek to gain momentum for reform by exploiting their temporary powers of authority are taking a big risk. They may gain political support at large by demonstrating the willingness to make big decisions, but do so at the price of antagonizing many of the stakeholders they have to deal with on a day-to-day basis long after the crisis is gone.[58] When leaders are seen to abuse the centralized decision regime for a "crash-through" strategy of pushing controversial reform, the backlash can be strong.

6.5   The perils of opportunity: from crisis-induced reforms to reform-induced crises

To some leaders, some of the time, crises may be more of an opportunity than a threat. For leaders who are likely to remain untainted by the politics of blaming that accompanies most contemporary crises, these episodes open windows of opportunity. Crises enable such leaders to temporarily stop "muddling through" and actually push through reform packages that would be unimaginable during "normal" times. It is by no means guaranteed that they succeed: even in deep crises the resilience of the institutional status quo and its political, bureaucratic, and societal veto players should not be underestimated.

But even when long-established, deeply entrenched policy trajectories are reformed, this does not mean that learning has taken place. It does not mean policies have been adapted, specifically redesigned to help reduce crisis vulnerabilities or increase crisis-response capacities. A critical observer may well conclude that the flurry of immediate measures and organizational adjustments is more a product of political and bureaucratic needs to deflect blame, communicate resolve, and demonstrate competence than of careful and reflective learning from the perturbations that crises cause.

The urge to project political determination and to alter quickly the conditions that seemingly were linked to the occurrence of the crisis is perfectly understandable. Yet while reformers may be able to grasp the direct consequences of their own proposals, the potential second-order effects of big and sudden changes are rarely considered in the aftermath of political crisis management. As a result, governments may achieve some kind of readjustment in light of a recent, frame-breaking experience, but they forego the opportunity of having a more informed learning process aimed at upgrading crisis management performance in a more fundamental fashion.

It may be true that the great leaders in history are those who turned crisis into prosperity, but it should be remembered that many failed in the attempt. Explanations of the development of administrative and political systems often feature crises. For instance, one significant force propelling advances in European integration was the periodic occurrence of political crises. These episodes altered the political agendas and calculus of European leaders. More importantly, the need to respond to them often produced constructive innovations of collaborative institutions and programs. However, studies of imperial decline document the serial *mis*management of crises.

The relation between crisis and development thus remains a contentious one. This should come as no surprise if one realizes that the requirements of reformist leadership conflict with the best practices of conventional crisis management. In other words, the standard prescriptions for political reform craft are a dangerous guide for leaders in times of crisis.

Crises tend to cast long shadows upon the political systems in which they occur. It is only when we study these longer-term processes that we are able to assess their full impact. Unfortunately, such studies are quite rare.[59] In the wake of the 9/11 events, such investigations seem of significant relevance to society and to government leaders. Most studies of the "crisis aftermath" of emergencies have been about community reconstruction, individual and collective trauma, and legal battles. We need to complement these studies by taking a broader macro-social perspective that looks at collective "learning" for an entire nation, polity, or society in the aftermath of crisis. It remains an open question whether crises trigger systemic change or whether they forestall such change, and to what extent these processes can be channeled by good crisis governance.

Notes

1 The intelligence communities retained their autonomy, however. See Kettl (2004) for an analysis of this period in US politics.
2 We are keeping here with the two dimensions of political learning that Heclo (1974) discerns.
3 Brunsson and Olsen (1993); Olsen and Peters (1996); Peters and Pierre (2001).
4 Wildavsky (1984: 245).
5 Haas (1990); Hall (1993); Sabatier (1999); Busenberg (2001).
6 Rose (1993).
7 Stern (1997b).
8 Rose (1993).
9 See Vaughan (1996) for a detailed description of this system and a penetrating analysis of its shortcomings.
10 Old-fashioned scholarly research can add value to lesson-drawing efforts. Unfortunately, academic research tends to be a lengthy affair. Research reports are generally completed long after the political urge to learn or reform has passed. The passing of time has some advantages: it might, for example, help to cool the heat of the crisis experience, and create a climate more conducive to a reflective rather than an opportunistic use of investigation findings. In fact, the kind of instant analysis that we often see in the wake of a crisis is not unlike instant coffee: the first hurried sip reminds you of the real thing, while the last sip convinces you to invest the time to prepare the proper quality potion in the future.
11 For an overview, see Etheredge (1985); Fiol and Lyles (1985); and Stern (1997b). For case-based findings, see Jacobs (1989); Rosenthal and 't Hart (1989).
12 Staw et al. (1981).
13 Carrel (2000).
14 This literature is pessimistic with regard to *crisis* learning (see Carley and Harrald, 1997 for an interesting discussion; see also Sagan, 1993). It has slightly more upbeat news when it comes to the capacity to learn from routine events and policy delivery.
15 Turner (1976); Turner and Pidgeon (1997).

16 Pidgeon (1997).
17 To learn the right lessons, one would have to test hypotheses in organizations that have experienced crises and in organizations that have remained free from them (Turner, 1978; Perrow, 1994).
18 Vertzberger (1990).
19 Deutsch (1966: 166).
20 Sitkin (1992). See Hargrove (1994) for an intriguing analysis of this phenomenon.
21 Quarantelli (1996).
22 The paradox is introduced by Dekker and Hansén (2004).
23 Pidgeon (1997).
24 May (1972); Neustadt and May (1986); Rosenthal et al. (1989); Stern and Sundelius (1997).
25 Blight and Welch (1989).
26 See, for example, Scanlon (1989).
27 Argyris and Schön (1978).
28 van Duin (1992).
29 Argyris and Schön (1978: 24).
30 Argyris and Schön (1978: 22).
31 van Duin (1992); Birkland (1997); Thomas (1999); Busenberg (2001); Cobb and Primo (2003); Dekker and Hansén (2004).
32 Roberts (1993). Note the caution in LaPorte (1996). See Weick et al. (1999) for a discussion of potential lessons from HRO research. But also see Sagan (1993), Perrow (1994), and Marais et al. (2004) for penetrating criticisms of High Reliability Theory (HRT) findings.
33 Schwartz and Sulitzneanu-Kenan (2004).
34 Keeler (1993); Kingdon (1995); Cortell and Peterson (1999).
35 It is often observed that the Chinese character for crisis denotes both threat and opportunity.
36 Almond et al. (1973).
37 Baumgartner and Jones (1993).
38 We define reform here as an effort to structurally alter (the foundations of) policy or organizations, practices and structure according to a preconceived plan.
39 Leemans (1976); Caiden (1991); Wilsford (1994); Shepsle (2001).
40 Keeler (1993); Kingdon (1995); 't Hart and Goldfinch (2003).
41 See Boin and 't Hart (2000) for a set of hypotheses with regard to the process that gives rise to such a judgment.
42 Boin and 't Hart (2000). The legitimacy of a sector is the long-term resultant of societal, political, and legal support and acceptance. It cannot be measured in absolute terms. It is possible, however, to assess and detect significant alterations in levels of legitimacy. Steep declines in a fairly short time period are telltale signs of (impending) institutional crisis. Researchers can gauge these by examining the extent and content of media coverage, the amount and content of parliamentary attention for the sector, and the number and nature of administrative appeals, court and Ombudsman rulings concerning the sector.

43 We do not take a stance here in the question of whether the BBC acted rightly or wrongly; our point is that the very questioning of the BBC's reporting adequacy undermined its reputation and its institutional status.

44 This example is taken from Alink (forthcoming).

45 These core beliefs are also referred to in the literature as policy paradigms (Hall, 1993; see also Sabatier and Jenkins-Smith, 1993).

46 Selznick (1957); Suchman (1995); LaPorte (1996).

47 Pierson (2000); Hay (2001); Kuipers (2004).

48 Lipsky (1980); Wilson (1989).

49 This represents something of a departure from conventional wisdom. Early macro-political theories of crisis development were quite deterministic and optimistic. Crises were viewed as necessary breakdowns on the way to a better future (Almond et al., 1973). Even after structural functionalism's demise, the deterministic tendency among crisis theorists remained well alive in their emphasis on overloaded politics and limited administrative capacities as inherent crisis generators in contemporary governance. See, for example, Dror (1986); Kaase and Newton (1995). We beg to differ. Moreover, by treating the crisis management strategies of actors as a key factor, we depart from the political science mainstream which tells us that the institutional characteristics and historical legacies are all that matter, and that we should not assume "that the talkers and the legislators could ever straightforwardly shape outcomes" (Skocpol, 1985: 93; see also Dryzek, 1992).

50 Lanzara (1998) offers a very similar distinction between "exploitation" and "exploration" strategies.

51 't Hart and Goldfinch (2003).

52 Schön (1971); Terry (1995).

53 Counter-elites, especially oppositional forces, are far more likely to entertain that perception, but are often in a much less powerful position to determine policy (Tarrow, 1994).

54 On the former, see Janis and Mann (1977); Janis (1989); Staw (2003); on the latter, Lindblom (1979); Rose and Davies (1994).

55 Goldfinch and 't Hart (2003).

56 For the required skills of reform craft, see Bryson and Crosby (1992) and Moon (1995).

57 Schumpeter (1943).

58 Boin and Otten (1996).

59 But see Birkland (1997). See also a recent symposium on crisis management (Kurtz and Browne, 2004).

7 How to deal with crisis: lessons for prudent leadership

7.1 Introduction

In this book we have presented a number of empirical claims about leadership in crisis management. These are based on the findings of several decades of crisis research in various corners of the social sciences. In this final chapter, we take the lessons that emerge from theories and research findings on crisis management and translate these into recommendations for improving crisis management practices.

In the real world of crisis management, trade-offs must often be made among these various desirabilities. Policy makers face such challenges, make decisions, and have to live with the consequences of their actions or inactions. These consequences also matter to citizens who either suffer the results of governmental unpreparedness or reap the benefits secured by crisis-ready leaders and organizations.

This chapter attempts to transfer knowledge from academia to the corridors of public power. These research findings should prove helpful to those who have or take the public responsibility to deal with crises. A deeper and more comprehensive understanding of the subject enables public leaders to think about and engage in crisis management in a more reflective and responsible fashion. Our recommendations do not tell policy makers *what* to do and decide when they face the leadership challenges that emerge during crises. They do offer ideas and suggestions about *how* prudent leadership in crises might be exercised and organized.

7.2 Grasping the nature of crises

Let us begin with the nature of the beast. What is it that makes crises particular? And what should policy makers understand about crises when they seek to enhance their crisis leadership capacities?

One of the most important things to keep in mind is that crisis is a label, a semantic construction people use to characterize situations or epochs that they somehow regard as extraordinary, volatile, and potentially far-reaching in their negative implications. The intensity or scope of a crisis is thus not determined solely by the 'objective' nature of the threat, the level of uncertainty, or the time available to decision-makers. A crisis is to a considerable extent what people make of it.

Why people collectively label and experience a situation as a crisis remains something of a mystery. Physical facts, numbers, and other seemingly objective indicators are important factors, but they are not decisive. A flood that kills 200 people is a more or less routine emergency in Bangladesh, but it would be experienced as a major crisis in, let's say, New Jersey or Paris. Crises are in this sense in the eye of the beholder. It is people's frames of reference, experience, and memory, values and interests that determine their perceptions of crisis. A sense of "collective stress" results not just from some objective threat but also from the intricate interaction between events, individual perceptions, media representations, political reactions, and, as we have argued throughout the book, government efforts at "meaning making."

This process of collective understanding is one of escalation and de-escalation. It is subject to the influence of actors who have a stake in playing up a crisis mood, or playing it down. And this is exactly what happens when unexpected incidents or major disruptions are predicted or actually occur: not only will different political, bureaucratic, societal and international stakeholders form their own picture of the situation and classify it in terms of threats and opportunities, but many of them will actively seek to influence the public perception of the situation. Once a particular definition of the situation has taken hold in leaders' minds or in public discourse, it becomes a political reality that policy makers have to take into account and act upon.[1] Initial definitions tend to be persistent.

Policy makers should therefore actively consider what a particular, potentially crisis-triggering event means to them and their overall political strategies, and should take a proactive part in shaping the public understanding of it. If they don't, others will, leaving policy makers to respond to an agenda that is not necessarily favorable to their view of the common good or to the interests they cherish.

The second thing to keep in mind is that incidents and disturbances are much more likely today than ever before to be viewed not as unfortunate events that just "happen" but as the avoidable consequences of deficient political choices, government policies, and organizational practices. The "Act of God" argument or its mundane corollary ("shit happens") no longer suffices to account for the occurrence and severity of a crisis. In the Western world, citizens and opinion leaders expect comprehensive security and a comfortable degree of stability, even when they may recognize in the abstract that their world has become increasingly complex and risky. When the ordinary routines of life are disrupted severely, something must have gone wrong somewhere and somebody will have to answer for it.

Leadership in crisis response will inevitably require a two-pronged strategy: dealing with the events "on the ground" (whether literally as in civil emergencies or metaphorically as in a currency or stock market crisis) and dealing with the political upheaval and instability triggered by these events. Neglecting one or the other is detrimental to any attempt to exercise public leadership in a crisis.

Thirdly, one should accept that even the richest and most competent government imaginable can never guarantee that major disruptions won't occur. Policy makers cannot escape the dilemmas of crisis response by banking on crisis prevention. Crisis prevention is a necessary, indeed vital task, but it works best for familiar contingencies, such as those that have occurred previously and exhibit tell-tale signs at an early stage. Crises are the unique combination of system vulnerabilities, inherent "pathogens," and climate factors of a political and societal nature. Prevention is very difficult when it comes to the "unknowable" and "unimaginable" events at the heart of many crises. There is no alternative to investing serious time and energy in thinking in a more generic sense about the "rude surprises" that will inevitably occur: the unpleasant, undesirable, unexpected, unorthodox, uncertain, and often inconceivable contingencies that cannot be met by the available repertoires and resources of society and government.[2]

Policy makers do not like to think about potentially nasty and as yet purely hypothetical events, since it is so psychologically unsettling and because there are so many other pressing issues. However, if they do not lead the way in breaking through the natural tendency for organizations to ignore or minimize this kind of contingency planning by demonstrating personal and sustained commitment to it, they should not expect much to happen in this regard. It is politically prudent to think about future crises. In the wake of a crisis, a laissez-faire approach in the pre-crisis stage tends to be viewed as negligence, and can cause much trouble for the leaders who bear final responsibility.

This may all seem rather ominous. Yet leaders should keep an open mind to the fundamental ambiguity of crises: they entail threats, but they may also harbor opportunities. Leadership makes a crucial difference in our perspective. Let us recapitulate what we regard as the five key tasks of crisis leadership:

- sense making: making sure that policy makers get a firm grasp on what is going on and what might happen next;
- decision making and coordinating implementation: shaping the overall direction and coherence of the collective efforts to respond to the crisis;
- meaning making: actively shaping the public understanding of the crisis as much as is feasible in a democratic, mediatized political system, in order to align the collective definition of the crisis in such a way that it becomes possible to work purposefully toward a set of desirable crisis outcomes;
- accounting and ending: contributing to the democratic process of explaining one's ideas and actions to forums of "legitimate value judges,"[3] in order to achieve closure of the crisis and allow society to move on;
- learning: drawing lessons and grasping opportunities to reconsider and perhaps reform those features of existing institutions, policies, and practices that have been found wanting beyond repair in the crisis process.

In the sections that follow we summarize our recommendations for each of these critical leadership tasks in a number of maxims. Taken together, they constitute an agenda for developing leadership capacity in times of crisis.

7.3   Improving crisis sense making

There are many reasons why leaders do not see crises coming   Threats that policy makers and their organizations spot in time are the ones that can be managed best. An early-warning system that works gives them a chance to nip at least some evolving threats and risks in the bud. Moreover, accurate early warning of an impending crisis gives policy makers a chance to mitigate its consequences when it is too late or otherwise impossible to avert its occurrence. This buys them time to deal with the impact in a more orderly and effective fashion than is likely to happen in the case of a surprise. Speaking politically, effective warning gives leaders important advantages over those who do not see the crisis coming. It allows them to think in advance not only about threats to stave off but also about strategic or tactical opportunities that every crisis harbors.

This is something that leaders should get their staffers to do as a matter of routine: scan potential crises issues consistently for both threats and opportunities.[4] If leaders and their staffers fail to see them and act upon them, other players in the political arena might be more astute, and this may complicate rather than facilitate a leader's prospects of handling a crisis successfully.

Policy makers should be alert to factors that inhibit the flow of vital information and limit their capacity for early, flexible and imaginative threat assessments. More often than not, they are caught by surprise in the event of hostile attacks, large-scale accidents, or civil disorders. In spite of vast investments in information-gathering agencies, intelligence analysts, and a close reading of the daily news, senior officials appear genuinely baffled time and again.

Crises surprise leaders in various ways. In some cases, no one in their surroundings was looking in the right direction. Leaders should therefore take steps to reduce the likelihood of such blind spots, and be alert to what they are *not* told and what they might *not* get to see of the surrounding world. They should hone their intuition and develop their capacity for detecting the silences and omissions in the midst of the incoming flow of information and the talk of their advisers.[5] Leaders must make sure that their intelligence and advisory system operates on a principle of "managed diversity": diversity of technical expertise, of values, of cultural backgrounds, in short of predispositions and perspectives in scanning and interpreting the environment for possible major contingencies. If they do not actively organize diversity and redundancy in their advisory system, there is a real risk that existing policy paradigms and organizational traditions will reproduce a limited and sometimes outright biased view of the situation.

Secondly, surprise may occur because various officials and agencies have parts of the puzzle but fail to put the pieces together in time. Sharing information and joint sense making are by no means given, particularly not when organizations compete for turf, money, prestige, or simply the top official's attention. Policy makers must actively create strong incentives for hitherto separated, closed, competitive segments of the bureaucracy to share and compare information.

This does not mean they should demand uniform outlooks and consensus-based advice. They must simply nurture interaction. It is a leadership task to balance expert outlooks and recommendations, and weigh them against other equally important perspectives.[6] This leadership skill must be informed by a sensitivity to the wider political landscape. An ideologically based or personally constructed normative compass for any public action is a source of inner strength, but does not suffice. Leadership also requires the ability to grasp and connect with the fleeting public view of what constitutes a reasonable course of action in a given crisis.

Finally, a crisis may surprise a leader simply because no one had the guts to tell the leader the bad news of its suspected arrival. The inner circle around a chief executive may shield him from unpleasant news. The less sure advisers feel about their position in the corridors of power, and particularly *vis-à-vis* the leader, the stronger the incentives for them to tell the chief executive what they think he wants to hear – and thus to avoid mentioning anything that might be controversial or upsetting to him.

Consistently asking for *all* the news, including worst-case scenarios, is essential but not sufficient. Policy makers must also show by their attitudes and actions that they value those who bring them bad news or have the courage to argue unpopular viewpoints. In any system where hierarchy is the bottom line, anticipatory compliance and risk minimization are always right around the corner, even in seemingly informal, collegial, "professional" groupings. Leaders must be continuously aware of the distorting influence their presence might have on the frankness of discussion among their advisers. Sometimes the best leadership is not to provide vision and direction, indeed even not to be present, when advisers seek to ascertain threats and make sense of contingencies. Leaders are better off getting the fruits of their deliberation, including any important or persisting disagreements, before they engage with them directly.[7]

A crisis can become uncontrollable when leaders fails to develop a clear picture of the unfolding events   Crises generate a search for information by all parties involved. If one does not manage the flow of incoming information there is a serious risk that one will be swept away by a deluge of data, communications, and "news." The effects of this deluge are amplified by colleagues, staffers, and advisers who all diagnose the needs of the situation according to their personal inclinations, professional identities, and institutional roles.

To make sense of a crisis, leaders must make sure that robust systems of data collection and information verification are in place. They should secure and encourage staff to look methodically for the relevant facts in the explosion of data, yet remain aware of how information is filtered and summarized before it reaches their desk. They should probe behind the seductive phrasings in texts and the compelling charts in briefings, verify key facts, check assumptions underlying major intervention proposals, and test these assumptions against their own values and political objectives.

In the thick of a crisis, a leader should dare to take his time to evaluate the information in front of him and to contemplate the dilemmas that seem to emerge from that information. This does not mean leaders should procrastinate in the hope that the threat will evaporate or incremental improvement will occur. Only if the information flows have been properly organized – and this should be done in advance – can leaders afford the luxury to call a time out.

This is not to say that all information flows can be controlled. Rumors, for instance, are part and parcel of any crisis. Leaders should try to address them through developing (in advance) a rumor-control regime: proactive engagements with the mass media and direct channels of communication to the relevant publics should help them in their struggle with unfounded but widely accepted images of the situation. Leaders should remember that rumors are not purely dysfunctional: they may provide vital warnings or indicate key uncertainties. Rumors should be read as pointers for effective communication and action. Moreover, particularly in adversarial types of crises, the flip side of rumor control may be rumor diffusion: it sometimes helps to keep one's opponents guessing about one's state of mind, intentions, and capabilities.

Crises that challenge personal sense-making capacities are the ones leaders find particularly distressing Part of leadership mythology is that true leaders are impervious to stress. Crisis reality is that they are not. Images of devastation and loss can affect policy makers deeply. Some crises hurt their friends or loved ones directly. Some may present them with dilemmas that touch their deepest fears about holding high office and the awesome responsibilities it entails. Some crises are simply too demanding and last too long.

These kinds of crisis characteristics do more to people than just arouse them into maximum alertness. They wear policy makers down. Here we are reminded that leaders are humans too: they are not immune to stressors. It takes wisdom and courage to admit as much, particularly in the midst of an ongoing crisis, but this very awareness facilitates coping.

A leader who lacks the capacity for self-monitoring and has failed to assign it to deeply trusted others in their inner circle runs the risk of falling prey to high stress and fatigue, with potentially ruinous consequences. Distressed and weary leaders may slide into adopting simplistic images of the situation, stereotypes of other parties, and may be prone to either passivity or haste and recklessness. When that happens, their ability to make a sober diagnosis and provide a beacon of calmness and prudence diminishes.

Rigorous adherence to elementary rules of stress control is essential for leaders in times of crisis. This includes a suitable regime of waking, working, eating, drinking, and sleeping hours; a pre-arranged delegation of competence and trust to deputies so that they can act with authority; getting some of the most experienced and trusted advisers to monitor a leader's condition and performance during the crisis, with the explicit assignment to issue warnings when executive stress is beginning to take its toll. These rules should inform all efforts to prepare for crises.

7.4   Improving crisis decision making

The rhetoric of "the leader in charge" has little to do with the reality of effective crisis decision making and coordination   The effectiveness of the crisis response is *not* directly related to an all-or-nothing, do-or-die decision delivered by the crisis leader.[9] To be sure, crises are often best engaged through a combination of strategic choices and concerted action. But it is not always a single boss or a small team at the top of the governmental hierarchy who should make all decisions and who should coordinate each and every action. Crises produce control paradoxes: everybody assumes and expects leaders to be in charge, but the very circumstances of the crisis make it both very difficult and sometimes rather undesirable that they are.

However powerful they might seem, leaders are never wholly free agents. They are institutionally embedded rulers: the institutional features of administration shape the discretionary space for leaders in dealing with crises. Part of a proactive crisis management strategy is to reflect upon the institutional setting of crisis leadership and, if necessary, try to alter it. Crisis leadership is more than proactive crisis responses; it also involves fundamental questions of institutional design.

One such question concerns the division of labor between the various layers of authority and nodes of action in a governance system that is preparing for, or responding to, crisis: what should central, top-level executives delegate to other officials and organizations, and where should they insist upon close supervision of the full chain of command and execution? This is a perennial debate – and a rather complex one we might add – in public government. Easy answers do not exist; but during a crisis there is little time to resolve such issues.

A second design issue concerns the management of heterogeneity and conflict in crisis response systems. Crisis response operations mobilize many distinct, partly overlapping, and sometimes openly competing organizational units. Each draws upon its mandate, professional repertoire, and ethos in the fulfillment of the task at hand. Cooperation across such professional boundaries has proven to be at least as difficult as cooperation across geographical or institutional borders. When a crisis

hits, leaders are ill-served when significant parts of the response operation are marred by inter-organizational miscommunications and rivalries right down to the operational level. Trying to arbitrate such issues in
the midst of a crisis not only consumes an inordinate amount of a chief
executive's much-needed time and energy, it is also likely to leave deep
scars in organizations and among professionals whose passions are
already aroused by the pressure of events.

Both design issues are best addressed by intelligent decentralization.
When a crisis materializes, a leader must be able to rely on the capacity
of professional units to improvise and synchronize their actions with
others. Leaders should therefore invest in creating the institutional and
social conditions that facilitate effective network coordination during
crises. During a crisis, they should monitor if and how coordination
emerges, and they should be available to "trouble shoot" when fric-
tions do occur – as they surely will no matter how solid the pre-crisis
network formation. Inadequacies must be swiftly addressed, even if that
entails serious departures from pre-crisis planning (see further below).

> *. . . But the buck of making the critical decisions goes all the way up
>   to the top leader(s)*   History is filled with examples of leaders
who failed to rise to the responsibility of high office when no one else
could make the call. The craft of governing requires a judgment call:
leaders must resist the temptation of impetuous moves in the heat
of crisis, but they cannot endlessly postpone decisions just because
of lingering uncertainty or irreversibility of consequences. Somewhere
between the irresponsible flight into symbolic action and the paralysis
prompted by fear, leaders must identify the critical decisions that they
alone can make.

Among the toughest decisions in crises are those that force leaders to
choose between whether or not to take draconic measures. Effective
intervention in a crisis may require the relaxation of the conventional
constraints that come with democratic governance and the rule of law.
When a leader decides to take that route, and gets results in reducing the
threat and restabilizing the situation, he may at first be heralded by the
media as a courageous and forceful leader. But as is bound to happen in
a democracy, soon after stakeholders and accountability forums (including these very same mass media) will scrutinize his actions. A few key
questions are certain to emerge. Did leaders exercise good judgment, or
did they allow themselves to be captured by some hard-line faction
among their advisers? Did they try to protect the general interest or did
they seek to exploit the opportunities offered by the crisis to strike out
against political enemies?

If short-term considerations prevail over longer-term ones, leaders set the stage for a critical discussion on their performance. The core question, then, is: at what cost to public values, civil liberties, freedom of the press, and reputation abroad do leaders seek to gain the upper hand in crises by means of rash moves? Even in the heat of crisis, broader strategic and normative considerations must prevail in leaders' reasoning and choices. One such consideration must be how various actions taken during peak moments in the crisis process will play out in the long run. When the ordinary grind of political life takes hold again, draconic crisis measures will appear in another light. The trade-offs leaders made between effectiveness and appropriateness will be reframed and reassessed by pivotal forces in their political environment.

Crisis planning helps more than crisis plans ever will in coordinating crisis response operations   Even if all possible crises could be imagined, and even if money were not an issue, governments would still experience many problems in the implementation of their crisis contingency plans. This is not surprising: students of public administration have stocked libraries with their research findings identifying the various inherent shortcomings of modern government. Hence leaders should *assume* that even if their associates correctly identify and agree on the nature of future threats, they are likely to fail at properly designing the right plan, securing the required funding, training the officials who should do the job, controlling the entire process, or correcting deviations when they occur. In other words: the crisis plan may be really good, but it is unlikely that real crisis response patterns will follow it.

As Russell Dynes observed for disaster management: "The composition of the emerging structure seldom fits neatly with the pre-disaster patterns of community organization or with the images of coordination which are specified in planning."[10] This observation rings true for most of the crisis cases we have studied. Whether we look at textbook examples of perfect response or devastating failures, crisis plans rarely occupy centre stage in the heat of the moment. A crisis plan may exert some influence in the establishment of a crisis center, but the existence and use of a formal plan do not by any means determine the effectiveness of the crisis response.[11]

There is a good reason why detailed plans tend not to work well when implemented religiously. A fundamental tension exists between the idea of planning and the nature of crisis decision making. Planning presupposes knowledge of what will happen. In routine and rather stable environments, we may be able to predict with a certain degree of precision how many people will require medical attention, attend school, draw unemployment, or commit crimes. Planning can thus begin. A crisis, by definition, disturbs stable environments and creates uncertainty. It presents authorities with unfamiliar challenges that can never fully be dealt with in preconceived plans. Any crisis response operation will therefore necessarily contain elements of improvisation, which require flexibility and resilience rather than paper plans.

Crisis decision making and coordination are much more effective when they are not dictated by detailed plans and allow for a healthy degree of improvisation. In most crises, lives are saved and interests are protected because of alert and decisive individuals and because organizations worked together in innovative ways. Lives are, of course, also lost because of individual errors and organizational miscommunications, but it is hard to see how an excessively detailed and constraining plan would have improved coordination. Indeed, it is much easier to see how a plan would suffocate individual initiative and spontaneous, organic cooperation. Moreover, the absence of some planning dictate allows for new organizational forms to emerge, replacing overloaded, disgraced, or demolished public organizations originally tasked with crisis management. This is a vital development underlying many effective crisis management operations, and one that should be facilitated by keeping contingency plans simple. These plans should formulate clear principles about aims to be achieved and the core preconditions that apply; they should be flexible and low on details about how the various professionals are supposed to do their jobs.

To be sure, planning the organization of crisis decision making and implementation can benefit the effectiveness of crisis management efforts. The secret lies in the planning *process*: by working on response issues, participants become sensitive to problems that may emerge during a crisis. They develop an understanding for the needs and capacities of other potential crisis management actors. This helps to build social capital that facilitates smooth interactions in the heat of crisis. When planning is viewed in terms of social capital building, the use of simulations immediately comes to mind. Well designed and implemented simulations are an elementary tool to foster realistic expectations and build mutual trust, precisely the characteristics that inform effective coordination. The Mayor of New York City, Rudolph Giuliani, referred directly to a series of simulation exercises held in the years before September 2001 in his explanation of the relatively coordinated response to the World Trade Center collapse.

The real secret of coordinated crisis networks is found in the shared values that guide the actions of the various actors involved.[12] This explains why coordination initially seems to evolve quite naturally in the early phases of many crises (the value of saving lives becoming powerfully dominant), only to dissolve as the various actors begin to champion different values (as the threat to life recedes). This insight also helps to think through issues of preparation and planning. Leaders may thus be better off in using crisis-planning processes to explore what binds actors together and try to codify that in institutionalized coordination arrangements rather than trying to heal factional conflict once it erupts in the heat of a crisis.

7.5   Improving crisis meaning making

Leaders who lack the ability to communicate cannot lead in crises   A crisis never speaks for itself. In the uncertainty that such a period of discontinuity provokes, people will try to attach meaning to their plight. They will want to know why this happened and why it was not prevented. They will want to find out what their leaders did to prevent or at least minimize the scope of the crisis. Through a process of collective meaning making, in which many different actors promote their version of the events, some sort of shared (or contested) assessment will arise.

Nor can leaders rely upon their crisis management performance to speak for itself. If they want to be favorably assessed – in democracies a condition *sine qua non* for a post-crisis leadership career – they will have to "market" their version of events. This may be a humbling and perhaps humiliating experience if it is approached as a chore to be performed to satisfy the ungrateful. But leaders who understand that crisis management is nothing more than governance under extreme conditions will see this as an opportunity to explain the past and define possible futures. The ability to shape images of recent adversity is extremely helpful in charting new courses. Leaders must therefore build on their crisis performance and surf the wave it provides for them.

Policy makers who seek to influence the process of meaning making in crises must tell their story to the public, the media, and the politicians in a convincing way. Crisis communication is one of the most effective yet least understood means of imposing a degree of order on a highly dynamic environment. Through effective communication leaders can shape perceptions that channel behavior. That is why sloppy or clumsy communications may have perverse effects: the behavior of individuals will be informed by some alternative picture of the situation – a frame that may motivate people to act in contraproductive ways. This should not be read as a cue for Machiavellian leadership. It just reminds leaders not to take for granted that their interpretation of the situation will match the dominant one among stakeholders or the general public. Leaders must therefore become skilled in the art of crisis communication before they must deal with crisis. In the absence of these skills, crisis leaders become dangerously dependent on media advisers, spin doctors, spokespersons or other surrogates.

Meaning making, however, entails more than effective media management, a sound public relations policy, or a spin-doctoring wizard. To be sure, media management requires a Herculean effort if one wants to do it well. And yes, having a "spin doctor" in the team certainly helps to package the message the right way. But thinking in terms of media management and "spin" evokes a tactical approach from leaders where a strategic one is required. Meaning making requires a philosophy of crisis management, which reminds leaders of core values that must be preserved, structural weaknesses that must be repaired, and opportunities to be explored.

Leader credibility is a particularly helpful resource in times of crisis. Under threatening uncertainty, people look toward leaders and will gladly put their fate in the hands of those they trust. Few leaders, however, are trusted to this extent.

Leaders are easily tempted to make up for this "trust deficit" by making tall promises and delivering assuring explanations. This is a mistake. Credibility is won the hard way but is lost easily. A leader who enters a crisis with low credibility status is facing an uphill struggle. He will have to earn credits under trying conditions. This can only be done by performing well. Giuliani, again, constitutes a good example: highly controversial and all but written off prior to 9/11; a national hero after it – by virtue of his determined, dignified, and honest leadership style during the crisis. In contrast, empty promises and false assurances will be exposed by at least some segments of the mass media army that congregates around the story of a major crisis, and will then be fully exploited by political opponents to erode the support base on which a leader depends.

7.6   Improving crisis termination

Crises do not end of their own accord – they must be terminated   It is tempting to consider the cessation of operational crisis management activities as the end of the crisis. It usually does not work that way because the political aftermath assumes its own dynamics. Different actors explore the aftermath for opportunities to attack opponents, attract praise, initiate reform – or gain in any other way from the temporary state of "unfreezed" structures. All these activities nurture a process of escalation, which leads surprised and exhausted leaders into what is known as the "crisis after the crisis."

Crisis leaders must therefore manage both the operational and the political dimensions of crisis. They cannot afford to view operational crisis management purely or even predominantly in functional terms – they should "delegate" this perspective to senior officials who are further removed from the political domain and stand closer to the operational heat. A crisis leader must play the political game throughout the crisis, starting the moment a crisis begins. That means operating in the political domain, which inevitably takes away from operational command duties. Leaders should engage in high politics even if normal politics have been suspended because of the crisis.

Rendering account after a crisis is desirable and inevitable – yet also politically risky Crises cast long shadows. And so they should, to some extent. Major breakdowns in public order, safety, health, and prosperity do not occur every day in most Western societies. Their very occurrence should provoke serious reflection, and should – as a matter of democratic principle – compel leaders to account for their actions and those of the people and agencies in their sphere of responsibility prior to, during, and following a crisis. Crises require an open and active accountability process, one that makes it possible to release tensions, to re-equilibrate the social and political system, and to engage in meaningful learning.

The massive media onslaught that is the hallmark of contemporary crises guarantees that questions of responsibility, accountability, blame, and compensation will be on the agenda. All actors involved are likely to continuously assess and perhaps even defend their positions, in particular those who bear final responsibility. Apart from the mass media, many formal, institutional accountability practices will be set in motion in judicial, political, and professional arenas. These various and sometimes closely intertwined accountability processes need not necessarily escalate into tough, aggressive blame games, but they do often enough for any leader to take that option into account.

Leaders should therefore prepare themselves and their staff for the cascading political and possibly legal developments that may feature in the wake of a crisis. Throughout the crisis, they should carefully document the crisis response as well as the process which produced it. In addition, they should closely monitor the events and the stances taken by major political actors for possible long-run, second-order consequences, those that come back to haunt leaders if they ignore them. They should check how the media report the crisis and the government's handling of it. Fluid images of success or fiasco are framed through media reports of what leaders seemingly did and did not do during the crisis.

The evolution of the crisis narrative during the accountability process can deprive leaders of control and drive them out of office. Leaders should therefore beware not to immediately disband their crisis team as the acute crisis stages seem to pass. They should stay proactive with their organization, the media, and the principal political stakeholders. The crisis aftermath is not a time to take a low profile or return to "business as usual." Leaders should remain visibly on top and be proactive in rendering account: open and forthright if possible, alert and disciplined, repentant if necessary. Leaders should not render their political fate dependent upon interpretations of the crisis put forward by their critics and other stakeholders who may not necessarily have an interest in a fair and balanced evaluation of the crisis process.

. . . But to treat it by definition as a blame game would create a self-fulfilling prophecy It is sometimes said that in an earlier era, governmental leaders could count on public sympathy in times of trouble. If bad things happened, these were attributed to exogenous factors (enemies, nature, or Acts of God). Today, this is certainly no longer the case. Leaders must battle to (re-)obtain public support. So instead of assuming that most crises generate the rally-around-the-flag effect as seen in the United States following the 9/11 attacks, leaders must seriously entertain the alternative scenario: that they become scapegoats. In times where governments are often already deeply unpopular, leaders run a serious risk of bearing the brunt of a societal blaming process.[13]

When they come under fire in the wake of a crisis, it may be comforting for a leader to point the finger at somebody or something else. They can try to claim, for example, that it was the mass media that inflamed a difficult situation into a crisis. With a more responsible media, the crisis would not have erupted at all, or their ability to manage the situation would have been much better, or so they may argue. Unfortunately, the chances of success for this type of blame-shifting strategy are slim. Experience suggests that it is counterproductive for public leaders to blame the media for what can easily be construed as their own shortcomings.

Finding scapegoats lower down the bureaucratic hierarchy or across the partisan divide may also seem an expedient blame-avoidance strategy for an embattled leader. Here the chances of getting away with it are somewhat bigger. History is filled with examples of how mid-level officials face charges linked to crises, while the top leadership escapes from being held liable. Yet this strategy may come at a hefty price. It earns a leader the lasting distrust if not enmity of the people and organizations that must work for him in years to come; some of these "lightning rods" might not take their victimization lying down. When they put up a fight, a blame game is started that is likely to feed on itself and escalate into a situation where everybody loses.

By denying his role in the crisis, a leader misses a rare opportunity for true self-evaluation and reflection. A leader would be well advised to seize upon that opportunity, especially in the absence of a natural "Teflon" coating that prevents crisis-induced blame from sticking to him. In the end, buck passing only undermines one's authority, whereas proactive and well-communicated responsibility taking serves to reinforce it.

7.7   Improving crisis learning and reform craft

Drawing lessons from crises should involve more than unreflective copying of seemingly successful policies and categoric rejections of seemingly failed practices   Over the course of their careers, seasoned policy makers gather experiential lessons. When they face a new crisis, they may assume it resembles previous ones, and rely upon a tried-and-tested repertoire of techniques and stratagems. To the extent that the current challenge resembles the recollected past, this is a sensible thing to do. It reduces a policy maker's sense of uncertainty and may increase the speed and efficiency of crisis responses.

The present is not a carbon copy of any past, however. Policy makers are easily led astray rather than helped by a strong reliance upon historical analogies with past crises. Direct personal experiences with crises are valuable, but scarce and inherently ambivalent diagnostic resources. It is naturally tempting for people to over-generalize from the experience of one or two vividly remembered personal experiences to the neglect of the wider experience base. For this reason alone, personal experiences of crisis can and should be complemented by knowledge of the experiences of others. This experience may be drawn from the history of one's own country or organization, or be vicarious – drawn from the experience of other organizations in one's own country or from that of organizations in other countries. Before they draw lessons, policy makers should make sure they are informed by multiple, systematic, and unbiased accounts and analyses of not just the most recent but a range of relevant crisis experiences.

If learning is to be more than the idiosyncratic use of analogies or the unreflective copying of best practices, it should entail an intelligent investigation of a range of past crises. Commissions, investigation boards, and consulting firms play a role. The research on so-called high-reliability organizations suggests that there are ways to build a safety culture that facilitates effective learning. Moreover, the blossoming field of crisis consultancy has developed several techniques – such as executive debriefings, post-mortem analyses, and the use of scenarios – that may facilitate crisis learning.[14]

If they are to have any impact upon future public performance, the findings of such systematic examinations, the lessons learned, must be transmitted among individuals and embedded within the collective learning dynamics of governments. The lessons must become part of a shared and institutionalized memory bank, maintained by organizational units close enough to the heart of the policy-making machinery to be relevant, but shielded as much as possible from post-crisis politicking. From this reservoir of experience-based crisis management knowledge, guidelines for future governmental action can be formulated and disseminated. Hence a pivotal leadership task is to make sure the institutional preconditions for this to happen exist. They should win top-level support for the way lessons are formulated, even when the resulting lessons are controversial. Crisis-aware public leaders stimulate the quest for meta-learning (i.e. "learning to learn") in the public sector.[15]

Crisis-induced learning involves proactive, interactive, and ongoing crisis-planning processes   Crisis management requires cooperative arrangements across different types of boundaries. Such working networks must be built prior to being thrown into the hot seat. Public-private partnerships are needed as many vital resources are in private hands. Operational activities must be shaped in conjunction with a general philosophy of crisis management, which itself is the outcome of strategic and political-symbolic deliberations.

Chief executives should foster crisis planning as an ongoing process. They should espouse a holistic view of the requirements for crisis management performance, in contrast to narrow, sector-based, and mechanistic perspectives grounded in distinct professions. Such a shared paradigm for professional coordination can only be built in advance of the next major crisis. This leaders can do by showing personal commitment to crisis preparedness. Without leadership commitment, the work toward improving organizational crisis capacity will soon slide into a low-prestige ritual without adequate staff motivation. Leaders must free up some of their own time and allocate ample resources for joint socialization and concerted action among the organizations most likely to form the nucleus of crisis response operations. Joint training and rigorously designed and executed exercises must become institutionalized rather than incidental occurrences in the government system.

Leaders must stimulate their organizations to launch an enduring awareness-raising and training program, which engages many parts of the leadership and their immediate staffs. This will demand considerable resources including costly personnel time and executive attention. A chief executive could motivate this strategy by imagining a crisis and having to admit that the organization was inadequately prepared for the situation because the policy makers gave a higher priority to other responsibilities. A much better incentive is found in the fruits of active involvement: a leader develops an intimate knowledge of operational vulnerabilities and strategic concerns at the various levels of the policy cycle. Employees are more likely to respect leaders who are willing to engage, showing their own doubts and weaknesses. Insecure leaders tend to stay away from crisis management – until it is forced upon them, of course.

Sweeping reforms are not necessarily the best expression of crisis-induced learning   Deep crises often generate strong media and political pressures for sweeping overhauls of pre-existing policies and organizations. If things went wrong so badly, the institutional fabric must have been really vulnerable. This line of thinking is predicated on the premise that big events must have big causes. It is supported by the long lists of missed signals, unheeded warnings, and response problems that post hoc examinations tend to produce. But the more sophisticated of these examinations also reveal another truth: crises are all too often the result of escalated chain reactions in policy systems or high-risk technologies. Moreover, crises are labels that do not correspond one-on-one with the performance of organizations or operators.

Sweeping reforms do look good from a political perspective. They reassert the capacity to lead and they hold the promise of serendipitous gains from adversity. But sweeping reforms inevitably come with down sides, which are only noted in the longer run long after the crisis has faded. Reforms suggest that policies and organizations did not function well, which disregards the efforts of policy makers and operators to deal with the crisis in question. This nurtures so-called "appreciative gaps" that so often separate leaders from operational reality. In addition, sweeping reforms tend to be hastily construed and therefore ill conceived. The performance capacity may therefore be undermined rather than bolstered. Leaders are well advised to subject large-scale reform to the scrutiny accorded to such proposals in normal times, even if this makes for a tedious and compromise-filled process.

In fact, there is something to be said for the idea that in many instances the worst-case situation (the entire system has failed, therefore everything must change) does not exist, and that more effective crisis-induced learning is better guided by a leadership strategy of "dynamic conservatism."[16] This strategy prioritizes the defense of core values and institutional commitments. It urges leaders to flexibly adapt policy-making structures and modus operandi of public organizations to the high-pressure context of crisis rather than to succumb to the temptation of grand reform rhetoric.

It is, of course, not easy to determine what must change so that the rest can remain the same. Leaders therefore need some kind of policy compass or roadmap, which helps them negotiate this inherent tension between stewardship and change mastership. They must have a clear idea of what is worth preserving in their society, policy field, or organization. This can guide them once they are forced into the unfamiliar, chaotic terrain of a major crisis. Such a philosophy of crisis management should help to prevent from occurring common crisis response modes such as ad hocery, improvisation, and stress-induced rigidity. It should prevent leaders from making immediate, "knee-jerk" decisions; it focuses attention on long-term consequences of any reform plans.

The implementation of reform programs is a long-term process that generates complex problems. Contrary to popular expectations, as we have shown, crisis-induced reforms do not escape this iron law; quite the contrary. Crisis-induced reform is often a product of centralized and opportunistic policy management (matching pre-existing reform packages to now-salient critical problems). In this context of "seizing the moment," due process and deliberative democracy make way for procedural shortcuts, and forceful crisis rhetoric masks the implementation dilemmas attached to the reforms advocated.

The German reunification brokered so brilliantly by Helmut Kohl and others in the wake of the collapse of the Berlin Wall will remain a textbook case for years to come: a political success when it was decided upon, it became an implementation nightmare in the years after – economically, socially, and politically.[16] Whereas successful reform leaders take an inclusive approach and co-opt key officials and groups who will become involved during the implementation process, rapid-fire reform strategies in crisis decision making tend to hinge upon exclusive, inner-circle modes of making policy. As a consequence, the appreciative gap that separates policy makers from implementers is not bridged, but widened.[17] As soon as the sense of crisis urgency passes, leaders will have to deal with this gap. Hence the paradox: crisis-induced reforms are likely to produce reform-induced crises.

7.8   Preparing for crises: concluding reflections

Citizens expect many things of their leaders. Being an effective crisis manager is not always at the top of the mental checklists that voters use to evaluate candidates for high office, but many political executives will find out during the course of their tenure that it is a crucial quality they must possess if they want to stay in office and remain effective. In crises, the leadership potential of public office-holders is put to the test, and the testing is done in full public view thanks to the relentless media scrutiny that crises generate.

Many government leaders have failed to live up to the multifaceted requirement of successful crisis management: being effective, being moral, respecting democratic constraints – and being seen to be this way. Often, short-term imperatives for visible, forceful, and symbolic action have won out over considerations of democratic legitimacy. In other instances, a legalistic drive to adhere strictly to the book has generated a public impression of a timid, ineffectual, or insensitive government in the face of grave threats. Effective leadership requires policy makers to devise, enact and legitimize a workable balance between these contradictory imperatives.

Moreover, leaders should also display an awareness of the fact that crisis management is situated on the dividing line between stability and change in policies and polities. Many historic revolutions, for instance, began as public order crises that escalated due to ineffectual leadership. Many revolutions were then shaped by leaders who well understood the dynamics of crisis.

For public leaders, taking the time for strategic reflection on their crisis management capacity is a good investment in a political future. It prepares them for their role in this unfolding script of turmoil between stability and change. It forces them to consider their legacy: what is worth defending and for what change can a crisis be exploited?

Crises are often turning points between different social and political orders. A pivotal strategic question of crisis leadership is where a reasonable defense of incumbency and stability ends and a debilitating, and potentially self-defeating, posture of rigidity begins. When may imminent threats justifiably be met by what will seem disproportionate measures to at least some people? How far can crisis management responses go before democracy itself is fatally wounded? These questions were topical in the tumultuous years of the 1960s; they have been rediscovered after the 9/11 events and will be with us in the near and distant future. The attacks on Madrid and London have revived these pertinent questions in Europe as well.

These are no doubt difficult questions. They surely are a far cry from the reassuring "ten principles of effective crisis management" found in best-selling crisis management handbooks, many of which sell an illusion of control (top-down, linear, straightforward) which does not fit particularly well with the context of contemporary crises. Difficult questions and dilemmas of leadership in crises need to be faced, not shunned.

Notes

1 Hermann and Hagan (1998).
2 The term "rude surprises" was coined by LaPorte (2003).
3 The term is taken from Dror (1986).
4 Regester and Larkin (1997).
5 Malcolm Gladwell (2005).
6 George and Stern (2002).
7 Janis (1989).
8 To understand the dynamics and effects of crisis response, we must cast our net wider and consider the institutional context in which leaders operate and crisis decision making takes place. For such an approach, see Stern and Sundelius (2002).
9 Dynes (1970: 208).
10 For a discussion of the symbolic value of planning, see Clarke (1999).
11 All this should not be interpreted as a postmodern rejection of bureaucratic structures. Bureaucracies – think of the Salvation Army or a local transportation company – can prove a powerful source of improvisation during a crisis. The secret of these types of organizations is that their structure revolves around commonly shared values. In routine situations, bureaucratic structure helps to optimize efficiency; during a crisis, these structures can be temporarily abandoned as the shared values guide improvisation.
12 Douglas (1992).
13 Lagadec (1997); Boin et al. (2004). Following a crisis, it is common to initiate exercises in formulating lessons learned from such an episode. However, the step from observing the recent performances of oneself and others in the heat of a crisis to formulating lessons learned of enduring value is quite formidable. For one, one needs to distinguish between the many lessons observed and the fewer lessons learned.
14 For a theoretical introduction see Argyris and Schön (1978); Weick and Sutcliffe (2002).
15 Schön (1971).
16 See also Zelikow and Rice (1995).
17 Boin and Otten (1996).

References

Adomeit, H. (1982) *Soviet Risk-taking and Crisis Behavior: A theoretical and empirical analysis.* Boston: Allen & Unwin.

Aguirre, B. E. (2004) "Homeland security warnings: Lessons learned and unlearned," *International Journal of Mass Emergencies and Disasters* 22: 103–15.

Alink, F. (forthcoming) *Crisis als kans?* Dissertation. Department of Public Administration, Leiden University.

Alink, F., Boin, R. A., and 't Hart, P. (2001) "Institutional crises and reforms in policy sectors: The case of refugee policy in Europe," *Journal of European Public Policy* 8: 286–306.

Allison, G. T. (1971) *Essence of Decision: Explaining the Cuban missile crisis.* Boston: Little Brown.

Almond, G. A., Flanagan, S., and Mundt, R. (eds.) (1973) *Crisis, Choice and Change: Historical studies of political development.* Boston: Little Brown.

Argyris, C. and Schön, D. A. (1978) *Organizational Learning: A theory of action perspective.* Amsterdam: Addison-Wesley.

Axelrod, R. and Cohen, M. D. (2000) *Harnessing Complexity.* New York: Basic Books.

Baggot, R. (1998) "The BSE crisis: Public health and the 'risk society'," in Gray, P. D. and 't Hart, P. (eds.) *Public Policy Disasters in Western Europe.* London: Routledge, pp. 61–78.

Bardach, E. (2001) "Development dynamics: Interagency collaboration as an emergent phenomenon," *Journal of Public Administration Research and Theory* 2: 149–64.

Barnard, C. (1938) *The Functions of the Executive.* Cambridge: Harvard University Press.

Barton, A. H. (1969) *Communities in Disaster: A sociological analysis of collective stress situations.* New York: Doubleday.

Barton, L. (1993) *Crisis in Organizations: Managing and communicating in the heat of chaos.* Cincinnati: South-Western Publishing Co.

Baumgartner, F. R. and Jones, B. D. (1993) *Agendas and Instability in American Politics.* Chicago: University of Chicago Press.

Beck, U. (1992) *Risk Society: Toward a new modernity.* London: Sage Publications.

Bennett, A. (1999) *Condemned to Repetition? The rise, fall and reprise of Soviet-Russian military interventionism, 1973–1996.* Cambridge: The MIT Press.

Bennett, W. L. (1980) "Myth, ritual and political control," *Journal of Communication* 30: 166–79.

Bennett, W. L. and Entman, R. M. (eds.) (2001) *Mediated Politics: Communication in the future of democracy.* Cambridge: Cambridge University Press.

Bernardsdottir, A. E. and Svedin, L. (2004) *Small-state Crisis Management: The Icelandic way.* Stockholm: Swedish National Defence College.

Bernstein, S., Lebow, R. N., Stein, J. G., and Weber, S. (2000) "God gave physics the easy problems: Adapting social science to an unpredictable world", *European Journal of International Relations* 6: 43–76.

Binder, L., Coleman, J. S., LaPalombar, J., Pye, L. W., Verba, S., and Weiner, M. (1971) *Crisis and Sequences in Political Development.* Princeton: Princeton University Press.

Birkland, T. (1997) *After Disaster: Agenda-setting, public policy, and focusing events.* Washington: Georgetown University Press.

Blight, J. G. and Welch, D. A. (1989) *On the Brink: Americans and Soviets reexamine the Cuban missile crisis.* New York: Hill and Wang.

Blix, H. (2004) *Disarming Iraq.* New York: Pantheon.

Blumer, J. G. and Gurevitch, M. (1995) *The Crisis of Public Communication.* London: Routledge.

Boin, R. A. (2005) "From crisis to disaster: Toward an integrative perspective", in Quarantelli and Perry (eds.) *What is a Disaster? New answers to old questions.* Philadelphia: Xlibris Press, pp. 153–72.

Boin, R. A. and 't Hart, P. (2000) "Institutional crises in policy sectors: An exploration of characteristics, conditions and consequences," in Wagenaar, H. (ed.) *Government Institutions: Effects, changes and normative foundations.* Dordrecht: Kluwer Press, pp. 9–31.

Boin, R. A., Kofman-Bos, C., and Overdijk, W. I. E. (2004) "Crisis simulations: Exploring tomorrow's vulnerabilities and threats," *Simulation and Gaming: An International Journal of Theory, Practice and Research* 35: 378–93.

Boin, R. A., Lagadec, P., Kerjan, E. M., and Overdijk, W. I. E. (2003) "Critical infrastructures under threat: Learning from the anthrax scare," *Journal of Contingencies and Crisis Management* 11: 99–104.

Boin, R. A. and Otten, M. H. P. (1996) "Beyond the crisis window for reform: Some ramifications for implementation," *Journal of Contingencies and Crisis Management* 4: 149–61.

Boin, R. A. and Rattray, W. A. R. (2004) "Understanding prison riots: Toward a threshold theory", *Punishment & Society* 6: 47–65.

Bovens, M. and 't Hart, P. (1996) *Understanding Policy Fiascoes.* New Brunswick: Transaction Publishers.

Bovens, M., 't Hart, P., Dekker, S., and Verheuvel, G. (1999) "The politics of blame avoidance: Defensive tactics in a Dutch crime-fighting fiasco," in Anheier, H. K. (ed.) *When Things Go Wrong: Organizational failures and breakdowns.* London: Sage, pp. 123–47.

Bracken, P. (1983) *The Command and Control of Nuclear Forces.* New Haven: Yale University Press.

Braithwaite, V. and Levi, M. (eds.) (1998) *Trust and Governance.* New York: Russell Sage Foundation.

Brändström, A. (2000) *Minks or Submarines: The dilemma in the Swedish hunt for submarines*. Stockholm: Swedish National Defence College.

Brändström, A., Bynander, F., and 't Hart, P. (2004) "Governing by looking back: Historical analogies in crisis management," *Public Administration* 82: 191–210.

Brändström, A. and Kuipers, S. L. (2003) "From 'normal incidents' to political crises: Understanding the selective politicization of policy failures," *Government and Opposition* 38: 279–305.

Brändström, A. and Malesic, M. (eds.) (2004) *Crisis Management in Slovenia: Comparative perspectives*. Stockholm: Swedish National Defence College.

Brandt, N. (2003) *Chicago Death Trap: The Iroquois theatre fire of 1903*. Carbondale: Southern Illinois University Press.

Brecher, M. (ed.) (1979a) *Studies in Crisis Behavior*. New Brunswick: Transaction Books.

Brecher, M. (1979b) "'Vertical' case studies: A summary of findings," in Brecher (ed.) *Studies in Crisis Behavior*, pp. 267–72.

Brecher, M. (1979c) "State behavior in international crisis: A model," *Journal of Conflict Resolution* 23: 446–80.

Brecher, M. (1980) *Decisions in Crisis: Israel's choices 1967 and 1973*. Berkeley: University of California Press.

Brecher, M. (1993) *Crises in World Politics: Theory and reality*. Oxford: Pergamon Press.

Breed, W. (1955) "Social control in the newsroom: A functional analysis," *Social Forces* 33: 326–35.

Bruner, J. S. (1957) "On perceptual readiness," *Psychological Review* 64: 123–52.

Brunsson, N. and Olsen, J. P. (1993) *The Reforming Organization*. London: Routledge.

Bryson, B. (2003) *A Short History of Nearly Everything*. New York: Broadway Books.

Bryson, J. M. and Crosby, B. C. (1992) *Leadership for the Common Good: Tackling public problems in a shared-power world*. San Francisco: Jossey-Bass.

Buchanan, M. (2000) *Ubiquity: Why catastrophes happen*. New York: Three Rivers Press.

Burke, J. P., Greenstein, F. I., Berman, L., and Immerman, R. H. (1989) *How Presidents Test Reality: Decisions on Vietnam, 1954 and 1965*. New York: Russell Sage Foundation.

Busenberg, G. J. (2001) "Learning in organizations and public policy," *Journal of Public Policy* 21: 173–89.

Buzan, B., Waever, O., and de Wilde, J. (1998) *Security: A new framework for analysis*. London: Lynne Rienner.

Bynander, F. (1998) "The 1982 Swedish Hårsfjärden submarine incident: A decision making analysis," *Cooperation and Conflict* 33: 367–407.

Bynander, F. (2003) *Rise and Fall of the Submarine Threat: Threat politics and submarine intrusions in Sweden 1980–2002*. Uppsala: Uppsala University Press.

Caiden, G. E. (1991) *Administrative Reform Comes of Age*. New York: Walter de Gruyter.

Carley, K. M. and Harrald, J. R. (1997) "Organizational learning under fire: Theory and practice," *American Behavioral Scientist* 40: 310–32.

Carrel, L. F. (2000) "Training civil servants for crisis management," *Journal of Contingencies and Crisis Management* 8: 192–6.

Charles, M. T. (2001) "The fall of TWA flight 800," in Rosenthal, Boin, and Comfort (eds.) *Managing Crises*, pp. 216–34.

Chisholm, D. (1989) *Coordination Without Hierarchy: Informal structures in multi-organizational systems*. Berkeley: University of California Press.

Clarke, L. B. (1999) *Mission Improbable: Using fantasy documents to tame disasters*. Chicago: The University of Chicago Press.

Clarke, R. A. (2004) *Against All Enemies: Inside America's war on terror*. New York: The Free Press.

Cobb, R. W. and Primo, D. M. (2003) *The Plane Truth: Airline crashes, the media and transportation policy*. Washington: Brookings Institution.

Columbia Accident Investigation Board (2003) *Columbia Accident Investigation Report 1*. Burlington: Apogee Books.

Combs, J. E. (1980) *Dimensions of Political Drama*. Santa Monica: Goodyear.

Committee of Privy Counsellors (2004) *Review on Intelligence of Weapons of Mass Destruction*. London: The Stationery Office.

Cook, R. F. (2004) *The Point of Departure: Diaries from the front bench*. New York: Simon and Schuster.

Cortell, A. P. and Peterson, S. (1999) "Altered states: Explaining domestic institutional change," *British Journal of Political Science* 29: 177–203.

Crisis Onderzoek Team (1994) *Crisismanagement bij Nevcin Polymers: Een reconstructie van de gebeurtenissen na 8 juli 1992*. Leiden: COT.

Cuny, F. L. (1983) *Disasters and Development*. New York: Oxford University Press.

Cyert R. M., March J. G., and Clarkson, G. P. E. (1963) *A Behavioral Theory of the Firm*. Englewood Cliffs: Prentice-Hall.

David, C. P. (1993) *Foreign Policy Failure in the White House: Reappraising the fall of the Shah and the Iran-Contra affair*. Lanham: University Press of America.

Davidson, A. (1990) *In the Wake of the Exxon Valdez: The devastating impact of the oil spill*. San Francisco: Sierra Club Books.

Dekker, S. (forthcoming) *Commissions as Troubleshooters: Crisis and the politics of inquiries*. Dissertation. Department of Public Administration, Leiden University.

Dekker, S. and Hansén, D. (2004) "Learning under pressure: The effects of politicization on organizational learning in public bureaucracies," *Journal of Public Administration Research and Theory* 14: 211–30.

Deutsch, K. W. (1966) *The Nerves of Government: Models for political communication and control*. New York: The Free Press.

Devine, P. G., Hamilton, D. L., and Ostrom, T. M. (eds.) (1994) *Social Cognition: Impact on social psychology*. San Diego: Academic Press.

DiIulio, J. J., Alpert, G. P., Moore, M. H., Cole, G. F., Petersilia, J., Logan, C. H., and Wilson, J. Q. (1993) *Performance Measures for the Criminal Justice System*. Discussion papers from the BJS-Princeton Project, Princeton University.

Douglas, M. (1992) *Risk and Blame: Essays in cultural theory*. London: Routledge.

Douglas, M. and Wildavsky, A. (1982) *Risk and Culture: An essay on the selection of environmental dangers*. Berkeley: California University Press.

Dowty, A. (1984) *Middle East Crisis: US decision making in 1958, 1970 and 1973*. Berkeley: University of California Press.

Drabek, T. E. (1985) "Managing the emergency response," *Public Administration Review* 45: 85–92.

Drabek, T. E. and Quarantelli, E. L. (1967) "Scapegoats, villains, and disasters", *Transaction* 4: 12–17.

Dror, Y. (1986) *Policymaking Under Adversity*. New Brunswick: Transaction Books.

Dryzek, J. S. (1992) "The good society versus the state: Freedom and necessity in political innovation," *Journal of Politics* 54: 518–40.

Dunsire, A. (1978) *Control in a Bureaucracy*. Oxford: Martin Robertson.

Dynes, R. R. (1970) *Organized Behaviour in Disaster*. Lexington: D. C. Heath and Company.

Dyson, S. B. and Preston, T. (2003) *Lenses for Leaders: The role of complexity and prior expertise in shaping the use of analogy in foreign policy decision making*. Washington: Department of Political Science, Washington State University.

Edelman, M. J. (1964) *The Symbolic Uses of Politics*. Urbana: University of Illinois Press.

Edelman, M. J. (1971) *Politics as Symbolic Action: Mass arousal and quiescence*. Chicago: Markham.

Edelman, M. J. (1977) *Political Language: Words that succeed and policies that fail*. New York: Academic Press.

Edelman, M. J. (1988) *Constructing the Political Spectacle*. Chicago: The University of Chicago Press.

Eichengreen, B. (2002) *Financial Crises: And what to do about them*. New York: Oxford University Press.

Eisenhower, D. D. (1966) *The White House Years: Waging peace, 1956–1961*. London: Heinemann.

Ekengren, M. and Sundelius, B. (2004) "National foreign policy co-ordination," in Sjursen, H., Carlsnaes, W., and White, B. (eds.) *Contemporary European Foreign Policy*. London: Sage Publications, pp. 110–22.

Elder, C. D. and Cobb, R. W. (1983) *The Political Uses of Symbols*. New York: Longman.

Entman, R. M. (1993) "Framing: Toward a clarification of a fractured paradigm," *Journal of Communication* 43: 51–8.

Erikson, K. T. (1976) *Everything in its Path: Destruction of community in the Buffalo Creek Flood*. New York: Simon and Schuster.

Erikson, K. T. (1994) *A New Species of Trouble: Explorations in disaster, trauma and community*. New York: Norton.

Eriksson, J. (2001) "Introduction", in Eriksson, J. (ed.) *Threat Politics: New perspectives on security, risk and crisis management*. Aldershot: Ashgate, pp. 8–16.

Etheredge, L. S. (1985) *Can Governments Learn? American foreign policy and Central American revolutions*. New York: Pergamon Press.

Fearn-Banks, K. (1996) *Crisis Communications: A casebook approach*. Mahwah: Lawrence Erlbaum Associates.

Feldman, M. S. and March, J. G. (1981) "Information in organizations as signal and symbol," *Administrative Science Quarterly* 26: 174–86.

Feldman, M. S. and March, J. G. (1988) "Information in organizations as signal and symbol," in March, J. G. (ed.) *Decisions and Organizations*. Oxford: Blackwell, pp. 409–28.

Fiol, C. M. and Lyles, M. A. (1985) "Organizational learning," *Academy of Management Review* 10: 803–13.

Flin, R. (1996) *Sitting in the Hot Seat: Leaders and teams for critical incidents*. Chichester: Wiley.

Flin, R. (2001) "Decision making in crises: The Piper Alpha disaster", in Rosenthal, Boin, and Comfort (eds.) *Managing Crises*, pp. 103–18.

Flin R. and Arbuthnot, K. (eds.) (2002) *Incident Command: Tales from the hot seat*. Aldershot: Ashgate Publishing.

Gabriel, R. T. (1985) *Military Incompetence: Why the American military doesn't win*. New York: Hill and Wang.

George, A. L. (1993) *Bridging the Gap: Theory and practice in foreign policy*. Washington: United States Institute of Peace Press.

George, A. L. and Stern, E. K. (2002) "Harnessing conflict in foreign policy making: From devil's to multiple advocacy," *Presidential Studies Quarterly* 32: 484–508.

Glad, B. (1980) *Jimmy Carter: In search of the great White House*. New York: W. W. Norton.

Gladwell, Malcolm, (2005) *Blink: The Power of Thinking Without Thinking*. New York: Brown & Co.

Goldfinch, S. and 't Hart, P. (2003) "Leadership and institutional reform: Engineering macroeconomic policy change in Australia", *Governance* 16: 235–70.

Goldstone, J. A. and Useem, B. (1999) "Prison riots as microrevolutions: An extension of state-centered theories of revolution," *American Journal of Sociology* 104: 985–1029.

Goode, E. and Ben-Yehuda, N. (1994) *Moral Panics: The social construction of deviance*. Oxford: Blackwell.

Gormley, W. T. and Weimer, D. L. (1999) *Organizational Report Cards*. Cambridge: Harvard University Press.

Graber, D. A., McQuail, D., and Norris, P. (1998) "Introduction: political communication in a democracy," in Graber, D. A., McQuail, D., and Norris, P. (eds.) *The Politics of News: The news of politics*. Washington: CQ Press.

Haas, E. R. (1990) *When Knowledge is Power: Three models of change in international organizations*. Berkeley: University of California Press.

Habermas, J. (1975) *Legitimation Crisis*. Boston: Beacon Press.

Haldeman, H. R. and Ambrose, S. E. (1994). *The Haldeman Diaries: Inside the Nixon White House*. New York: Putnam.

Hall, P. A. (1993) "Policy paradigms, social learning and the state: The case of economic policy making in Britain," *Comparative Politics* 35: 275–96.

Halper, T. (1971) *Foreign Policy Crises: Appearance and reality in decision making*. Columbus: Charles E. Merrill.

Hansén, D. and Stern, E. K. (2001) "From crisis to trauma: The Palme assassination case," in Rosenthal, Boin, and Comfort (eds.) *Managing Crises*, pp. 177–99.

Hargrove, E. C. (1994) *Prisoners of Myth: The leadership of the Tennessee Valley Authority*. Princeton: Princeton University Press.

't Hart, P. (1993) "Symbols, rituals and power: The lost dimension in crisis management," *Journal of Contingencies and Crisis Management* 1: 36–50.

't Hart, P. (1994) *Groupthink in Government: A study of small groups and policy failure*. Baltimore: Johns Hopkins University Press.

't Hart, P. and Boin, R. A. (2001) "Between crisis and normalcy: The long shadow of post-crisis politics," in Rosenthal, Boin, and Comfort (eds.) *Managing Crises*, pp. 28–46.

't Hart, P. and Pijnenburg, B. (1988) *Het Heizeldrama: Rampzalig organiseren en kritieke beslissingen*. Alphen aan de Rijn: Samsom.

't Hart, P. and Rijpma, J. (eds.) (1997) *Crises in het Nieuws: Samenspel en tegenspel tussen overheid en media*. Alphen aan den Rijn: Samsom.

't Hart, P., Rosenthal, U., and Kouzmin, A. (1993) "Crisis decision making: The centralization thesis revisited," *Administration and Society* 25: 12–45.

't Hart, P., Stern, E. K. and Sundelius, B. (eds.) (1997) *Beyond Groupthink: Political group dynamics and foreign policy making*. Ann Arbor: University of Michigan Press.

Hay, C. (2001) "The 'crisis' of Keynesianism and the rise of neoliberalism in Britain: An ideational institutionalist approach," in Campbell, J. L. and Pedersen, O. K. (eds.) *The Rise of Neoliberalism and Institutional Analysis*. Princeton: Princeton University Press, pp. 193–218.

Heath, R. L. (2004) "Telling a story: A narrative approach to communication during crisis," in Millar and Heath (eds.) *Responding to Crisis*, pp. 167–87.

Heclo, H. (1974) *Modern Social Politics in Britain and Sweden*. New Haven: Yale University Press.

Henry, R. A. (2000) *You'd Better Have a Hose if You Want to Put Out the Fire*. Windsor: Gollywobbler Productions.

Herek, G. M., Janis, I. L. and Huth, P. (1987) "Decision making during international crisis: Is quality of process related to outcome?," *Journal of Conflict Resolution* 31: 203–26.

Hermann, C. F. (1963) "Some consequences of crisis which limit the viability of organizations," *Administrative Science Quarterly* 8: 61–82.

Hermann, C. F. (ed.) (1972) *International Crises: Insights from behavioral research*. New York: The Free Press.

Hermann, M. G. (1979) "Indicators of stress in policy makers during foreign policy crises," *Political Psychology* 1: 27–46.

Hermann, M. G. and Hagan, J. (1998) "International Decision Making: Leadership Matters" *Foreign Policy* 110: 124–137.

Hodgkinson, P. E. and Stewart, M. (1991) *Coping with Catastrophe: A handbook of disaster management*. London: Routledge.

Holsti, O. R. (1972) *Crisis, Escalation and War*. Montreal: McGill-Queens University Press.

Holsti, O. R. (1979) "Theories of crisis decisionmaking," in Lauren, P. G. (ed.) *Diplomacy: New approaches in history, theory, and policy*. New York: The Free Press, pp. 99–136.

Honig, J. W. (2001) "Avoiding war, inviting defeat: The Srebrenica crisis, July 1995," in Rosenthal, Boin, and Comfort (eds.) *Managing Crises*, pp. 61–73.

Honig, J. W. and Both, N. (1997) *Srebrenica: Record of a war crime*. New York: Penguin.

Hood, C. C. (1976) *The Limits of Administration*. London: John Wiley.

Hood, C. C. (2002) "The risk game and the blame game," *Government and Opposition* 37: 15–37.

Hood, C. C., James, O., Peters, G., and Scott, C. (eds.) (2004) *Controlling Modern Government: Oversight, competition, mutuality and randomness in three public policy domains*. Cheltenham: Edgar Elgar.

Hoyt, P. D. and Garrison, J. A. (1997) "Political manipulation within the small group of foreign policy advisers in the Carter administration," in 't Hart, Stern, and Sundelius (eds.) *Beyond Groupthink*, pp. 249–74.

Iyengar, S. (1996) "Framing responsibility for political issues," *Annals of the American Academy of Political and Social Sciences* 546: 59–70.

Jacobs, B. D. (1989) "The Brixton riots: London 1981," in Rosenthal, Charles, and 't Hart (eds.) *Coping with Crisis*, pp. 340–66.

Jacobs, B. D. and Boin, R. A. (2001) "The Stephen Lawrence case: The London metropolitan police in crisis," in Rosenthal, Boin, and Comfort (eds.) *Managing Crises*, pp. 74–88.

Jacobs, B. D. and 't Hart, P. (1992) "Disaster at Hillsborough stadium: A comparative analysis," in Parker, D. J. and Handmer, J. W. (eds.) *Hazard Management and Emergency Planning: Perspectives on Britain*. London: James and James, pp. 127–51.

Janis, I. L. (1982) *Groupthink*. Boston: Houghton Mifflin.

Janis, I. L. (1989) *Crucial Decisions: Leadership in policymaking and crisis management*. New York: The Free Press.

Janis, I. L. and Mann, L. (1977) *Decision-making: A psychological analysis of conflict, choice and commitment*. New York: The Free Press.

Jasanoff, S. (ed.) (1994) *Learning from Disaster: Risk management after Bhopal*. Philadelphia: University of Pennsylvania Press.

Jervis, R. (1976) *Perception and Misperception in International Politics*. Princeton: Princeton University Press.

Jervis, R. (1992) "Political implications of loss aversion," *Political Psychology* 13: 187–204.

Jervis, R. (1997) *System Effects: Complexity in political and social life*. Princeton: Princeton University Press.

Kaase, M. and Newton, K. (1995) *Beliefs in Government*. Oxford: Oxford University Press.

Kam, E. (1988) *Surprise Attack*. Cambridge: Harvard University Press.

Keeler, J. T. S. (1993) "Opening the window for reform: Mandates, crises and extraordinary policy making," *Comparative Political Studies* 25: 433–86.

Kertzer, D. I. (1988) *Ritual, Politics and Power*. New Haven: Yale University Press.

Kettl, D. F. (2003) "Contingent coordination: Practical and theoretical puzzles for homeland security," *American Review of Public Administration* 33: 253–77.

Kettl, D. F. (2004) *System Under Stress: Homeland security and American politics.* Washington: CQ Press.

Key, V. O. (1961) *Public Opinion and American Democracy.* New York: Knopf.

Key, V. O. (1966) *The Responsible Electorate: Rationality in presidential voting.* Cambridge: Harvard University Press.

Keys, D. (1999) *Catastrophe: An investigation into the origins of the modern world.* London: Century Keys.

Khong, Y. F. (1992) *Analogies at War: Korea, Munich, Dien Bien Phu, and the Vietnam decisions of 1965.* Princeton: Princeton University Press.

Kingdon, J. W. (1995) *Agendas, Alternatives, and Public Policies.* 2nd ed. New York: HarperCollins.

Klein, G. (2001) *Sources of Power: How people make decisions.* 7th ed. London: The MIT Press.

Kletz, T. A. (1994) *Learning From Accidents.* London: Butterworth-Heinemann.

Klinenberg, E. (2002) *Heat Wave: A social autopsy of disaster in Chicago.* Chicago: University of Chicago Press.

Kroon, M. B. R., 't Hart, P., and van Kreveld, D. (1991) "Managing group decision making processes: Individual versus collective accountability and groupthink," *International Journal of Conflict Management* 2: 91–115.

Kuipers, S. L. (2004) *Cast in Concrete? The institutional dynamics of Belgian and Dutch social policy reform.* Dissertation. Delft: Eburon.

Kurtz, R. S. and Browne, W. P. (2004) "Crisis management, crisis response: An introduction to the symposium", *Review of Policy Research* 21: 141–3.

Lagadec, P. (1990) *States of Emergency: Technological failures and social destabilization.* London: Butterworth-Heinemann.

Lagadec, P. (1997) "Learning processes for crisis management in complex organizations," *Journal of Contingencies and Crisis Management* 5: 24–31.

Lagadec, P. (2004) "Understanding the French 2003 heat wave experience: Beyond the heat, a multi-layered challenge," *Journal of Contingencies and Crisis Management* 12: 160–9.

Landau, M. (1973) "On the concept of a self-correcting organization," *Public Administration Review* 33: 533–42.

Lanzara, G. F. (1998) "Self-destructive processes in institution building and some modest countervailing mechanisms," *European Journal of Political Research* 33: 1–39.

LaPorte, T. R. (1996) "High reliability organizations: Unlikely, demanding, and at risk," *Journal of Contingencies and Crisis Management* 4: 60–71.

LaPorte, T. R. (2003) "Anticipating Rude Surprises: Reflections on 'crisis management' without end." EU/US Crisis Management Conference: Minnowbrook Conference Center, 6–10 August.

Larsson, S., Olsson, E. K., and Ramberg, B. (eds.) (2005) *Crisis Decision Making in the European Union.* Stockholm: Swedish National Defence College.

Lazarus, R. S. (1966) *Psychological Stress and the Coping Process.* New York: McGraw-Hill.

Lebow, R. N. (1981) *Between Peace and War: The nature of international crisis.* Baltimore: Johns Hopkins University Press.

Lebow, R. N. and Stein, J. G. (1994) *We All Lost the Cold War.* Princeton: Princeton University Press.

Leemans, A. F. (1976) *The Management of Change in Government*. The Hague: Martinus Nijhoff.

Leveson, N. (1995) *Safeware: System safety and computers*. Reading: Addison Wesley.

Lewis, D. (1997) *Hidden Agendas: Politics, law and disorder*. London: Hamish Hamilton.

Libertore, A. (1993) "Chernobyl comes to Italy: The reciprocal relationships of radiation experts, government policies, and the media," in Barker, A. and Peters, G. (eds.) *The Politics of Expert Advice: Creating, using and manipulating scientific knowledge for public policy*. Edinburgh: University of Edinburgh Press, pp. 33–48.

Lindblom, C. E. (1979) "Still muddling, not yet through," *Public Administration Review* 39: 517–29.

Lindgren, K. (2003) 'Vad Styr Ledaren? Om beslutsfattare och policyforandring i sakerhetspolitiska kriser.' Dissertation, Uppsala University.

Linz, J. J. (1978) "Crisis, breakdown and reequilibration," in Linz and Stepan (eds.) *The Breakdown of Democratic Regimes*.

Linz, J. J. and Stepan, A. C. (eds.) (1978) *The Breakdown of Democratic Regimes*. Baltimore: Johns Hopkins University Press.

Lipsky, M. (1980) *Street-level Bureaucracy: Dilemmas of the individual in public service*. New York: Russell Sage Foundation.

Lipsky, M. and Olson, D. J. (1977) *Commission Politics: The processing of racial crisis in America*. New Brunswick: Transaction Books.

Lloyd, J. (2004) *What the Media are Doing to Our Politics*. London: Constable.

Lombardi, W. J., Higgins, E. F., and Bargh, J. A. (1987) "The role of consciousness in priming effects on categorization: Assimilation versus contrast as a function of awareness of the priming task," *Personality and Social Psychology Bulletin* 13: 411–29.

Longley, J. and Pruitt, D. G. (1980) "Groupthink: A critique of Janis's theory," *Review of Personality and Social Psychology* 1: 74–93.

MacGregor Burns, J. (1978) *Leadership*. New York: Harper and Row.

Maoz, Z. (1990) *National Choices and International Processes*. Cambridge: Cambridge University Press.

Marais, K., Dulac, N., and Leveson, N. (2004) "Beyond normal accidents and high reliability organizations: The need for an alternative approach to safety in complex systems." Paper presented at the Engineering Systems Division Symposium. Cambridge: The MIT Press.

March, J. G. (ed.) (1988) *Decisions and Organizations*. Oxford: Blackwell.

March, J. G. (1994) *A Primer on Decision Making: How decisions happen*. New York: The Free Press.

May, E. R. (1972) *"Lessons" of the Past*. New York: Oxford University Press.

McCauley, C. (1989) "The nature of social influence in groupthink: Compliance and internalization," *Journal of Personality and Social Psychology* 22: 250–60.

McConnell, A. (2003) "Overview: Crisis management, influences, responses and evaluation," *Parliamentary Affairs* 56: 363–409.

Meltsner, A. J. (1990) *Rules for Rulers: The politics of advice*. Philadelphia: Temple University Press.

Meyer, T. (2002) *Media Democracy: How the media colonize politics.* Cambridge: Polity Press.

Meyers, G. C. (1986) *When It Hits the Fan: Managing the nine crises of business.* Boston: Houghton Mifflin.

Milburn, T. (1972) "The management of crisis," in Hermann (ed.) *International Crises*, pp. 259–80.

Millar, D. P. and Heath, R. L. (ed.) (2004) *Responding to Crisis: A rhetorical approach to crisis communication.* Mahwah: Lawrence Erlbaum.

Millar, F. E. and Beck, D. B. (2004) "Metaphors of crisis," in Millar and Heath (eds.) *Responding to Crises*, pp. 153–66.

Miller, A. (2001) "The Los Angeles Riots: A study in crisis paralysis," in Rosenthal, Boin and Comfort (eds.) *Managing Crises*, pp. 49–60.

Mitroff, I. I. and Pauchant, T. C. (1990) *We're So Big and Powerful Nothing Bad Can Happen to Us.* New York: Carol Publishing Corporation.

Moon, J. (1995) "Innovative leadership and policy change: Lessons from Thatcher," *Governance* 8: 1–25.

Murray, C. and Cox, C. B. (1989) *Apollo: Race to the moon.* New York: Simon and Schuster.

Nacos, B. L. (2002) *Terrorism and the Media: From the Iran hostage crisis to the World Trade Center bombing.* 3rd ed. New York: Columbia University Press.

National Commission on Terrorist Attacks (2004) *The 9/11 Commission Report.* New York: W. W. Norton & Company.

Neustadt, R. N. and May, E. R. (1986) *Thinking in Time: The uses of history for decision-makers.* New York: The Free Press.

Nimmo, D. and Combs, J. E. (1985) *Nightly Horrors: Crisis coverage in television network news.* Knoxville: University of Tennessee Press.

Nimmo, D. and Combs, J. E. (1990) *Mediated Political Realities.* 2nd ed. New York: Longman.

Nisbett, R. and Ross, L. (1980) *Human Inference: Strategies and shortcomings of social judgment.* Englewood Cliffs: Prentice-Hall.

Nohrstedt, S. (1991) "The information crisis in Sweden after Chernobyl," *Media, Culture and Society* 13: 477–97.

Northouse, P. G. (2001) *Leadership: Theory and research.* Thousand Oaks: Sage Publications.

Nudell, M. and Antokol, N. (1988) *The Handbook for Effective Emergency and Crisis Management.* Lexington: Lexington Books.

OECD (2003) *Emerging Risks in the 21st Century: An agenda for action.* Paris: OECD.

Ohanian, R. (1991) "The impact of celebrity spokespersons' perceived image on consumers' intention to purchase," *Journal of Advertising Research* 31: 46–54.

Olsen, J. P. and Peters, B. G. (eds.) (1996) *Lessons From Experience: Experiential learning in administrative reforms in eight democracies.* Oslo: Scandinavian University Press.

Paige, G. D. (1968) *The Korean Decision: June 24–30, 1950.* New York: The Free Press.

Parker, C. and Stern, E. K. (2002) "Blindsided? September 11 and the origins of strategic surprise," *Political Psychology* 23: 601–30.

Patterson, P. (1989) "Reporting Chernobyl: Cutting the government fog to cover the nuclear cloud," in Walters, Wilkins, and Walters (eds.) *Bad Tidings*, pp. 131–48.

Pauchant, T. C. and Mitroff, I. I. (1992) *Transforming the Crisis-prone Organization: Preventing individual, organizational and environmental tragedies.* San Francisco: Jossey-Bass.

Pearce, T. and Fortune, J. (1995) "Command and control in policing: A systems assessment of the gold, silver and bronze structure," *Journal of Contingencies and Crisis Management* 3: 181–7.

Perrow, C. (1984) *Normal Accidents: Living with high-risk technologies.* New York: Basic Books.

Perrow, C. (1994) "The limits of safety: The enhancement of a theory of accidents", *Journal of Contingencies and Crisis Management* 2: 212–20.

Perrow, C. (1999) *Normal Accidents: Living with high-risk technologies.* 2nd ed. Princeton: Princeton University Press.

Perrow, C. and Guillen, M. F. (1990) *The AIDS Disaster: The failure of organizations in New York and the nation.* New Haven: Yale University Press.

Perry, R. W. and Lindell, M. K. (1997) "Principles for managing community relocation as hazard mitigation measure," *Journal of Contingencies and Crisis Management* 5: 49–59.

Petak, W. J. (ed.) (1985) "Emergency management: A challenge for public administration," *Public Administration Review* 45: 3–7.

Peters, B. G. and Pierre, J. (eds.) (2001) *Politicians, Bureaucrats, and Administrative Reform.* London: Routledge.

Petroski, H. (1992) *To Engineer is Human: The role of failure in successful design.* New York: Vintage Books.

Pfetsch, B. (1998) "Government news management," in Graber, D., McQuail, D., and Norris, P. (eds.) *The Politics of News: The news of politics.* Washington: CQ Press, pp. 70–93.

Pidgeon, N. (1997) "The limits to safety? Culture, politics, learning and man-made disasters," *Journal of Contingencies and Crisis Management* 5: 1–14.

Pierson, P. (2000) "Increasing returns, path dependence, and the study of politics," *American Political Science Review* 94: 251–67.

Platt, A. (ed.) (1971) *The Politics of Riot Commissions, 1917–1970: A collection of official reports and critical essays.* New York: Macmillan.

Pollitt, C. (1993) *Managerialism and the Public Services: Cuts or cultural change in the 1990s?* 2nd ed. Oxford: Blackwell.

Posner, R. A. (2004) "The 9/11 report: A dissent," *New York Times*, 29 August.

Post, J. M. (1991) "The impact of crisis-induced stress on policy makers," in George, A. (ed.) *Avoiding War: Problems of crisis management.* Boulder: Westview Press, pp. 471–94.

Preston T. (2001) *The President and His Inner Circle: Leadership style and the advisory process in foreign affairs.* New York: Columbia University Press.

Preston, T. and 't Hart, P. (1999) "Understanding and evaluating bureaucratic politics: The nexus between political leaders and advisory systems," *Political Psychology* 20: 49–98.

Price, M. (1995) *Television, the Public Sphere and National Identity*. Oxford: Clarendon Press.

Quarantelli, E. L. (1954) "The nature and conditions of panic," *American Journal of Sociology* 60: 267–75.

Quarantelli, E. L. (1996) "The future is not the past repeated: Projecting disasters in the 21st century from present trends," *Journal of Contingencies and Crisis Management* 4: 228–40.

Quarantelli, E. L. (ed.) (1998) *What is a Disaster? Perspectives on the question*. London: Routledge.

Quarantelli, E. L. and Perry, R. W. (eds.) (2005). *What is a Disaster? New answers to old questions*. Philadelphia: Xlibris Press.

Raphael, B. (1986) *When Disaster Strikes: How individuals and communities cope with catastrophe*. New York: Basic Books.

Reason, J. (1990) *Human Error*. New York: Cambridge University Press.

Regester, M. and Larkin, J. (1997) *Risk Issues and Crisis Management: A casebook of best practice*. London: Kogan Page.

Resodihardjo, S. L. (forthcoming) *Institutional Crises and Reform: Constrained opportunities*. Dissertation. Department of Public Administration, Leiden University.

Reyntjens, F. (2001) "From ethnicity to genocide in Rwanda," in Rosenthal, Boin, and Comfort (eds.) *Managing Crises*, pp. 89–100.

Rijpma, J. A. (1997) "Complexity, tight-coupling and reliability: Connecting normal accidents theory and high reliability theory," *Journal of Contingencies and Crisis Management* 5: 15–23.

Rijpma, J. A. and van Duin, M. J. (2001) "From accident to disaster: The response to the Hercules crash," in Rosenthal, Boin, and Comfort (eds.) *Managing Crises*, pp. 143–54.

Roberts, J. M. (1988) *Decisionmaking During International Crises*. London: MacMillan.

Roberts, K. (ed.) (1993) *New Challenges to Understanding Organizations*. New York: MacMillan.

Robertson, A. (2001) "Mediated threats," in Eriksson, J. (ed.) *Threat Politics: New perspectives on security, risk and crisis management*. Aldershot: Ashgate, pp. 61–83.

Rochlin, G. I. (1996) "Reliable organizations: Present research and future directions," *Journal of Contingencies and Crisis Management* 4: 55–9.

Rose, R. (1993) *Lesson-drawing in Public Policy: A guide to learning across time and space*. Chatham: Chatham House Publishers.

Rose, R. and Davies, P. L. (1994) *Inheritance in Public Policy: Change without choice in Britain*. New Haven: Yale University Press.

Rosenthal, U. (1978) *Political Order: Rewards, punishments and political stability*. Meppel: Krips Repro.

Rosenthal, U. (1998) "Future disasters, future definitions", in Quarantelli, E. (ed.) *What is a Disaster? Perspectives on the question*. London: Routledge, pp. 146–60.

Rosenthal, U., Boin, R. A., and Bos, C. J. (2001) "Shifting identities: The reconstructive mode of the Bijlmer plane crash," in Rosenthal, Boin, and Comfort (eds.) *Managing Crises*, pp. 200–15.

Rosenthal, U., Boin, R. A., and Comfort, L. K. (eds.) (2001) *Managing Crises: Threats, dilemmas, opportunities.* Springfield: Charles C. Thomas.

Rosenthal, U., Charles, M. T., and 't Hart, P. (eds.) (1989) *Coping With Crisis: The management of disasters, riots and terrorism.* Springfield: Charles C. Thomas.

Rosenthal, U., Charles, M. T., 't Hart, P., Kouzmin, A. and Jarman, A. (1989) "From case studies to theory and recommendations," in Rosenthal, Charles and 't Hart (eds.) *Coping with Crisis,* pp. 466–67.

Rosenthal, U. and 't Hart, P. (1989) "Managing terrorism: The South Moluccan hostage takings," in Rosenthal, Charles, and 't Hart (eds.) *Coping with Crisis,* pp. 367–93.

Rosenthal, U., 't Hart, P., and Kouzmin, A. (1991) "The bureau-politics of crisis management," *Public Administration* 69: 211–33.

Rosenthal, U., 't Hart, P., van Duin, M. J., Boin, R. A., Kroon, M. B. R., Otten, M. H. P., Overdijk, W. I. E. (1994) *Complexity in Urban Crisis Management: Amsterdam's response to the Bijlmer air disaster.* London: James & James.

Rutherford, P. (2004) *Weapons of Mass Persuasion: Marketing the war against Iraq.* Toronto: University of Toronto Press.

Sabatier, P. A. (ed.) (1999) *Theories of the Policy Process.* Boulder: Westview Press.

Sabatier, P. A. and Jenkins-Smith, H. (1993) *Policy Change and Learning: An advocacy coalition approach.* Boulder: Westview Press.

Sagan, S. D. (1993) *The Limits of Safety: Organizations, accidents and nuclear weapons.* Princeton: Princeton University Press.

Sarangi, S. (2002) "Crimes of Bhopal and the global campaign for justice," *Social Justice* 29: 47–52.

Scanlon, J. (1989) "Toxic chemicals and emergency management: The evacuation of Mississauga, Ontario, Canada," in Rosenthal, Charles, and 't Hart (eds.) *Coping With Crisis,* pp. 303–21.

Scanlon, J. (1994) "The role of EOCs in emergency management: A comparison of American and Canadian experience," *International Journal of Mass Emergencies and Disasters* 12: 51–75.

Schneider, S. K. (1993) *Flirting With Disaster: Public management in crisis situations.* Armonk: Sharpe.

Schön, D. A. (1971) *Beyond the Stable State.* New York: Random House.

Schön, D. A. and Rein, M. (1994). *Frame Reflection: Toward the resolution of intractable policy controversies.* New York: Basic Books.

Schumpeter, J. A. (1943) *Capitalism, Socialism and Democracy.* London: Allen & Unwin.

Schwartz, P. and Randall, D. (2003) *Abrupt Climate Change Scenario and its Implications for United States National Security.* Report commissioned by the US Defense Department. Washington: United States Department of Defense.

Schwartz, R. and Sulitzneanu-Kenan, R. (2004) "Managerial values and accountability pressures: Challenges of crisis and disaster," *Journal of Public Administration Research and Theory* 14: 79–102.

Seeger, M. W., Sellnow, T. L., and Ulmer, R. R. (2003) *Communication and Organizational Crisis.* Westport: Praeger.

Selznick, P. (1957) *Leadership in Administration: A sociological interpretation.* New York: Row-Peterson.

Senate Intelligence Committee (2004) *Report on the U.S. Intelligence Community's Prewar Intelligence Assessments on Iraq.* Washington: US Senate.

Seymour-Ure, C. (2003) *Prime Ministers and the Media: Issues of power and control.* Malden: Blackwell.

Shepsle, K. A. (2001) "A comment on institutional change," *Journal of Theoretical Politics* 13: 321–5.

Shibutani, T. (1966) *Improvised News: A sociological study of rumor.* New York: Bobbs-Merrill.

Shils, E. A. (1968) "Ritual and crisis," in Cutler, D. R. (ed.) *The Religious Situation.* Boston: Beacon Press, pp. 730–40.

Shilts, R. (1987) *And the Band Played On: Politics, people and the AIDS epidemic.* New York: St. Martin's Press.

Shrivastava, P. (1987) *Bhopal: Anatomy of a crisis.* Cambridge: Ballinger.

Sick, G. G. (1985) *All Fall Down: America's tragic encounter with Iran.* New York: Random House.

Silverstein, A. M. (1981) *Pure Politics and Impure Science: The swine flu affair.* Baltimore: Johns Hopkins University Press.

Simon, H. A. (1976) *Administrative Behavior: A study of decision making processes in administrative organization.* 3rd ed. New York: The Free Press.

Simon, H. A. (1981) *The Sciences of the Artificial.* 2nd ed. Cambridge: The MIT Press.

Sitkin, S. B. (1992) "Learning through failure: The strategy of small losses," *Research in Organizational Behavior* 14: 231–66.

Skocpol, T. (1985) "Bringing the state back in: Strategies of analysis in current research," in Evans, P. B., Rueschemeyer, D., and Skocpol, T. (eds.) *Bringing the State Back in.* Cambridge: Cambridge University Press, pp. 3–37.

Slatter, S. (1984) *Corporate Recovery: Successful turnaround strategies and their implementation.* Harmondsworth: Penguin Books.

Smart, C. and Vertinsky, I. (1977) "Designs for crisis decision units," *Administrative Science Quarterly* 22: 640–57.

Smelser, N. J. (1962) *Theory of Collective Behavior.* London: Routledge.

Smith, D. (2005) "Through a glass darkly: A response to Stallings' 'Disaster, crisis, collective stress, and mass deprivation'", in Quarantelli and Perry (eds.) *What is a Disaster?*, pp. 292–307.

Smith, H. (1989) *The Power Game: How Washington works.* New York: Ballantine Books.

Smith, S. (1985) "Groupthink and the hostage rescue mission," *British Journal of Political Science* 15: 117–23.

Snider, L. (2004) "Resisting neo-liberalism: The poisoned water in Walkerton, Ontario," *Social and Legal Studies* 13: 265–89.

Sorokin, P. A. (1943) *Man and Society in Calamity: The effects of war, revolution, famine, pestilence upon human mind, behavior, social organization and cultural life.* 3rd ed. New York: Dutton.

Stallings, R. A. (1995) *Promoting Risk: Constructing the earthquake threat.* New York: Aldine De Gruyter.

Staw, B. M. (2003) *Psychological Foundations of Organizational Behavior.* Englewood Cliffs: Prentice Hall.

Staw, B. M., Sandelands, L. E., and Dutton J. E. (1981) "Threat rigidity effects in organizational behaviour: A multilevel analysis," *Administrative Science Quarterly* 26: 501–24.

Steinberg, T. (2000) *Acts of God: The unnatural history of natural disaster in America*. New York: Oxford University Press.

Stephens, M. (1980) *Three Mile Island*. New York: Random House.

Stern, E. K. (1997a) "Probing the plausibility of newgroup syndrome: Kennedy and the Bay of Pigs," in 't Hart, Stern, and Sundelius (eds.) *Beyond Groupthink: Political group dynamics and foreign policymaking*. Ann Arbor: University of Michigan Press, pp. 153–89.

Stern, E. K. (1997b) "Crisis and learning: A balance sheet," *Journal of Contingencies and Crisis Management* 5: 69–86.

Stern, E. K. (1999) *Crisis Decisionmaking: A cognitive-institutional approach*. Stockholm: Department of Political Science, Stockholm University.

Stern, E. K. (2003) "Crisis Studies and Foreign Policy Analysis: Insights, Synergies, and Challenges" *International Studies Review* 5: 183–202.

Stern, E. K. and Hansén, D. (eds.) (2000) *Crisis Management in a Transitional Society: The Latvian experience*. Stockholm: Swedish National Defence College.

Stern, E. K. and Nohrstedt, D. (eds.) (1999) *Crisis Management in Estonia: Case studies and comparative perspectives*. Stockholm: Swedish National Defence College.

Stern, E. K. and Sundelius, B. (1997) "Sweden's twin monetary crises of 1992: Rigidity and learning in crisis decision making," *Journal of Contingencies and Crisis Management* 5: 32–48.

Stern, E. K. and Sundelius, B. (2002) "Crisis management Europe: An integrated regional research and training program," *International Studies Perspectives* 3: 771–88.

Stern, E. K., Sundelius, B., Nohrstedt, D., Hansén, D., Newlove, L., and 't Hart, P. (2002) "Crisis management in transitional democracies: The Baltic experience," *Government and Opposition* 37: 524–50.

Suchman, M. C. (1995) "Managing legitimacy: Strategies and institutional approaches," *Academy of Management Review* 20: 571–610.

Sundelius, B. and Grönvall, J. (2004) "Strategic dilemmas of biosecurity in the European Union," *Biosecurity and Bioterrorism* 2: 17–23.

Sylves, R. and Cumming, W. R. (2004) "FEMA's path to homeland security: 1979–2003," *Journal of Homeland Security and Emergency Management* 1: 1–21.

Tarrow, S. G. (1994) *Power in Movement: Social movements, collective action and politics*. Cambridge: Cambridge University Press.

Terry, L. (1995) *Leadership of Public Bureaucracies: The administrator as conservator*. Thousand Oaks: Sage Publications.

Thomas, G. (1999) "External shocks, conflict and learning as interactive sources of change in US security policy," *Journal of Public Policy* 19: 209–31.

Thomas, W. and Thomas, D. (1928) *The Child in America: Behavior problems and programs*. New York: A. A. Knopf.

Thompson, J. D. (1967) *Organizations in Action: Social science bases of administrative theory*. New York: McGraw-Hill.

Tierney K., Lindell, M. K. and Perry, R. W. (2001) *Facing the Unexpected: Disaster preparedness and response in the United States*. Washington: Joseph Henry Press.

Tilly, C. and Stinchcombe, A. L. (1997) *Roads From Past to Future*. Lanham: Rowman & Littlefield.

Turner, B. A. (1976) "The organizational and interorganizational development of disasters," *Administrative Science Quarterly* 21: 378–97.

Turner, B. A. (1978) *Man-made Disasters*. London: Wykeham.

Turner, B. A. and Pidgeon, N. (1997) *Man-made Disasters*. 2nd ed. London: Butterworth Heinemann.

Turner, J. C. and Giles, H. (eds.) (1981) *Intergroup Behaviour*. Oxford: Blackwell.

Useem, B. and Kimball, P. A. (1989) *States of Siege: U.S. prison riots, 1971–1986*. New York: Oxford University Press.

van Duin, M. J. (1992) *Van Rampen Leren: Een vergelijkend onderzoek naar de lessen uit spoorwegongevallen, hotelbranden en industriële ongelukken*. Dissertation. Department of Public Administration, Leiden University.

Vandenbroucke, L. S. (1993) *Perilous Options: Special operations as an instrument of U.S. foreign policy*. New York: Oxford University Press.

Vasterman, P. L. M. (2004) *Mediahype*. Amsterdam: Aksant.

Vaughan, D. (1996) *The Challenger Launch Decision: Risky technology, culture and deviance at NASA*. Chicago: University of Chicago Press.

Verbeek, B. (2003) *Decision-making in Great Britain During the Suez Crisis: Small groups and a persistent leader*. Aldershot: Ashgate.

Vertzberger, Y. Y. I. (1990) *The World in their Minds: Information processing, cognition and perception in foreign policy decisionmaking*. Stanford: Stanford University Press.

Vizzard, W. J. (1997) *In the Crossfire: A political history of the Bureau of Alcohol, Tobacco, and Firearms*. Boulder: Lynne Rienner.

Wachtendorf, T. (2004) *Improvising 9/11: Organizational improvisation following the World Trade Center disaster*. Dissertation. Delaware: University of Delaware.

Waddington, D. P. (1992) *Contemporary Issues in Public Disorder: A comparative and historical approach*. London: Routledge.

Walters, L. M., Wilkins, L., and Walters, T. (eds.) (1989) *Bad Tidings: Communication and catastrophe*. Hillsdale: Lawrence Erlbaum Associates.

Waugh, W. L. (1990) *Terrorism and Emergency Management: Policy and administration*. New York: Marcel Dekker Inc.

Weick, K. E. (1988) "Enacted sense making in crisis situations," *Journal of Management Studies* 25: 305–17.

Weick, K. E. (1995) *Sense Making in Organizations*. Thousand Oaks: Sage Publications.

Weick, K. E. and Sutcliffe, K. M. (2002) *Managing the Unexpected: Assuring high performance in an age of complexity*. San Francisco: Jossey-Bass.

Weick, K. E., Sutcliffe, K. M., and Obstfeld, D. (1999) "Organizing for high reliability: Processes of collective mindfulness," in Sutton, R. S. and Staw, B. M. (eds.) *Research in Organizational Behavior* 21: 81–123. Stanford: Jai Press.

Wenger, D., Quarantelli, E. L. and Dynes, R. R. (1986) *Disaster Analysis: Local emergency management offices and arrangements.* Newark: University of Delaware.

White, R. K. (ed.) (1986) *Psychology and the Prevention of Nuclear War.* New York: New York University Press.

Wildavsky, A. B. (1984) *Speaking Truth to Power: The art and craft of policy analysis.* New Brunswick: Transaction.

Wildavsky, A. B. (1988) *Searching for Safety.* Berkeley: University of California Press.

Wildavsky, A. B. (1995) *But Is It True? A citizen's guide to environmental health and safety issues.* Cambridge: Harvard University Press.

Wildavsky, A. B. and Dake, K. (1991) "Theories of risk perception: Who fears what and why?," *Daedalus: Journal of the American Academy of Arts and Sciences* 119: 41–59.

Wilensky, H. L. (1967) *Organizational Intelligence: Knowledge and policy in government and industry.* New York: The Free Press.

Wilkins, L. (1989) "Bhopal: The politics of mediated risk," in Walters, L.M, Wilkins, L., and Walters, T. (eds.) *Bad Tidings: Communication and catastrophe.* Hillsdale: Lawrence Erlbaum Associates, pp. 21–34.

Wilsford, D. (1994) "Path-dependency, or why history makes it difficult, but not impossible to reform health care services in a big way," *Journal of Public Policy* 14: 251–83.

Wilson, D. S. (2002) *Darwin's Cathedral.* Chicago: University of Chicago Press.

Wilson, J. Q. (1989) *Bureaucracy.* New York: The Free Press.

Woodward, B. (2004) *Plan of Attack.* New York: Simon and Schuster.

Woodward, B. and Bernstein, C. (1994) *All the President's Men.* New York: Simon and Schuster.

Zartman, I. W. (ed.) (1994) *International Multilateral Negotiations: Approaches to the management of complexity.* San Francisco: Jossey-Bass.

Zelikow, P. and Rice, C. (1995) *Germany Unified and Europe Transformed: A Study of Statecraft.* Cambridge, MA: Harvard University Press.

Index